Patriarch Photios of Constantinople

THE ARCHBISHOP IAKOVOS LIBRARY
OF ECCLESIASTICAL AND HISTORICAL SOURCES NO. 5

N. M. Vaporis, General Editor

Patriarch Photios of Constantinople

His Life, Scholarly Contributions, and Correspondence Together with a Translation of Fifty-two of His Letters

by
Despina Stratoudaki White

HOLY CROSS ORTHODOX PRESS
Brookline, Massachusetts 02146
1981

Funds for the publication of **Patriarch Photios of Constantinople** were generously provided by the ST. PHOTIOS FOUNDATION St. Augustine, Florida

Published by the Holy Cross Orthodox Press.

BX
395
.P5
W48
1982

Cover design by **Mary Vaporis**

Library of Congress Cataloging in Publication Data

White, Despina Stratoudaki.
    Patriarch Photios of Constantinople.

    (The Archbishop Iakovos library of ecclesiastical and historical sources; no. 5)
    Bibliography: p.
    Includes index.
    1. Photios I, Saint, Patriarch of Constantinople, ca. 820-ca. 891.
2. Christian saints — Turkey — Biography. I. Photius I, Saint, Patriarch of Constantinople, ca. 820-ca. 891. II. Title. III. Series.
BX395.P5W48   270.3'092'4 [B]   82-1004
ISBN 0-916586-26-X   AACR2
ISBN 0-916586-21-9 (pbk.)

Dedicated to the memory
of my beloved husband

CONTENTS

7

FOREWORD

Patriarch Photios of Constantinople is one of the outstanding churchmen of all time. Revered by the Orthodox Church as a saint and champion of Orthodoxy, Patriarch Photios has been studied hitherto primarily in light of the events of the ninth-century controversy between the Orthodox and Latin Churches.

In the present volume, as well as in her other book (authored with Joseph R. Berrigan, Jr.): *The Patriarch and the Prince*, Brookline: Holy Cross Orthodox Press, 1982, Professor Despina S. White studies Patriarch Photios as "an intellectual, an encyclopedist, a teacher...a voracious student of anything that books could offer...a strong upholder of Orthodoxy, the savior of Constantinople, the father of his flock," and a person of enormous compassion. More than anything else, it is the Patriarch's humanity that shines forth from his letters which Professor White presents here for the first time in English translation.

It is, therefore, with a great deal of pleasure that the present volume has been accepted in the series, "The Archbishop Iakovos Library of Ecclesiastical and Historical Sources."

N. M. Vaporis
General Editor

9

ACKNOWLEDGEMENTS

I wish to express my thanks and appreciation to the following individuals:

Professor Dionysios Zakythinos (University of Athens, Greece) for suggesting the topic;

Professor Anastasios Bandy (University of California at Riverside) for reading the entire manuscript and offering many valuable suggestions and improvements;

Professors Joseph R. Berrigan, Jr. and Linda Piper (University of Georgia) for their guidance and moral support;

My friends Corawayne Wright (Wesleyan College) and Ben McClary (Middle Georgia College) for their constant help and encouragement;

The librarians and staff of the Bibliotheque National, Bodleian, Marciana, the Patriarchal Institute for Patristic Studies and Vatican Library of St. Louis University for their promptness in supplying microfilms of the manuscripts used and read for this study;

The editor of *Classical Folia* for permission to incorporate the "Letter to Eusebia" (June 1975, pp. 31-43), in this work;

The editor of *The Greek Orthodox Theological Review* for permission to incorporate the "Letter to Tarasios on the Death of His Daughter" (GOTR 18 [1973], 47-58), and the "Letter to the Bishops in Exile" (GOTR 19 [1974], 113-30) in this work;

The editor of Holy Cross Orthodox Press and members of his staff: Sophia Caparisos, Donna Anton Nicklas, and April Suzanne Koenig for their cooperation and assistance;

And most of all, my late husband, my children, and mother for their patience and understanding.

D.S. White

ABBREVIATIONS

AB	*Analecta Bollandiana* (Paris and Brussels, 1882-).
B	*Byzantion. Revue Internationale des Etudes Byzantines.* (Paris and Liege, 1924-9; Paris and Brussels, 1930; Brussels, etc., 1931-).
BA	*Byzantinisches Archiv* (at intervals; Leipzig and Munich, 1898-).
BM	*Byzantina Metabyzantina,* 1 (New York, 1946); 2 (1949).
BZ	*Byzantinische Zeitschrift* (Leipzig, 1892-).
CMH	*Cambridge Medieval History* (Cambridge, 1913-).
CSEL	*Corpus scriptorum ecclesiasticorum Latinorum.*
CSHB	*Corpus scriptorum historiae Byzantinae.*
DOP	*Dumbarton Oaks Papers* (Cambridge, Mass., 1941-).
DZG	*Deutsche Zeitschrift für Geschichtswissenschaft* (Freiburg im. Breisgau, 1889-98) (continued as *Historische Vierteljahrsschrift*).
EB	*Etudes Byzantines,* 1-3 (Bucharest, 1943-5) (continued as *Revue des Etudes Byzantines*).
ECQ	*Eastern Churches Quarterly* (Ramsgate, 1936-).
EHR	*English Historical Review* (London, 1886-).
EO	*Echos d'Orient* (Constantinople and Paris, 1897-1942).
GOTR	*The Greek Orthodox Theological Review* (Brookline, Mass., 1954-).
Mansi	Mansi, J.D., *Sacrorum conciliorum collectio.*
MGH, EP	*Monumenta Germaniae Historica.* Epistolae.
OCA	*Orientalia Christiana Analecta* (Rome, 1935-).
PG	Migne, *Patrologiae cursus completus. Ser. graeco-latina.*
PL	Migne, *Patrologiae cursus completus. Ser. latina.*
REB	*Revue des études byzantines* (Bucharest and Paris, 1946-).
REG	*Revue des études grecques* (Paris, 1888-).
Sem. Kond.	*Seminarium Kondakovianum.*
Val.	Ionnes N. Valettas, Φωτίου ᾿Αγιωτάτου Πατριάρχου Κωνσταντινουπόλεως, ᾿Επιστολαί (London, 1864).

INTRODUCTION

There is no written *Vita* of Patriarch Photios until the nineteenth-century works in the West of Cardinal Hergenröther, Abbé Fauché and Abbé Jager. Thus, to reconstruct the life of the patriarch, one has to consult writers such as the Continuator of Theophanes, George Hamartolos, Symeon Metaphrastes, Leo the Grammarian, Genesios, Cedrenos, Zonaras, and, in some instances, the lives of certain saints. Last but not least, the letters of Patriarch Photios in which he makes references to his family and his own life provide invaluable source material.

While the life of Patriarch Photios is well documented after he became patriarch in 858 for the first time until his second expulsion by Leo VI in 886, his whereabouts before and after these dates are somewhat uncertain. Thus, his letters and other writings provide more of the background and character of this extraordinary man as comforter of and mentor to his four brothers, as a man of the cloth, as head of the church of Constantinople, and as a friend and confidant of emperors and high officials. More and more historians in recent years have turned to letters as a source of the history and civilization of a given period. It is so fortunate that so many of Patriarch Photios' personal letters to friends and relatives as well as epistles addressed to popes and other patriarchs of the East and to high-ranking officials have survived in the various manuscript traditions. Reading these letters, one can perceive the man as he really was and learn details about the ninth century heretofore inadequately revealed. What impresses the reader of Patriarch Photios is his extensive knowledge of classical as well as Christian writings, though he never forgets that he is first of all a Christian, and, when in need, he turns to the Scriptures for comfort and consolation.

13

Some of Photios' letters have been translated into Latin and some into French and German. As far as is known, this is the first English translation of any of his letters. Letters from the Byzantine period have not yet been extensively used as source for the study of Byzantine history. In the case of Patriarch Photios, this has resulted in his being subjected to constant attack by his critics, but he provides his own defense in his words of consolation, advice, reprimand, brotherly love, or admiration to his fellow human beings.

CHAPTER ONE

THE LIFE OF PATRIARCH PHOTIOS

Saint Photios was Patriarch of Constantinople from 858 to 867 and from 877 to 886. He was an intimate of the powerful, a courtier, an intellectual, an encyclopedist, a teacher, and a voracious student of anything that books could offer. At the same time he was a strong upholder of Orthodoxy, the savior of Constantinople, the father of his flock, and the spiritual adviser of kings. In his writings and activities Photios embodied the intellectual pattern which represented the Byzantine spirit in subsequent centuries.[1] In the ninth century, with Photios begins, as is correctly stated by Professor Zakythinos, "the orbis byzantinus."[2]

Photios came from a well-to-do upper-class family. His father was Sergios, a *spatharios* in the palace;[3] his mother's name was Irene. It seems that a member of his family — it is not clear who — married into the imperial family; thus Photios was distantly related to the Amorian dynasty.[4] He had four brothers; Sergios and Constantine who became *protospatharii;* Tarasios who became a patrikios and Theodoros who probably was the youngest and who is called by Photios simply "brother."[5] His father was related to Patriarch Tarasios whom Photios called "uncle from his father's side."[6] In his writings Photios constantly refers to the sufferings of his parents for their beliefs, sufferings which they undoubtedly endured during the iconoclastic persecutions of the first part of the ninth century.[7]

The exact dates of the birth and death of St. Photios are not known. The various biographers of the patriarch set the date of his birth sometime in the first quarter of the ninth century, with the generally accepted date, according to Beck, around 820.[8] Regarding his age, Photios occasionally gave indirect references. He called Patriarch Nikephoros his "contemporary."[9] In another passage he stated that he was very young when he started to write his *Lexicon*,[10] and very old and tired when he finished the *Amphilochia* between 867-869 during his first exile. The later work was addressed to Amphilochios, the metropolitan of Kyzikos, and he refers to the time as "the times of evils."[11] Also a very significant point in establishing the age of Photios is the information furnished by him concerning the anathema pronounced upon his father, his uncle Tarasios, and himself by the last iconoclastic synod, which took place in 837.[12]

From an early age Photios dedicated himself to scholarship. Until recently the prevailing opinion was that Photios was self-taught because he made no mention of his teachers.[13] Today, however, as we learn more about Byzantine education, especially from the lives of the saints, we can follow Photios' education in greater detail.[14] It has now been established that Byzantium had a basic system of education comprised of grammar, rhetoric, logic, the trivium; and arithmetic, geometry, astronomy, and music, the quadrivium.[15] The student who desired higher education had, in all probability, to go to Constantinople. There one would go either to the school for higher education of the clergy, the Patriarchal Academy, or to the university, which was subsidized by the government.[16] Niketas, the biographer of Ignatios, says that Photios "was versed in grammar, philosophy, poetry, and rhetoric."[17]

In a letter to Protospatharios Michael, Photios himself defined what education meant to him. He advised his friend "to educate the children in such a way that it would be a source of pleasure to them while young and an enduring companion in their later years."[18] In these words, according to Professor Tatakis, it is not Photios the patriarch or the theologian who is speaking, but Photios the lover of knowledge.[19] He is in the tradition of Aulus Gellius, of Cicero, of Isocrates, an admirer of antiquity, a humanist.[20] As is evident from his life and from the information we have, Photios knew always, whether as a private citizen, as an important official in the imperial government, as patriarch during the peaceful years of his life, and later during the years of exile and hardship, how to offer his knowledge to everyone who came in contact with him. Krumbacher calls him "the great teacher of his nation."[21] In his enthusiasm as a teacher, Photios resembles one of the great educators of early Christian times, St. Basil of Cappadocia.

Before he became a patriarch, and after his return from exile, Photios was a professor of philosophy and dialectics at the university at the Magnaura Palace. He was a young man at the time of his first appointment; this we surmise from the writings of some critics on the young teacher.[22] Frequently a group of students awaited the teacher's return from his state duties, and Photios looked forward to that pleasant moment with anticipation.[23] He exerted great influence over his young disciples and his aim in educating them was always, as it had been for Origen, to guide their minds towards religious reverence.

Many of the lectures which he delivered during this period have survived.[24] In the same period, Photios continued the literary correspondence from which many letters survive. The topics he covered were as diverse as their recipients: To a historian he wrote "About Roman Titles";[25] to scientists "About Medical Matters" and "What is Called a Magnet";[26] to Leo the Philosopher, when he was head of the Magnaura University, Photios wrote a letter "On the Verb 'to be.'"[27]

In ninth-century Byzantium, Aristotelian logic and the Aristotelian method of research were the only accepted scientific ways. Regarding his philosophical preferences, Photios is considered an "avowed Aristotelian," but Plato was no stranger to him. He wrote on the *Categories of Aristotle,*[28] and while he disagreed with Plato's *Republic,*[29] he absorbed his ideas about images.

The Platonic influence is suggested in the text of his seventeenth Homily, written on the occasion of the dedication of the icon of the Virgin Mary (*Panagia*) at Hagia Sophia. It reads in part:

> These things are conveyed both by stories and pictures, but it is the spectators rather than the hearers who are drawn to emulation. The Virgin is holding the Creator, as an infant in her arms. Who is there who would not marvel upon seeing it rather than upon hearing about it, at the magnitude of the mystery, and who would not rise up to laud the condescension that surpasses all words.[30]

After the death of the last iconoclastic emperor, Theophilos (820-842), a regency was set up consisting of Empress Theodora,[31] the logothete of the *drome*, Theoktistos; the patrician Bardas, the brother of Theodora; and her uncle, the magister Emmanuel the Armenian.[32]

Theodora wished to restore icon veneration.[33] However, it took the regency a year to ease out the iconoclastic patriarch, John the Grammarian, and to elect a new patriarch, Methodios, from the party of the iconophiles.[34] Unlike Empress Irene (797-802), who was hampered by military opposition at the summoning of the Seventh Ecumenical Synod in 787, Theodora had the support of the army on convoking a synod in March of 843, which revoked the iconoclastic decrees and reaffirmed the canons of the Synod of Nicaea of 787. In memory of this event, the first Sunday of Great Lent is called the Sunday of Orthodoxy, still observed annually by the Eastern Orthodox Church throughout the world with special church services and hymns.[35] The new patriarch, Methodios, recalled the bishops who had been exiled because of their iconophile beliefs and had suffered during the iconoclastic upheavals. At the same time, however, he was very careful not to appoint as bishops men with extremist views in order to avoid any increase in resistance by the Zealots to his efforts to bring peace into the Church.[36]

In the government, however, the real power gradually passed to Theoktistos, as Theodora favored him most among the members of the regency. Theoktistos had proved to be a very competent and, at the same time, a very faithful servant. He had served Michael II, Theophilos' father, and Emperor Theophilos, who had appointed him to the regency council for his son Michael.[37] He served Theodora with the same zeal and devotion. Theoktistos, recognizing Photios' administrative abilities, named him protoasecretis around 851, with the rank also of protospatharios. This meant that Photios was the director of the imperial chancellery, or, according to Anastasios Bibliothekarios, "director of the office of asecretis."[38] Some scholars believe that the appointment of Photios as protoasecretis was much earlier, probably around 843, and that Photios succeeded the iconoclastic Zelix. Mystery still surrounds the figure of Zelix, who occupied this high position in Byzantium.[39] The next man we know to have held the office of protoasecretis is Photios. Photios, Theoktistos, and Bardas together initiated a far-reaching educational program. It was during the regency that Leo the Mathematician, Photios, and later Constantine-Cyril taught at the university. In the words of Father Dvornik:

> The regime of Theoktistos represents the continuation of the literary and scientific movement which in Byzantium continues from the learned Patriarch John the Grammarian to Leo the Mathematician and from Theophilos to Photios and their school.[40]

Unfortunately, in 847, the fourth year of his elevation,[41] Patriarch Methodios died and was succeeded by Ignatios from the party of the extremists. Ignatios, or Niketas, as he was baptized, was the son of Emperor Michael I Rangave (811-813).[42] He was tonsured after the death of his father and retired as abbot of the monasteries which he had founded on the island of Terebinthos. Ignatios, in contrast to Photios, disliked secular learning and spent most of his life up to his appointment as patriarch seeking monastic perfection.

It seems that a faction of the iconophile clergy headed by the monks of Studion, in their zeal to preserve traditional Christianity, were opposed to government controls as well as to any kind of secular learning. Those were the ultra-conservatives, who held that church orders and writings should be followed in all circumstances with the utmost vigor. The rest of the iconodules, on the other hand, favored "economia," that is, a policy of compromise in matters not concerning the fundamentals of the faith and also with the iconoclastic clergy. The moderates wished to forget the events of the iconoclastic period, which had kept Byzantium in internal turmoil for almost a century and a half. Among this group were Bardas, Photios (before he became patriarch), Constantine-Cyril, and other men of letters. The Patriarch Ignatios belonged to the ultra-conservative die-hard party and was the choice of the pious iconodule Empress Theodora. Niketas, Ignatios' biographer, insinuates that the empress played a leading part in Ignatios' elevation to the patriarchal throne.[43] Anastasios the Librarian, who was sent by the Pope to examine Ignatios' position, acknowledges in his preface to the Acts of the Eighth Synod the fact that Ignatios treated profane learning with the upmost contempt.[44] In this respect, he shared the feelings of the die-hard monks and zealots, in sharp contrast to the long line of men of learning who sat on the patriarchal throne of Byzantium, men such as the Patriarchs Nikephoros, Tarasios, John the Grammarian, and Methodios.

However, there was no apparent opposition by the episcopate towards the new patriarch, as evidenced by the homage paid to Ignatios from the friends of the deceased Patriarch Methodios.[45] The leader of the group was the bishop of Syracuse, Gregorios Asbestas, who himself had been considered for patriarch. Gregorios, it seems, had been accused of some indiscretion regarding the ordination of a priest and his case had not been cleared at that time by the church.[46] Ready to accept the new patriarch, Gregorios led his followers to the church to pay homage to Ignatios at his enthronement. But the uncompromising Ignatios ordered Gregorios out of the Church of Hagia Sophia.[47] The quarrel between the new patriarch and Gregorios intensified as it became a quarrel between the moderates, represented by Gregorios and his followers and friends, and the extremists of the Ignatian party. Gregorios appealed to Rome, and Pope Leo IV sent a letter to Ignatios reprimanding him for his decision.[48] There are three contemporary sources for these events, but all are partisans of Ignatios, and thus it is rather difficult to reconstruct the case objectively.[49] Nevertheless, the fact is that Ignatios lacked the temperament and diplomatic ability needed to unify the Church; on the contrary, he brought on an internal schism among the clergy.

Meanwhile Bardas, who had gained his nephew's confidence, was elevated by the young emperor to magister and was also appointed domestic of the schools, that is, the head of the imperial guard. Soon he also was made *curopalates,* a dignity conferred only upon close relatives of the emperor. Bardas and Theoktistos both wanted to run the government, and both had different ideas as to how it should be done, the first being a moderate, while the latter was a reactionary. One of the two had to go. On 13 March 856, Michael III came of age and turned the control of the government over to his uncle Bardas, raising him to the highest rank—that of caesar. It was then that Bardas and Michael decided to eliminate Theoktistos.[50] Bardas murdered Theoktistos with the approval of the emperor, and Theodora and her daughters were restricted to the palace for some time before being sent to a convent.[51] The senate, on the other hand, applauded the decision of Michael to rule without the regency-council.[52] The hopes of the moderates were high again. The extremists, however, with Patriarch Ignatios as their leader, were ready to act. The signal was given when, on the feast of the Epiphany in 858, Patriarch Ignatios refused, in the presence of all the dignitaries, to administer the sacrament of the Holy Eucharist to Bardas in Hagia Sophia. He based his action on the rumors concerning Bardas' illicit relations with the young wife of his dead son.[53] Bardas waited his turn. The moment came when he decided to confine his sister, Empress Theo-

dora, and her daughters to a convent, and he asked the patriarch to bless their veils. Ignatios refused to do so and also
protested the execution of a certain Gedeon, who, posing as
the empress' son, had instigated a plot against Bardas. Ignatios
was accused of high treason and was exiled to his monasteries
on the island of Terebinthos. It is not clear whether or not
the patriarch actually resigned. Until recently the view of the
partisans of Ignatios prevailed, based on the information
given by Niketas, the biographer of Ignatios. They believed
that Ignatios did not resign. However, after a careful reading
of the Niketas text, it is evident that Ignatios must have resigned, probably under duress, or his followers might have
had a stronger case. The text reads:

> Would you not think that the unlawfulness of the investiture had
> come from the fact that after Ignatios did not agree to resign honor-
> ably, they took it upon themselves — certain men around the em-
> peror — to take care of the rest of the matter.... They ordained the
> *spatharios* and protoasecretis Photios as patriarch of Constanti-
> nople. [54]

The resignation of Ignatios is very significant in regard to
the canonicity of Photios' position. Photios himself in his
enthronement epistles to the patriarchs of the East (Antioch,
Jerusalem, and Alexandria) refers to Ignatios' resignation. [55]
Also in his letter to Pope Nicholas I, Photios writes: "I received this high position from the one who was patriarch before me." [56]

Emperor Michael III and Bardas chose Photios as patriarch.
As head of the imperial chancery, Photios had exhibited an
unusual talent for practical and administrative matters, and
while he was at the university he had been admired among
the learned circles. The offer came as a surprise to Photios because of his lay status. [57] This was not, however, an unusual
procedure in Byzantium. Three other patriarchs, Paul III
(688-694), Tarasios (died 806), and Nikephoros (died 815),
were, like Photios, laymen before being elevated to the see of
Constantinople, and each had served as protoasecretis. After

much hesitation, Photios accepted the appointment; in five successive days he received all the offices and degrees of the priesthood: lector, subdeacon, and priest, and was consecrated bishop and enthroned as Patriarch of Constantinople on Christmas Day 858.[58]

All but five of those bishops present in Constantinople for the enthronement service acknowledged Photios as the new patriarch.[59] Photios' first effort as patriarch was to bring peace within the Church. This is evident from the text he chose for his first sermon, which he delivered on the day of his consecration from the pulpit of Hagia Sophia, entitled "Peace on earth, good will among men."

Also upon his accession, as was customary, Photios sent a letter to Pope Nicholas I in Rome and to the three other patriarchs in the East.[60] In the letter to the pope, Photios, after confessing his dedication to Orthodoxy, stated that he would have preferred to stay with his books and his eager pupils, but had agreed to become patriarch in "obedience to the will of God, who was thus punishing him for his transgressions."[61] In another epistle to Bardas, Photios complained again that he was forced by Bardas to take the see against his will.[62] Photios' letter to the pope reached Rome in the beginning of the year 860. The pope's reply to the patriarch was brief but friendly. He was satisfied, the pope wrote, with the new patriarch's profession of faith, but was somewhat disturbed by the manner of his ordination. For this reason, he added, he was sending two legates to Constantinople to examine the circumstances of Ignatios' resignation.

The two papal legates, Rodoald and Zacharias, arrived in Constantinople and attended the synod called by Photios in 861. They were also commissioned to request the return of the patrimonies of Sicily and Calabria, as well as those of Illyricum, to the jurisdiction of Rome.[63] These patrimonies had been taken away from the pope by the iconoclastic emperors the previous century. On this mission, however, the papal legates were not successful with the patriarch. Nevertheless, they found that the election of Photios was legal and canonical, and after completing their mission they returned to Rome. Disappointed because the patrimonies were not restored to Rome, Pope Nicholas rejected the findings of his legates and in 863 convoked a synod at the Lateran in Rome, which deposed Photios and reinstated Ignatios.

Meanwhile, the church of Constantinople entered a period of great missionary activity under Photios' leadership (858-867). The first contact with Rhos came during Photios' second year as patriarch, on 18 June 869, when a fleet of 200 slipped through the Bosporos and attacked Constantinople.[64] The Rhos, or Rus, a Scandinavian people, made their first appearance in history in 839, when on the eighteenth of May of that a year a Byzantine embassy was received by Louis the Pious in Ingelheim. In the *Annales Bertiniani*, it is said that the Greek ambassadors had with them some men "qui se, id est gentem suam, Rhos vocari dicebant." They had come to see the emperor in Constantinople in order to negotiate a trade agreement, but because it was not safe for them to return by road to the East, Theophilos sent them with the embassy, asking Louis to see that they returned safely to their country.[65] The Rhos settled in two centers, in Kiev around 840 and in Novgorod about the middle of the ninth century. They lived there peacefully and traded with the Byzantines until 860 when they attacked Constantinople. At that time the emperor was away from the capital on a campaign against the Arabs in Asia Minor and the imperial fleet was engaging the Arabs in the Mediterranean. The city of Constantinople was completely defenseless. The Rhos pillaged the suburbs and the small islands in the straits.[66] The prefect of the city and the patriarch were in charge of the city's defense. Photios, in two memorable sermons preached in the Church of Hagia Sophia, encouraged the frightened inhabitants in Constantinople to put their faith in God and stand against the attackers.[67] The siege was suddenly raised and the invaders left the city after the 'holy robe' of the Virgin was carried by the patriarch in procession around the walls of the city and the garment was dipped in water, creating a great storm.[68] We learn of the miraculous salvation of Constantinople from Photios' sermon.

The important aftermath of this attack was that, soon after, ambassadors from the Rhos were baptized in Constantinople by the patriarch. In his encyclical of 867, Photios announced to the patriarchs of the East that the Rhos were living now as citizens and ambassadors of the empire.[69] Although more than a century passed before the final conversion of the "Kievan Rus" to Christianity, which took place in 987/988 with Prince Vladimir's acceptance of Christianity and marriage to a Byzantine Porphyrogeneta princess, the actual Christianization of the Rhos began at the time of Photios.

Toward the end of 860, Emperor Michael III and Patriarch Photios decided to renew contacts with the Khazars, a Turkish people who had emerged north of the Caucasus about the end of the sixth century. By the middle of the seventh century they had occupied the area between the Volga and the Dnieper rivers as far north as the forest belt of Central Russia and the Upper Oka. Emperor Heraklios in 627 had entered into an agreement with the Khazars, who promised to guard the north Caucasian front against the Persians. In 733 the son of Leo III, the future Emperor Constantine V, married Irene, the daughter of the Khagan of the Khazars. It was this Khazar princess who introduced the *tzitzakion* — her national dress — into the court of Byzantium. The importance of the Khazars to the Byzantines is evident in the tenth-century *Book of Ceremonies*, where the Khazar ruler ranked second only to the caliph of Baghdad in the diplomatic protocol among non-Christian rulers.[70]

Attempts had been made in the past by Constantinople to Christianize the Khazars, but these met with very little success. It seemed that the Khazars were more eager to trade their shamanistic religion for Judaism or Islam. In fact, the

Jewish religion was dominant among the upperclass, and Jewish rabbis were very influential at the Khazar court.

In spite of their religious preferences, however, the Khazars remained allies of Byzantium. The embassy which was sent late in 860 from Constantinople to the Khazar Court was headed by Constantine-Cyril, a long-time friend of Photios' from the university, and by his brother Methodios. Constantine-Cyril and his brother Methodios were born in Thessalonike to an upper-class Greek family. Their father was *droungarios* in the army; that is, a commander of five battalions.[71] Both brothers received their primary education in Thessalonike, where they had the opportunity to come in contact with the numerous Slavs who lived in that city and learn the various Slavic tongues. When Constantine-Cyril was about seventeen years old, he went to Constantinople, where under the protection of Theoktistos he worked and studied at the University of Magnaura and met Photios. His brother Methodios, at a young age, was appointed by Emperor Michael III as head of one of the Slavic provinces because of his knowledge of Slavic languages. Methodios soon withdrew from his post and entered a monastery on Mount Olympos in Bithynia. Constantine-Cyril, even though he had the chance to obtain a high position in the government, chose when he was twenty-three years of age (according to the legend), to become a priest. At the end of 850 or at the beginning of 851 he was appointed teacher at the university, where he joined, as a colleague, Photios and Leo the Philosopher, his former teachers. Thus, it is not strange that Constantine was chosen to head the embassy to the Khazars. Constantine, accompanied by his brother, spent the winter in Cherson in the Crimea, where Constantine improved his knowledge of Hebrew and even learned the Samaritan dialect in order to debate the Mosaic law with the powerful rabbis at the court of the Khazar ruler, probably at Samander on the lower Terek, or at the Derbent the following summer.[72] The converts to Christianity during this particular embassy were not very numerous, about two hundred, but the alliance with the Khazars was strengthened and remained close until the decline of their power in the beginning of the tenth century.

The Byzantine Church, however, continued its missionary activity in the Black Sea area during the decade of the 860s, which prompted Patriarch Photios to express his satisfaction in a letter to the archbishop of Bosporos. He said that the Black Sea from "an inhospitable sea had now become indeed a hospitable sea," the latter being the old name for the Black Sea. [73]

Soon after the embassy returned from the land of the Khazars, another mission of great importance was entrusted to the brothers, Constantine-Cyril and Methodios, in Moravia. The long treaty between Bulgaria and Byzantium signed in 814 by Khan Omortag and Emperor Leo V expired in 845 and was not renewed. Soon afterwards the Bulgarian armies invaded Macedonia around the areas of the Strymon and Nestos rivers. During this period the Byzantine armies were engaged in the struggle against the Arabs in Asia Minor and the fleet in the Mediterranean. The regency government of Theodora, in order to have peace in the northern frontier, made some concessions to the Bulgars. Thus, soon after 852, when Boris succeeded to the throne in Bulgaria, he received from the Byzantines a belt of territory some 25 miles wide, south of the old frontier of Thrace, including the ruined fortresses of Develotos and Anchialos. [74] Boris, sensing the weakness of the Byzantines at this time, wanted to attack them. [75] But instead he changed his mind and turned westward against the Serbians and the Croatians. The Serbians, however, captured his son Vladimir with twelve of his great boyards. Boris had to submit to terms of peace and returned to his capital, where he lived quietly for a few years. In the west Boris' kingdom now stretched as far as the Tisza River, where it met with the Frankish kingdom, for the Avars, who lived in Pannonia, had been completely defeated by Charlemagne's son Pepin in 796. The then king of the Franks, Louis the German, wanting to secure the eastern flank of his domain while he battled against the rebellion of his son Carloman, made overtures to Boris.

Previously, the Franks had been enemies of the Bulgars. During the war between the Franks and the kingdom of the Moravians, Boris at first had allied himself with the prince of the Moravians, Ratislav, in an unsuccessful war against the Franks in 853. When, however, Louis' son Carloman revolted against his father with the help of Ratislav, Boris went over to Louis' side and formally signed a treaty with him in 862. During the negotiations, Boris had probably been approached by the Franks to accept Christianity and he must have been receptive to the idea. Louis, without losing any time, wrote to Pope Nicholas I and received a letter from him congratulating him on his achievement. [76] Ratislav, viewing with alarm the rapprochement between the Bulgars and the Franks, sent an embassy to Constantinople to offer an alliance with them in order to counterbalance the pact between Boris and Louis. Ratislav at the same time requested Emperor Michael III to send to Moravia a teacher who knew Slavonic and could instruct his people in the Christian religion. Patriarch Photios saw the opportunity of extending the influence of the Greek Church to the far regions of the Danube. Without losing any time he sent the two brothers, Constantine and Methodios, to Moravia. We are in the dark as to how the arrangements were made. The fact is that by the summer of 864, the two brothers set out on their journey to the land of Ratislav and stayed there no more than four years. [77] Meanwhile, Constantine used a Glagolitic alphabet (probably invented by him) and translated the Scriptures into the dialect of Macedonian Slavonic, which was completely different from the Slavic language spoken in Moravia, but easy to understand and to learn. [78] The attempt by the two brothers to Christianize the Moravians was, however, a failure. They probably returned to Constantinople around the end of the year 867, and in the following year they went to Rome. Moravia was too far away from Constantinople and too difficult to reach for the Byzantines to exert their influence there. Bulgaria, on the other hand, was an immediate neighbor, and there things turned out better for Photios and the Greek Church.

The head of Byzantine affairs at this time, as we have seen, was Bardas. Being an expert diplomat, Bardas understood the dangers of a Bulgar-Frankish alliance and immediately concluded a treaty with the Moravians in 863. What Bardas could clearly foresee was that along with the Frankish influence in Bulgaria, there was also going to be increasing influence from Rome. Rome and the Frankish kingdom had become close since the time of Pope Stephen III, who had personally gone to meet King Pepin at Ponthion on 6 January 754. This meeting was an outgrowth of the pressures and policies of the iconoclastic emperors in Constantinople. The papacy had been losing ground and influence in Byzantium; therefore, the popes were forced to search for powerful allies in the West.

Also, the Lombards who had established a kingdom in northern Italy were threatening Rome. According to the *Annales*, Pope Stephen met King Pepin in the villa which is called Quierzy (Aisne) and suggested that the king should defend him and the Roman Church from attack by the Lombards.[79] The pope, after the king granted his request, consecrated him and his two sons Charles and Carloman with holy oil. Later, in 800, Charles (Charlemagne) was crowned Holy Roman Emperor of the West by Pope Leo III.[80]

Charlemagne died in 814 after a long reign and was succeeded by Louis I the Pious as emperor. In turn, in 825 his son Louis the German took over the government of Bavaria and gradually enlarged his domain all over Carolingian Germany. Next he turned eastward against the Moravians, and for that he needed the help of the Bulgars. He also, as we have seen, had trouble with his son Carloman. This effort resulted in the Franco-Bulgarian pact on the one hand, and in the Byzantine-Moravian alliance on the other. Following these events in the spring of 864, a Byzantine army invaded

Bulgaria from the south while their Moravian allies moved in from the north.

The Byzantine fleet also appeared on the Bulgarian coast, blockading the harbors. During this time the Bulgars were suffering from a terrible famine.[81] Boris capitulated quickly, gave up his idea for an alliance with the Franks, and promised to be baptized by the patriarch of Constantinople. The pope's prayers were thus realized, with a slight difference: instead of Roman and Frankish missionaries, the Greeks had been chosen to be God's instruments for the conversion of the Bulgars.

Boris was baptized and given the name Michael after the Byzantine emperor who stood as his sponsor. It is stated in some sources that Patriarch Photios performed the ceremony.[82] On this occasion Photios sent Boris-Michael a long and very interesting letter, in which he explained how a Christian prince should behave in his private and public life. This letter, a lengthy masterpiece of composition, is considered one of the best samples of Byzantine epistolography.[83] It is a part of the genre of the 'Furstenspiegeln,' so well known in classical Greece and Byzantium. There also survives another much shorter letter, which was written also by Photios for Boris. While this letter is preserved only in the manuscript Iviron 684 of the sixteenth century, the former has been copied in a number of codices from the tenth to the eighteenth centuries. The long letter of Boris is divided into two parts: one dealing with the duties of a Christian prince, while the other gives a brief analysis of the seven Ecumenical Synods.[84]

Boris, however, remained undecided between Rome and Constantinople. Finally, he turned to his former ally, the German emperor Louis II, and in 866 asked him to send a bishop and priests to Bulgaria. At the same time he requested a bishop from Rome.[85]

Pope Nicholas I decided to make the most of the opportunity offered by Boris' request. Immediatley, he sent as papal legates two bishops, Paul of Populania and Formosus of

Porto, with missionaries, and for some time everything went well in Bulgaria for the Roman Church.[86] Boris was so pleased with the new missionaries that he took a solemn oath to remain the faithful servant of the successor of Saint Peter forever.[87] At the same time, the pope wrote a long letter explaining in detail the everyday duties of a Christian under 106 headings.[88] Nicholas finally saw his hopes and dreams materializing.

To the Byzantines, this was a serious and threatening situation. The armies of the Bulgars could invade the borders of Byzantium at any time. Furthermore, the situation in Constantinople was very serious. Caesar Bardas, who actually ruled the empire, had been assassinated. The murderer was Basil, a favorite of Michael III's, who had risen from a stable boy to become the emperor's constant companion and eventually was named co-emperor. There is evidence that the emperor himself was an accomplice in the murder of Bardas.[89]

The Byzantines had to win the Bulgars back, but the task was not easily accomplished. The Greek missionaries, who had been forced to leave Bulgaria, had made complaints about certain innovations which their Western rivals were introducing in Bulgaria. The Latins, for instance, allowed the Bulgars to drink milk and eat cheese during Lent, a practice forbidden by the Eastern Church. The Western Church forbade their priests to be married, while in the East a priest could get married before his ordination. What was even more serious, the Latins taught that the Holy Spirit proceeded not only from the Father, as was stated in the Nicene Creed, but also from the Son. The procession of the Holy Spirit had occupied the Fathers of the Eastern and Western Churches from the early centuries of Christianity. The First Ecumenical Synod in Nicaea (325) in composing the creed, simply stated: "And in the Holy Spirit, the Lord and the Giver of Life, who proceeds from the Father, who together with the Father and Son is worshipped and glorified."[90] The Third Ecumenical Synod in Ephesos (431) and the Fourth in

Chalcedon (451) forbade any additions or alterations to the Nicaean-Constantinoplitan creed.[91] The Eastern Church has retained the creed unaltered since then. In the West, first in Spain because of the Arian heresies, the Council of Toledo in 589 added the *Filioque*, that is, that the Spirit proceeded also from the Son. Richard Haugh believes that the addition was not intentional but from ignorance.[92] The Visigoth king Recared, in pronouncing the *Filioque*, thought he was following the Nicene Creed. From Spain the *Filioque* was adopted by the Carolingian theologians. Patriarch Paulinus of Aquileia at the synod of Friuli in 796 wrote: "and in the Holy Spirit, the Lord and giver of life, who proceeds from the Father and the Son."[93] A few years later, in 809, Charlemagne convoked a council at Aachen which approved the addition of the *Filioque* to the creed. When, however, he asked Pope Leo III to include it in the text of the Nicene Creed, Leo refused.[94] Later Pope Nicholas I, in correspondence with Patriarch Photios, defended the addition, saying that several "illustrious men, especially Latins, had written about the procession of the Holy Spirit from the Father and the Son." He also pointed out that "the truth did not come only from the Greeks."[96]

The Eastern Church has continued to abide by the decrees of the ecumenical synods and by the teachings of the Cappadocian Fathers and Athanasios the Great, especially as to the consubstantiality of the Spirit with the Father and the Son. Father Meyendorff[96] expressed the Eastern concept of the Trinity in the words of Saint Athanasios: "The Father does all things by the Word in the Holy Spirit."[97]

Patriarch Photios, with the consent of Emperor Michael III and his co-emperor Basil, sent an encyclical letter to the patriarchs of Antioch, Alexandria and Jerusalem summoning a general synod in the summer of 867 in Constantinople.[98] The purpose of this synod was to examine and condemn the above-mentioned practices of the Latins in Bulgaria, as well as the doctrine of the procession of the Holy Spirit from the

Son as well as the Father. Unfortunately, very little of what occurred at this synod has reached us, and the meager information we have comes exclusively from anti-Photian sources.[99] What can be inferred with certainty is that the synod did take place and was attended by many bishops. Pope Nicholas was condemned for the Latin practices in Bulgaria; the Roman doctrine of the procession of the Holy Spirit from the Father *and* the Son was rejected as heretical and Roman interference in the affairs of the Byzantine Church was pronounced unlawful;[100] iconoclasm was condemned once more and Louis II was recognized as emperor of the West at the closing of the synod. Patriarch Photios for many years occupied himself with the *Filioque* question. In consequence, in 883 he sent the famous letter to the metropolitan of Aquileia, in which at great length he defended the position of the Eastern Church on this issue. Very upset, the patriarch wrote:

> It has come to our ears that some of those who live in the West, either because they have not been fully satisfied with the Lord's utterance, or because they have no understanding of the definitions and dogmas of both the Fathers and synods, or because they overlook the precisions therefrom, or because they have minds that are insensible to such matters, not knowing how else one would state it; nevertheless, surreptitiously introduce the teaching (would that they had not) that the Divine and all-Holy Spirit proceeds not only from God, that is, the Father, but also from the Son, and through such an utterance produce extensive harm to those who believe it.[101]

Again in 885 he wrote the long treatise on the *Mystagogy of the Holy Spirit.*[102]

Pope Nicholas died on 13 November 867 without hearing the sentence passed on him by the Eastern bishops and was succeeded by Adrian II. Meanwhile, in Constantinople, more dramatic events were happening. On the night of 23 September 867, Emperor Michael III was murdered in his quarters by his 'friend' Basil, whom he had elevated to co-emperor and who then assumed the sole power as Emperor Basil I (867-886) and became the founder of the so-called Macedonian Dynasty.[103] Upon his ascent to the throne Basil sided with the party of the extremists and decided to heal the breach with Rome. According to the account of Georgios the Monk and others, Photios, probably on the day of the Feast of St. Demetrios on 26 October 867, criticized the recent actions of the emperor and refused him Holy Communion.[104] By November of that same year Patriarch Photios had been deposed and was restricted to the Monastery of Skepe.[105] In the interim, Basil sent Admiral Helias to the island of Terebinthos, where Ignatios resided, to escort him back to the capital with great honors and pomp. Upon his return to Constantinople, Ignatios began his second term as patriarch.[106] Immediately, in the winter of 868, Basil sent Spatharios Euthymios to Rome to announce the changes in Constantinople.[107] Pope Adrian II in return sent Euthymios back with Theognostos carrying two letters — one addressed to the emperor, in which he commended him for replacing Photios with Ignatios, and another to Patriarch Ignatios. The pope also requested that representatives be sent from Constantinople to participate in the Roman synod which he planned to call the following year.

Emperor Basil I, accommodating the request, sent the embassy to Rome, probably in the spring of 869. Among the emissaries were Basil the spatharios; one representative of Ignatios, John of Lilaison; and one of Photios', Peter of Sardes.[108] A letter was also sent by the emperor asking for fairness in the verdict and for a special delegation from Rome to Constantinople to announce it.[109]

The Byzantine embassy was received by the pope at the Church of Santa Maria Maggiore, where the acts of the Synod of 867 were read. Subsequently, a synod took place, probably at the beginning of June, since a letter sent by the pope to the emperor referring to the findings is dated 10 June 869.[110] The synod condemned and anathematized Photios, including all his acts and all the bishops and churches that he had consecrated.[111] At the end of the meeting, the acts of the Synod of 867 were burned in front of St. Peter's Cathedral in a

pouring rain. In his letter to the emperor the pope asked that
the minutes of the Synod of 867 be burned also in Constantinople. [112]

The synod in Constantinople opened on 5 October 869,
but the attendance was very meager, as only twelve bishops
were present at the first session. The papal legates were the
bishops Donatos and Stephanos and the Deacon Marinos, as
well as Anastasios Bibliothekarios. [113] By the sixth session,
some 102 bishops condemned Photios and approved 27
canons. [114] The synod is numbered in the West as the Eighth
Ecumenical Synod, but it is not so recognized by the Greek
Orthodox Church because it did not make any dogmatic decisions. In the Western Church the Synod of 869-870 was first
called ecumenical by the canonists of Pope Gregory VII at
the end of the eleventh century. Patriarch Photios, following
his sentence, was sent into exile and Ignatios was reinstated
as patriarch.

It was during these long years of exile and confinement in
a monastery outside of Constantinople that most of the letters translated in this study were written. One of the most
moving of Photios' letters is addressed to Emperor Basil I,
asking the ruler to allow him at least the company of his
books, as life without books was unbearable to him. [115]

With regard to the Bulgars, Ignatios followed the same
policy as Photios. In fact, while the meeting was in session
and the papal legates were still in Constantinople, an embassy
came from Boris-Michael asking for a meeting with the emperor and the patriarch. The meeting was held in the presence
of Basil I. Anastasios, the papal legate, has recorded this
meeting in detail even though he was not asked to attend, a
slight for which he never forgave the emperor. [116] The Bulgars
decided to join the Church of Constantinople again and to
break relations with Rome.

In spite of the many changes and decisions, the clergy in
Constantinople remained faithful to the exiled Patriarch Photios. Subsequently Basil I, realizing that his overtures to the

extremist party did not produce the advantages which he had anticipated, changed his policy and transferred his friendship to the moderate faction. In 873 Photios returned to Constantinople, was given an apartment in the imperial palace, and was entrusted by the emperor with the education of his sons, Leo and Alexander.[117] Photios also resumed his lectures at the University of Magnaura.[118] Three days after the death of Ignatios, on 26 October 877, Photios became Patriarch of Constantinople for the second time.[119]

Meanwhile, Pope Adrian II died in Rome in 872 and his successor, John VIII (872-882), was eager to maintain peaceful relations with Constantinople. At the request of Basil I, Pope John VIII sent legates again to the East, but by the time they arrived in Constantinople Patriarch Ignatios had died and had been succeeded by Photios. The Synod of 879-880, sometimes referred to as the "Synod of Union," reinstated Photios. The patriarch in return promised to give up all claims in Bulgaria.[120]

Thus, once more there was peace between East and West. Patriarch Photios held office until 886, when he was forced to resign by the new emperor, Leo the Wise (886-912).[121] Leo appointed as patriarch his brother, Stephanos, already predestined for that honor by his father, Basil I. Photios was ordered into exile to the monastery of the Armonians or Armenians, also called Bordonos.[122]

In his vast correspondence Photios says nothing about the circumstances that provoked a quarrel between him and his former pupil, Emperor Leo VI. Thus, the story of Photios' second resignation remains wrapped in mystery. The biographer of Leo VI, the monk Euthymios, who was also Leo's spiritual mentor, is the only one who mentions the resignation of Photios; the other chroniclers of the time are silent. Euthymios writes: "Regarding Photios, he [Leo] immediately relieved him of his office by dismissing him."[123] It is certain that the change was a matter of internal policy. In short Leo VI underwent the same change of mind Basil I did, who courted extremists at the beginning of his reign but later turned to the moderates. Evidence of change in attitude of the young monarch is found in the funeral oration which he delivered in honor of his father after Basil's death.[124]

Thus, Photios, after a year of hardship, was sent to a better place, where he lived quietly, devoting himself to writing and reading.

In spite of his hardships, Patriarch Photios lived to be almost a centenarian. The exact date of his death is not known, but according to some accounts, he is believed to have died on 6 February 897 at the place of his exile in the monastery of the Armonians. Immediately, his remains were brought to the Church of Hagia Sophia in Constantinople and there, in the presence of Emperor Leo VI and all the dignitaries, his name was commemorated together with that of Patriarch Ignatios: "Ignatios and Photios, the Orthodox patriarchs, in everlasting memory."[125] Finally, his body was put to rest in the Monastery of Eremias which had been built by him somewhere in the outskirts of Constantinople.

CHAPTER ONE

1. B.N. Tatakis, "Φώτιος ὁ μεγάλος ἀνθρωπιστής," ΚΥΡΙΛΛΟΥ ΚΑΙ ΜΕΘΟΔΙΟΥ ΤΟΜΟΣ ΕΟΡΤΙΟΣ ΕΠΙ ΤΗ ΧΙΛΙΟΣΤΗ ΚΑΙ ΕΚΑΤΟΣΤΗ ΕΠΕΤΗΡΙΔΙ (Thessalonike, 1968), p. 83.

2. Dionysios Zakythinos, "Κωνσταντῖνος ὁ Φιλόσοφος καί ἡ διαμόρφωσις τῶν σλαβικῶν γλωσσῶν," ΠΡΑΚΤΙΚΑ ΤΗΣ ΑΚΑΔΗΜΙΑΣ ΑΘΗΝΩΝ 45 (1970), 76.

3. For explanation of the Byzantine nobility and titles see, J.B. Bury, The Imperial Administrative System in the Ninth Century (London, 1911), pp. 45-78; also Louis Brehier, "L'Origine des titres impériaux à Byzance," BZ 15 (1906), 161-72; and R. Guiland, "La Noblesse byzantine: remarques," REB 24 (1966), 40-49.

4. J.B. Bury, "The Relationship of Photios to the Empress Theodora," *EHR* 5 (1890), 255-258; Theophanes Continuatus, *Chronographia*, ed. I. Bekker (Bonn, 1838), 4, 175, writes that a sister of the empress named Irene married the brother of Photios' mother.

5. Val. Epistles 7, 8, 9, 10 and 11 are addressed to Sergios; 12, 13, 14, 142, 143, 220, 223, and 224 to Tarasios; 15 and 16 to Constantine; and 17 to Theodoros.

6. Val. p. 180.

7. *PG* 102: 972; Val. pp. 145, 159.

8. H. G. Beck, *Kirche und theologische Literatur im byzantinische Reiche* (Munich, 1959), p. 520; J. Hergenröther, *Photius Patriarch von Konstantinopel. Sein Leben, seine Schriften und das griechische Schisma* (Regensburg, 1867-1869), 1, 315-16, places the date of his birth circa A.D. 827; Papadopoulos-Kerameus, "Ὁ Πατριάρχης Φώτιος ὡς πατήρ ἅγιος τῆς Ὀρθοδόξου Καθολικῆς Ἐκκλησίας," *BZ* 8 (1899), 658, puts the date closer to 800. Of the same opinion is the late metropolitan of Athens, Chrysostom Papadopoulos, ΠΕΡΙ ΤΗΣ ΕΠΙΣΤΗΜΟΝΙΚΗΣ ΔΡΑΣΕΩΣ ΤΟΥ ΜΕΓΑΛΟΥ ΦΩΤΙΟΥ ΠΑΤΡΙΑΡΧΟΥ ΚΩΝΣΤΑΝΤΙΝΟΥΠΟΛΕΩΣ (Athens, 1912), p. 10. Others put the date circa 819; see Hélène Ahrweiler, "Sur la carrière de Photius avant son patriarcat," *BZ* 58 (1965), 359.

9. Stavros Aristarches, ΤΟΥ ΕΝ ΑΓΙΟΙΣ ΠΑΤΡΟΣ ΗΜΩΝ ΦΩΤΙΟΥ ΠΑΤΡΙΑΡΧΟΥ ΚΩΝΣΤΑΝΤΙΝΟΥΠΟΛΕΩΣ ΛΟΓΟΙ ΚΑΙ ΟΜΙΛΙΑΙ (Constantinople, 1901), p. 256. It is possible, however, that Photios referring to Nikephoros as "τόν ἡμῶν Νικηφόρον" meant belonging to the iconophile faction.

10. *PG* 101:152.

11. In the letter to the Bishops in Exile, Photios also complains of the difficult time, *PG* 101:145; Val. pp. 471-85. For a recent translation of the "Letter to the Bishops in Exile," see Despina Stratoudaki White, "Photios' Letter to the Bishops in Exile," *GOTR* 19 (1974), 113-29.

12. V. Grumel, *Les Regestes des actes du patriarcat de Constantinople*, 2, nos. 536 and 413; *PG* 102:877; Ahrweiler, "Sur la carrière," p. 352; Papadopoulos-Kerameus, among others, is of the opinion that the anathema was pronounced in 815, "Πατριάρχης Φώτιος," p. 548.

13. Hergenröther 1:322, supports this position; the late father Francis Dvornik, "The Patriarch Photios in the Light of Recent Research," *Berichte zum XI Internationalen Byzantinisten-Kongress* (Munich, 1958), pp. 2-4, is of a different opinion.

14. Ignatios the Deacon, *Life of St. Nicephoros*, ed. C. DeBoor (Leipzig, 1880), pp. 144, 149 ff., gives details on higher education in Byzantium. Also a good study is that of Friedrich Fuchs, "Die höheren Schulen von Konstantinopel im Mittelalter," *Byzantinisches Archiv* 8 (1962), 1-43.

15. Frequently, Constantinople is mentioned as the center for higher education; nevertheless, Saint Kosmas was educated in Damascus (*PG* 94:445, 448), and Saint Methodios had most of his education in Syracuse (*PG*, 100:1245). Leo the Philosopher went to school on the Island of Andros and when he went to Constantinople, the schools had nothing new to offer him, Theophanes Continuatus, *Chronographia*, 4:192.

16. The university in Constantinople existed from the time of Constantine the Great and operated, with some reserves, until the ninth century. Louis Bréhier, "Notes sur l'histoire de l'enseignement superieur a Constantinople," *B* 3 (1927), 73-94. Also see M.J. Kyriakis, "The University: Origin and Early Phases in Constantinople," *B* 41 (1971), 161-82. Ioannes Anastasiou, ''Ἡ κατάστασις τῆς παιδείας εἰς τό Βυζάντιον,'' ΚΥΡΙΛΛΟΥ ΚΑΙ ΜΕΘΟΔΙΟΥ ΤΟΜΟΣ ΕΟΡΤΙΟΣ ΕΠΙ ΤΗ ΧΙΛΙΟΣΤΗ ΚΑΙ ΕΚΑΤΟΣΤΗ ΕΠΕΤΗΡΙΔΙ (Thessalonike, 1968), p. 54.

17. David Paphlagon (Niketas), ΤΟΥ ΕΝ ΑΓΙΟΙΣ ΗΜΩΝ ΙΓΝΑΤΙΟΥ ΑΡΧΙΕΠΙΣΚΟΠΟΥ ΚΩΝΣΤΑΝΤΙΝΟΥΠΟΛΕΩΣ: ΒΙΟΣ ΚΑΙ ΑΘΛΗΣΙΣ, *PG* 105:505 ff.

18. Val., Ep. 149.

19. Tatakis, ''Φώτιος,'' p. 89.

20. For the origin of the term "humanism" see *The Attic Nights of Aulus Gellius*, tr., J.C. Rolfe (London, 1927), pp. 45-47.

21. Karl Krumbacher, *Geschichte der byzantinischen Literatur (527-1453), (New York, 1958)*, 1:26.

22. Photios was called "Rabbi" despite his youth. Mansi, *Consiliarum generalium ecclesiae catholicae* (Rome, 1612), 16:412-414.

23. Val., Ep. 3; also *PG* 102:597.

24. They are incorporated in the *Amphilochia* (Athens, 1858), and in Aristarches, ΤΟΥ ΕΝ ΑΓΙΟΙΣ ΠΑΤΡΟΣ, 2:249-280.

25. Sophocles Economou, "About Roman Titles," *Amphilochia,* p. 186.

26. "Pertaining to Medicine," and "What is a Magnet?" Epistle of Photios "to the Most Saintly Philosopher," and "Anonymous Letter to Whoever Asks," *Amphilochia*, pp. 185, 215.

27. Val., Ep. 77, "To Leo the Philosopher."

28. Aristarches, ΤΟΥ ΕΝ ΑΓΙΟΙΣ ΠΑΤΡΟΣ, 1:96.

29. *PG* 103:69.

30. Cyril Mango, *The Homilies of Photios, Patriarch of Constantinople* (Cambridge, Mass., 1958), p. 294.

31. For an account of the life of Empress Theodora, see W. Regel, "Vita Sanctae Theodorae Imperatricis (893)," *Analecta Byzantino-Russica* 10 (1891), 1-44. Actually, Theodora was co-ruler with her oldest daughter Thekla and her son Michael. See Andreas Dikigoropoulos, "The Constantinopolitan Solidi of Theophilus," *DOP* 18 (1964), 353-61; also Warwick Worth, *Byzantine Coins of the British Museum* (London, 1908), p. 431, pl. 49. *In the Acta of the Forty-two Martyrs of Amorium*, ed. Vasiljevskij-Nitikin, the hierarchy is cited as follows: "The rulers of the Romans Michael, Theodora, and Thekla" (p. 52).

32. Theophanes Continuatus, *Chronographia*, 4:148. Theophanes is the only one who mentions Emmanuel as a member of the regency.

33. For the events of the first year of Theodora's regency, see Symeon Logothete, *Annales, PG* 109:708-13; Theophanes Continuatus, *Chronographia*, 4:148-51, and Genesios, p. 77. George Hamartolos, *Chronicon Breve, PG* 110:1029 ff.

34. On the strength of the iconoclastic party during this period, see Francis Dvornik, "The Patriarch Photios and Iconoclasm," *DOP* 7 (1953), 69-97; J. Gouillard, "Deux figures mal connues du second iconoclasme," *B* 31 (1961), 371-401; Mango, *The Homilies of Photios*, pp. 244-60.

35. A *synodicon* was read on the first Sunday of Great Lent. The oldest part of the *synodicon* deals with the final ruling of the question

of icons and in some ways compensates for the loss of the acts of the council of 843. *Synodicon for Orthodoxy Sunday*, ed., B. Uspenskii (Odessa, 1893), pp. 317-94, gives the text in Greek as well as in Bulgarian, Russian, and Serbian. See also R. Guilland, "Le Synodicon de l'Orthodoxie: édition et commentaire," *Travaux et Mémoires du Centre de Recherche d'Histoire et Civilization Byzantine*, 2 (1967), 1-316.

36. Theophanes Continuatus, *Chronographia*, 4:161; Ioannes Zonaras, *Epitome Historiarum*, ed. T. Buttner-Wobst, *CSHB* (1897), pp. 16 ff. George Hamartolos, *PG* 110:816. See also Peter Brown, "A Dark-Age Crisis: Aspects of the Iconoclastic Controversy," *EHR* 88 (1973), 1-34; *Vita Methodii, PG* 100:1244-61.

37. Theophanes Continuatus, *Chronographia*, 4:148.

38. Anastasios Bibliothekarios, *Prefatio octavae synodi (Consilium generalium)*, Mansi, 16:6.

39. Gouillard, "Deux figures mal connues," p. 380.

40. Francis Dvornik, *Les Légendes de Constantin et de Méthode vues de Byzance* (Hattiesburg, Miss., 1969), p. 45.

41. Theophanes Continuatus, *Chronographia*, 4:193, confirms that Methodios held the See of Constantinople for only four years. Also see A. A. Vasiliev, *Byzance et les Arabes; La Dynastie d'Amorium*, ed. H. Grégoire et al. (Brussels, 1935), p. 420. Upon Patriarch Methodios' death, Photios, who was still a layman, composed a poem praising the qualities of the departed Patriarch: "Here is the example of the high priest, the famous Methodios, who made his way to heaven." Aristarches, ΤΟΥ ΕΝ ΑΓΙΟΙΣ ΠΑΤΡΟΣ, 1:6.

42. George Hamartolos, *PG* 110:1040.

43. Niketas, *PG* 105:501.

44. "... qui scilicet viros exterioris sapientae repulisset," in Mansi, 16:6.

45. Niketas, *PG* 105:512.

46. Ibid.

47. Ibid.

48. Philip Jaffe, *Regesta pontificum romanorum* (Leipzig 1885-1888), 1, no. 2629; also *MGH*, Ep. 5, p. 589. A fragment of this letter

is in the collection *Britannica* in the British Museum, no. 8873, and belongs probably to the end of the eleventh century. Francis Dvornik, *Photian Schism* (Cambridge, 1970), p. 296.

49. Niketas, *PG* 105:489. Pseudo-Simeon, *Chronicon* (Bonn, 1838), p. 671. Stylianos of Neo-Caesarea, "Letter to Pope Stephen V," in Mansi, 16:232.

50. Joseph Genesios gives a very detailed picture of the plot of the murder and its execution, in *Regna*, ed. G. Lachmann (Bonn, 1834), pp. 88-89. Theophanes Continuatus, *Chronographia*, 4:171, gives a vivid picture of Theodora's grief.

51. First Thekla and her sister Anastasia were sent to the convent of Karianos, while Pulcheria and her mother Empress Theodora were sent to the monastery of Gastrion. Later, Thekla and Anastasia joined their mother and other sister and all took the veil. Simeon Logothetes (Continuator of George Hamartolos), *PG* 110:1048.

52. Ibid.

53. "It was all over town and came to the ears of the patriarch," writes Niketas, *PG* 105:224.

54. Ibid., col. 509.

55. Val. Ep. 2, p. 145.

56. Ibid., p. 136.

57. Patriarch Photios' letter "To Bardas, Magister, Patrician and Curopalates, " Val. Ep. 157, p. 492. Also in Hergenröther, 11:285. George Harmatolos writes that "Bardas appointed (as patriarch) Photios who was also the *protoasecretis* and a very erudite man," *PG* 110:1063. (Author's translation.)

58. Niketas, *PG* 105:235.

59. Pope Nicholas I expected six bishops to come from Constantinople to Rome to plead for Ignatios' cause (*MGH*, Ep. 6, p. 482).

60. Val. Epistles: 1, p. 133; 2, p. 143; 3, p. 146; 4, p. 165.

61. Val. Ep. 1, p. 133. (Author's translation.)

62. Ibid., Ep. 157, pp. 491-92.

63. Pope Nicholas' letter to Emperor Michael III and to Photios in *MGH*, Ep. 6, pp. 433-39. The pope states in his letter to the emperor

as one of the conditions the return to Roman jurisdiction of Illyricum, the patrimonies of Calabria and Sicily, and the right to consecrate the bishops of Syracuse.

64. A.A. Vasiliev, *The Russian Attack on Constantinople in 860* (Cambridge, Mass., 1946), pp. 188-228. Also C. DeBoor, "Der Angriff der Rhos auf Byzanz," *BZ* 4 (1895), 445-66.

65. Ibid., p. 64.

66. The exiled Patriarch Ignatios lived on one of these islands. Niketas, *PG* 105:516-17.

67. Greek text in Aristarches, ΤΟΥ ΕΝ ΑΓΙΟΙΣ ΠΑΤΡΟΣ ΗΜΩΝ ΦΩΤΙΟΥ, 2:5-27, 30-57; Basil Laourdas, ΦΩΤΙΟΥ ΠΑΤΡΙΑΡΧΟΥ ΚΩΝΣΤΑΝΤΙΝΟΥΠΟΛΕΩΣ ΟΜΙΛΙΑΙ (Thessalonike, 1970), pp. 29-39, 40-52; Photius, *De Rossorum incursione, homilia 1, Fragmenta historicorum graecorum,* ed. C. Muller (Paris, 1870), 5:162-67; Mango, *Homilies,* pp. 82-112.

68. The clothes of the Virgin had been discovered in a coffin at Blachernae in 619. J.B. Bury, *A History of the Eastern Roman Empire from the Fall of Irene to the Ascension of Basil I* (London, 1912), p. 95, n. 2.

69. Theophanes Continuatus, *Chronographia,* 4:196; Val., p. 178.

70. Constantine Porphyrogenitus, *De ceremoniis aulae byzantinae,* ed. J.J. Reiske, *CSHB* (Bonn, 1829), 7:3-807.

71. Dionysios Zakythinos, Η ΒΥΖΑΝΤΙΝΗ ΑΥΤΟΚΡΑΤΟΡΙΑ *(324-1071)* (Athens, 1969), p. 194.

72. Dvornik, *Les Legéndes,* p. 45 and 359.

73. *PG* 102:828; Val. Ep. 239; letter 42 of this study.

74. Robert Browning, *Byzantium and Bulgaria: A Comparative Study Across the Early Medieval Frontier* (Los Angeles, 1975), p. 54; Theophanes Continuatus, *Chronographia,* 4:165.

75. Genesios, *Regna,* pp. 85-86, writes that Empress Theodora answering the threats of Boris said: "It will be of no glory to you to defeat a woman; for if she defeats you, you will be ridiculed." (Author's translation.)

76. *Nicolai Papae I Epistolae et Decreta, PL* 119:875.

77. *The Vita Constantini*, Francis Dvornik, in his book *Les Legendes*, p. 374, says that they spent forty months in Moravia.

78. Regarding the new language in which Constantine wrote and taught in Moravia, the *Vita Constantini* reports that when Constantine went to Venice after Moravia he was questioned by the priests there as to how he dared write and teach the Scriptures in another language when "we know that only in three languages has God loaned us his books in Hebrew, Greek, and Latin." The response of Constantine among others was, "Does not the rain fall equally over everyone? Does not the sun light equally over the whole world? Are you not ashamed to recognize only three languages and leave the rest of the world in blindness and deafness? ... I had rather speak five words which people will understand than a thousand incomprehensible words," pp. 377-79.

79. *Annales regni Francorum*, ed. F. Kurze (Hannover, 1895), 4:11-753.

80. Ibid., p. 745.

81. Einhard, *The Life of Charlemagne*, ed. S. Painter (Ann Arbor, 1967), pp. 56-57.

82. Hamartolos' Continuator, *PG* 110:1048 states clearly that Emperor Michael III with Bardas attacked Bulgaria both from land and sea, while Bulgaria was suffering from a great famine, Also see F. Dvornik, *Les Slaves, Byzance et Rome au IXe siecle* (Paris, 1970), pp. 187.

83. *PG* 110:1048.

84. *PG* 102:665; Val. Ep. 6. See the forthcoming translation by Despina S. White and Joseph R. Berrigan, Jr., *The Patriarch and the Prince: The Letter of Patriarch Photios of Constantinople to Boris Khan of Bulgaria.*

85. *MGH* Ep. 7, p. 154, from Pope John VIII to Emperor Michael III.

86. *Liber pontificalis*, ed. Louis Duchnese (Paris, 1886-1892), 2:164.

87. Anastasios Bibliothecarios, *Ex acto consilii Constantinopolitano*, 4; Mansi, 16:2.

88. *Responsa Nicholai ad consulta Bulgarorum, PL* 119:978-1016.

89. H. Grégoire, "Etudes sur le IXe siecle," *B* 8 (1933), 524 ff. George Hamartolos *PG* 110:1060-61. "Basil killed Bardas while

Michael was watching."

90. *Nicene and Post-Nicene Fathers*, ed. Philip Schaff (Buffalo, 1886-1900), 16:163.

91. Ibid., pp. 231, 265.

92. Richard Haugh, *Photius and the Carolingians* (Belmont, Mass., 1975), pp. 28-29.

93. Paulinus of Aquileia, *Monumenta germaniae historica* 2 (Berlin, 1826), 287.

94. Leo III earlier had sent a letter to all the 'Churches of the East' in which he stated his belief in the procession of the Holy Spirit from both the "Father and the Son." *PL* 102:1031-32. But at the meeting between the Franks and Pope Leo III, he not only forbade them the addition of the *filioque* to the creed but also the singing of the creed, *PL* 102:971-76. A translation in English of the dialogue between the envoys and the pope in Haugh, *Photios and the Carolingians*, pp. 81-88.

95. *MGH*, Ep. 6, p. 605.

96. John Meyendorff, *Byzantine Theology* (New York, 1974), pp. 170-71.

97. *PG* 26:605a.

98. Val. Ep. 3.

99. The main anti-Photian sources are: *Liber pontificalis*, ed. L. Duchesne, 16 (Paris, 1886-1892): 178 ff. Anastasios Bibliothekarios, in *Mansi* 16:7, 8, 9; Metrophanes of Smyrna, in *Mansi* 16:143-220; Niketas, *PG* 105:537 ff; The Roman Synod of Adrian II, in *Mansi*, 16:125-28; Hergenröther, *Photius*, 1:649 ff.

100. Cyril Mango, "The Liquidation of Iconoclasm and the Patriarch Photios," *Iconoclasm* 1 (March, 1975):133-40, reexamines the motives of Patriarch Photios on the subject of iconoclasm.

101. Val. Ep. 5.

102. *PG* 102:262-91.

103. George Hamartolos gives details of the legend and truth about the background of Basil in *PG* 110:1041-61; on the coronation of Basil he writes "and the Patriarch [Photios] took the crown from the head of the King [Michael] and set it on the head of Basil," col. 1061; N.

Adontz, "L'Age et l'origine de Basil Ier," B 9 (1934); 259-60. Theophanes Continuatus writes that Basil was from Armenia, of the clan of the Arsakians; 4:212. The murder scene is described in detail by Hamartolos, *PG* 110:1069.

104. Hamartolos, *PG* 110:1076.

105. Anastasios Bibliothekarios states that "Basilius Photio sacro ministerio post depositionem irregulariter abutenti throno Constantinopolitano cedere persuader," Mansi, 16:6.

106. Niketas, *PG* 105:329-30.

107. According to Aristarches, ΛΟΓΟΙ ΚΑΙ ΟΜΙΛΙΑΙ, Euthymios left Constantinople in November 867 and arrived in Rome in the middle of the winter, in February 868; also in *Les Slaves, Byzance et Rome au IXe siecle*, p. 174.

108. The delegates met with unpredictable bad weather at sea and Peter drowned before reaching Italy. Mansi, 16:7; Niketas, *PG* 105:544.

109. Mansi, 16:96, 97.

110. *Liber pontificalis*, 2:178, describes in detail what happened at the session.

111. Mansi, 16:122-31, 372-80.

112. *Liber pontificalis*, 2:179.

113. Niketas, *PG* 105:331.

114. Mansi, 16:45.

115. Val. Ep. 218, pp. 530-34. See Letter 17 of this study.

116. *Liber pontificalis*, 2:182-84. George Hamartolos mentions Stephen only as pupil of Photios, not Leo, *PG* 110:1089.

117. Hamartolos, *PG* 110:1080.

118. Theophanes Continuatus, *Chronographia*, 4:276-77; Paul Lemerle, *Le Premier Humanisme byzantin* (Paris, 1971), p. 203, believes that Photios never taught at the university or had anything to do with the reorganization of the patriarchal academy.

119. Niketas, *PG* 105; George Hamartolos, *PG* 110:1081.

120. Epistle of Pope John VIII to Emperor Basil I (Mansi, 15:480-85, and 488-500); also, epistle to Photios (col. 505-509); V. Grumel,

"La Liquidation de la querelle photienne," *EO* 33 (1934), 154-88.

121. *Excerpta historica issu imperatori Constantini Porphyrogeniti*, ed. C. DeBoor (Berlin, 1903-1906), p. 5. George Hamartolos, *PG* 110: 1087.

122. Hamartolos, *PG* 110:1089.

123. *Vita Euthymii*, ed. C. DeBoor (Berlin, 1888), p. 5; also George Harmatolos, *PG* 110:1089.

124. A. Vogt and I. Hausherr, "L'Oraison funèbre de Basil Ier par son fils Leon le Sage," *Orientalia Christiana* 26 (1932), 502-13.

125. Papadopoulos-Kerameus, "Φώτιος," p. 657. The Greek Orthodox Church celebrates the memory of Saint Photios on February 6. A special acolouthia also exists under the title "'Ιερά ἀκολουθία τοῦ ἐν Ἀγίοις Πατρός ἡμῶν καί ' Ισαποστόλου Φωτίου Πατριάρχου Κωνσταντινουπόλεως τοῦ Ὁμολογητοῦ. Συνερανισθεῖσα ἐξ ἀρχαιοτέρων τῆς ἐκκλησίας ὕμνων καί συνταχθεῖσα ὑπό Κωνσταντίνου Μητροπολίτου Σταυρουπόλεως τοῦ Τυπάλδου," ed. John Karmires (Athens, 1951). The troparion (hymn) dedicated to Saint Photios reads: "Φώτιος ὁ Ἰσαπόστολος καί μέγιστος ἐν Πατράσι καί Ἱεράρχης, ὁ τῆς εὐσεβοῦς Πίστεως ἀτρόμητος ὁμολογητής καί τῆς ὀρθοδοξούσης οἰκουμένης ἀείξεως Πατριάρχης."

CHAPTER TWO

PHOTIOS' SCHOLARLY CONTRIBUTIONS

Photios' scholarly reputation is based primarily on his *Bibliotheca*, which is a collection of criticisms and extracts from 280 works of various authors from antiquity to his time.[1]

There are several speculations about when Photios wrote the *Bibliotheca*. Photios probably finished it circa 855.[2] Professor Edgar Martini has written a detailed history of it, trying to trace its fate from the time it left the author's hands to the end of the fifteenth century, when it became the common property of European humanists.[3] After long research Martini found that there are only two primary manuscripts of the *Bibliotheca*. Both were among the 482 Greek codices Cardinal Bessarion presented to the Venetian Republic in 1468 and both are now in the Bibliotheca Marciana in Venice. They are known as Codex A and Codex M. Codex A, which is the older, begins with the heading in majuscule: Φωτίου 'Αρχιεπισκόπου Κωνσταντινουπόλεως καί οἰκουμενικοῦ πατριάρχου, followed by a letter to Tarasios. The text itself has the heading: 'Απογραφή καί συναρίθμησις τῶν ἀνεγνωσμένων ἡμῖν βιβλίων, ὧν εἰς κεφαλαιώδη διάγνωσιν ὁ ἀγαπημένος ἡμῶν ἀδελφός ἐξητήσατο, ἔστι δέ ταῦτα εἴκοσι δεόντων ἐφ'ἑνί τριακόσια.[4] According to this original title page the number of books reviewed by Photios is 279. The titles *Myriobiblon* or *Bibliotheca*, the other names by which this work is known, are of a later date.

The next traces of the *Bibliotheca* are more extensive. Professor Stavros Kugeas has found two manuscripts with notes by Photios' pupil and friend, Arethas of Caesarea (850-935), written for him by the scribe Baanes circa 912.[5] This is the Codex M, which presumably was copied from a lost codex belonging to Arethas. Next, in the *Sylloge de historia animalum* written by Emperor Constantine VII Porphyrogenetos in the tenth century, is an excerpt on Agatharchides[6] from Photios' *Bibliotheca*. A few more traces of Photios' *Bibliotheca* appeared through the year 1261, when the Greeks recovered Constantinople from the Venetians. From this time on, traces of the *Bibliotheca* are frequent, but most of them derive from one or the other of the two old copies of Codex A and Codex M. By 1261 Codex M was in Thessalonike, but the location of Codex A was not known. Diller thinks it was in Constantinople, and that a Codex B was copied from A at the beginning of this period and remained also in Constantinople. Given this location, according to Diller, the proliferation of traces in the fourteenth century probably would be more from A than from M.[7] In the fifteenth century both A and M made their way to Italy, and finally in 1468, as mentioned before, came into the possession of Cardinal Bessarion.

Photios dedicated the *Bibliotheca* to his "dear brother, Tarasios" with a letter as preface to the work. He mentions that he was able to complete the work with the help of a secretary — γραφεύς — and it could serve as a consolation — παραμύθιον — and souvenir — ἐνθύμιον — during their separation while he was serving as ambassador to the Assyrians.[8] Professor Hélène Ahrweiler notes that Photios addresses his brother only as "dear brother," without his title of patrician, which indicates that Tarasios was still quite young and had not yet acquired his high position.[9] Photios also must have been very young, because he was not the principal dignitary during this mission. He was not yet protoasecretis, but only one member of this office.[10]

The *Bibliotheca* was the only work of this kind Byzantium produced in the literary field. Of the 279 works reviewed in the *Bibliotheca* 158 are of a religious nature. Among them are many histories of the Church (at least thirteen); many more works on the New Testament than the Old, but it does include works on the Old Testament such as Josephus' *Jewish Antiquities* and *The Jewish War*. Works by the evangelists and works of the Fathers of the Church are numerous. Most of the works are instructional; the kind that one would expect to be included in a theological seminary library.

The most contemporary works included are the *Abridged History* by the Patriarch of Constantinople, Nikephoros (810-815), covering events from 602-769, and a work by Sergios the Confessor chronicling the reign of Michael II (820-829), which can be considered as contemporary history. Unfortunately, this work has been lost and it is known only through Photios' analysis. [11]

The next largest group is composed of 37 historical works, followed by numerous romances of an adventurous nature. There are 16 philosophical discourses, of which 3 are on Jewish philosophy, 5 books on geography, 6 works on Western priests and popes, 6 on medicine, 3 works by women, several works on mythology and several on mathematics. Absent are the works of the major pagan philosophers, Plato and Aristotle, as well as of Homer and other poets, and the great tragedians. We know from the curriculum of the Byzantine schools that the ancient Greek authors were studied in the secular institutions of higher learning. [12]

The first work to be reviewed in the *Bibliotheca* is by a priest named Theodoros, who lived in the sixth century of our era. [13] The work examines the authenticity of the book of Saint Dionysios the Areopagite and, unfortunately, has been lost. The books reviewed next include those by Christian writers from the early Christian era. Origen is reviewed early in the *Bibliotheca*. Photios, however, is not fond of the Alexandrine scholar. In his words:

> In this book, Origen blasphemes greatly in declaring that the Son was created by the Father, the Holy Spirit by the Son, and while the Father rules over all of creation, the Son only over the logical beings

and the Holy Spirit only over those who are saved... ,And he wrote many more absurdities and many impieties. [14]

The acts of the first synod were written by Gelasios, who did not give a "documentary account," according to Photios. "The style also is common and base, but [there is] a detailed account of the events." [15] There is no account of the second synod, but Photios reviews in succession books on the third, fourth, fifth, sixth, and seventh synods. [16] Photios was a great admirer of the Cappadocians: he calls Saint Basil's *Canonical Letters* models of "epistolary style." [17] Other writings by Basil included in the *Bibliotheca* are: *On the Hexaemeron, Moral Discourses, The Letters,* and his *Rules on Asceticism.* [18] In reviewing the *Hexaemeron*, Photios noted that in order and clarity of thought Basil cannot be surpassed in stating that: "In the art of discourse and eloquence he does not need even the teaching of Plato or Demosthenes" [19]

Photios was particularly interested in John Chrysostom, whose many works he reviews. He respected the precision of his style and admitted that he was a great admirer of this "thrice blessed man." [20] Many works of church history by authors such as Eusebios, Sozomenos, Theodoretos, Socrates, Evagrios, and other Christian historians whose works have been lost, such as John of Aegea, Basilios of Cilicia, and Philostorgios, are reviewed in the *Bibliotheca.* [21] His favorite church historian was Theodoretos because of his sober, clear, and elevated style, which Photios finds "suitable for historical writings." [22]

The writings that are examined next are historical works, which at times are grouped together in a sequence. The oldest historian reviewed is Herodotos. His *History* is in nine books, the same as the number of Muses, for which the books were named, according to Photios. [23] Photios calls Herodotos' style of writing "a model of Ionic dialect." He continues: "He uses fables and makes digressions which, however, radiate the sweetness of his thought." Next chronologically comes the work of Ctesias, the doctor at the court of Artaxerxes around

405 to 397 B.C. who wrote a *History of the Persians* in twenty-three books. Photios reviews all of the books in great detail. He refers to certain peculiar things Ctesias wrote about
India such as: "the palm trees in India and their fruits are
twice as big as the ones in Babylon"; there is "a river whose
source is a rock, and, instead of water, honey flows." He
mentions also that the Indians do not eat pork; that they live
to be at least 120 years of age, and some reach 200; that they
never have headaches, ulcers, or pains in the eyes or teeth.[24]
Photios does not believe all the stories of Ctesias, but evi-
dently he was fascinated by them. Missing among the great
historians are Thucydides and Polybios; writers such as Hippocrates and Pausanias are left out. Of the historians of the
Hellenistic period, only Agatharchides is mentioned.[25] Photios
reviews his two books on Asia and forty-nine books on Europe;
he also reviews the five books of *On the Erythrean Sea.*

The Roman historians most read and criticized are those of
the Imperial period. He read all forty books of Diodorus Sicu-
lus, a contemporary of Augustus. Photios admires his style,
which is "clear without any trimmings, exactly what is suited
for history." He uses "neither old Attic nor the new spoken
language but something in between the two. He avoids mentioning heroes and gods of the ancient Greeks such as are
mentioned by the poets."[26] Photios reviews all of the twenty
books of the *Antiquities of Rome* of Dionysios of Halicarnas-
sos, thus producing an excellent study of literary criticism.[27]
Of more recent histories, he mentions a Byzantine history by
Melchos the Sophist, which ended with the year 480. This is
followed by the twenty-two books of the *History of Olym-
piodoros*, covering the years from 407-491.[28] Regarding the
later pagans, Photios read and criticized Plutarch's *Lives.*[29]
Included in his historical studies are the eighty books of Dio
Cassius' history of Rome, written in the third century.[30] Of
the eighty books, today only books 37-60 survive almost in
their entirety, and we are indebted to John Xiphilinos for a
review of Books 36-80. Constantine Porphyrogenetos and

Zonaras wrote extracts of Books 1-20.

The extensive analysis of the historical works shows Photios' well-developed sense of history. As a Christian, however, he applies the classical concepts of history to Christian historiography.[31]

In addition to history, the famous rhetors of ancient times are studied thoroughly. Photios mentions in detail the works of Andocides, Antiphon, Isocrates, Lysias, Demosthenes, Aeschines, Dinarchos, and Lycurgos, as well as the *Declamations* of Emperor Hadrian, which are now lost.[32] Among more recent rhetors he examines the works of Libanios, his pupil Aphthonios, Themistios, and Eusebios, who was martyred under Gallus and whose works are lost.[33]

Photios does not mention in the *Bibliotheca* works of the well-known philosophers, although he is well acquainted with their thought as it is apparent in his other writings. It seems that early in the Christian era Aristotelianism won over Platonism as a whole. Alexandria especially, until it was captured by the Arabs in 642, was a center of philosophical studies, and many commentaries on Aristotle were published there. Platonism nevertheless had its followers, which is evident in the works of Origen and Saint Clement. Works of Neoplatonists are also included in the *Bibliotheca*. Photios discusses at length *The Life of the Philosopher Isidoros* by Damascios, the last great teacher of Neoplatonism in Athens.[34]

Beginning in the sixth century Neoplatonism took hold of Byzantine mysticism through the works of Dionysios the Areopagite; and after the seventh century, as a result of the interpretations and writings of the great theologian Maximos the Confessor, the work of Dionysios was made easily accessible to Byzantine theologians. From the seventh century, however, until the eleventh, when Michael of Ephesos brought back philosophical speculation, the commentaries on the work of Aristotle ceased. It is not clear whether during these centuries Platonism was studied or the study of philosophy was abandoned. The philosophers and teachers reviewed by Photios are Libanios, Epiphanios, Lucian, Isocrates, and an anonymous Arab.[35]

Books on medicine also are reviewed. Many chapters of the *Bibliotheca* are dedicated to the study of maladies, since the art of medicine was quite advanced in Constantinople. Soon after Constantinople became New Rome, it surpassed even the City of Alexandria in the importance of its school of medicine. Gregory of Tours names a Frankish priest, Reovalis, who studied medicine in Constantinople. Another scholar, the famous Agapios, moved from Alexandria to Constantinople, "not to explain the Aristotelian or Platonic philosophy, but to explain medicine."[36] In the *Bibliotheca* Photios reviews the surgical methods of Galen, of the second century A.D.[37] Also, he reviews the four works of Oribasios, the personal physician of Julian the Apostate, on the subject of medicine.[38] "The first book of this author," according to Photios, "is an abridged edition of the writings of Galen; it is dedicated to Julian, who became an apostate from our faith," Photios continues in quoting the dedication. Oribasios, in the preamble, promises Julian that he will include in his writings only the things necessary to know about medicine. Then he goes on to say that the work will be done in so many books, but Photios in his review leaves out the number, and the final sentence is not finished. (In many other instances in the *Bibliotheca* Photios leaves his final sentence unfinished.) The second work by Oribasios, which contains seventy books on the subject of medicine, treats mainly of the quality of foods.[39] Also addressed to Julian, this study is very interesting to Photios and useful especially for its clear discussion of many topics and its medical terms.[40] The next work, again by Oribasios, is addressed to his son, Eustathios. This is a kind of first-aid instruction which excludes surgery. Its nine books contain advice on how to treat imaginary maladies with corporal exercises, and how to prepare certain pharmaceutical potions. Oribasios also includes certain recommendations to expectant mothers about their diet and also diets for older people.[41] The ninth book refers to the maladies of the chest, viscera, and discusses gout, arthritis, and sciatica.[42] In the next codex, Photios continues to review the works of Oribasios, whose fourth book, according to him, is dedicated to Eunapios and names many easy remedies. Photios describes the style of this treatise as "difficult and superfluous."[43] The next codex, under the title *The Man*, is the work of Theon, the chief doctor of Alexandria. Theon is known to us only from Photios' reference in the *Bibliotheca*. This work is of the same nature and serves the same purpose as the works of Oribasios, according to Photios.[44]

The last in the sequence is also a work on medicine in six books written by Aetios, and Photios writes a rather lengthy review of it. He finds the contents very useful because Aetios discusses in detail certain things pertaining to women, especially their diseases, and also venereal diseases.[45]

From the works on medicine Photios turns to a review of the long treatise of a monk of the sixth century named Job. It is a treatise on the Incarnation in nine books and forty-five chapters.[46] The author is already known to Photios by his other writings on the Holy Scriptures, and especially by a treatise against Severos which is lost to us. According to Photios, Job does not lack in vigor or piety even though his works are somewhat superficial. On the subject of agriculture, he reviews *A Collection on the Precepts of Agriculture,* written by Vindanios Anatolios from Beirut. This is also a lost work.[47]

The Hellenistic period is covered particularly well by references to books now lost. Photios gives an account of the *Narrations* by Conon, a work on Greek gods and heroes which was dedicated to King Archelaos Philopatris of Cappadocia.[48] In the *Bibliotheca* it is evident that the Byzantines studied Hellenistic literature and were well acquainted with it, especially the works of Lucian of Samosata of the second century of our era. Lucian, who was a Syrian, wrote in Greek and be-

came a master of Attic prose style. Though the great bulk of
Lucian's writings consisted of Platonic dialogues, he also
wrote a number of satires. With *The True History* and *Lucius;
or, The Ass*, he established a new genre of writing. His *True
History* is a parody of all travelers' tales from Odysseus to
Antonios Diogenes in *The Wonderful Things Beyond Thule*.
Though the works of Antonios Diogenes, Ctesias, and Iamblichos are lost, through Photios we learn that the romance of
Antonios Diogenes, *The Wonderful Things Beyond Thule*,
was the chief source of Lucian's *True History*. *Lucius, or,
The Ass*, of which we have only a fragment, is a parody of a
romance motivated by religion. Lucian's works provide
information about second-century society in a very realistic,
witty and ironic style.[49] Photios seemed to enjoy reviewing
romances and adventure stories; most of his comments are
extensive and agreeable. He read the *Aethiopica* of Heliodoros.[50] The study of the *Aethiopica*, which is the longest
and best constructed of the Greek novels extant, shows how
deeply the novel is infused with the religious and philosophical ideas of its author. According to Photios, this is the love
story of Chariclea and Theagenes. Chariclea was a priestess of
the temple in Athens and Theagenes was an athlete. They fell
in love and ran away to the island of Zakynthos. They were
pursued and after many adventures both lovers are forgiven
and finally marry. Heliodoros, the author, who was from
Emesa in Syria, later became a bishop.[51] As Lucian's work
reflects second-century life, so does Heliodoros' work reflect
in general the life and style of the third century. It describes
the splendor of the East and the power of the Oriental rulers
over the Greeks. The court of the great King of Persia, with
its absolutism and despotic powers, becomes the model for
other smaller courts. Eunuchs and other courtiers are at this
time the real power. War cry is in the air. Whole cities and
tribes revolt. Women as well as merchants and priests travel
widely. Women seem free to move about and to participate
in court and religious ceremonies. The times are also charac-

terized by a search for the new and the unknown, by scientific interest, as well as an interest in the arts, as there are many detailed descriptions of robes, jewels and other items.

The next romance, about the adventures of Leucippe and Clitophon, by Achilles from Alexandria, Photios finds daring and indecent.[52] He indicates marked similarities between it and the story of Chariclea and Theagenes. An epigram in the *Palatine Anthology*, attributed to Photios or to Leo the Philosopher, gives us a short review of the story:

> The story of Clitophon reveals to the eyes, as it were not a bitter love but a virtuous life. The very virtuous life of Leucippe puts all in ecstasy for the story tells how she was beaten and shorn of her hair and clothed pitiably, and — the greatest point — having died three times she endured to the end. And if you wish to be virtuous, friend, do not consider the side issues of the plot, for it joins in marriage those who love sanely.[53]

Next to be reviewed is a story by Iamblichos, and in comparing the three Photios finds Heliodoros the least indecent and ranks Iamblichos next and Achilles last. He finds the style of Iamblichos fluent and easy to follow; a style which he could use "in his writings of a more serious nature."[54] It is a love story about the beautiful Sinonis' refusal to marry the king because she is in love with Rhodanes. After many adventures there is a happy ending. Rhodanes becomes King of Babylon and is reunited with Sinonis. The story is written in sixteen books and Photios' review is long and detailed.

The story by Antonios Diogenes, *The Wonderful Things Beyond Thule*, whose twenty-five books have been lost, survives in Photios' lengthy review of the work.[55] In this story the hero, Dinas, accompanied by his son, disappears in the north end of the Caspian Sea on an island named Thule. Photios compares this story to others such as those of Lucian, Iamblichos, Achilles, and Damascios.[56] Photios gives only a short review of Damascios' writings, stating that his four books describe impossible, fantastic, incestuous, and impious acts. He finds Damascios' style concise and elegant. Stories of magic are not omitted from the *Bibliotheca*; the story by Theodoros on *Persian Magic* is known to us only through Photios' summary.[57]

Photios' extensive analysis of Hellenistic romances sheds light on this somewhat obscure period. In this respect he stands as a kind of bridge between the knowledge we have of Hellenistic romances from the works of Chariton of the second century A.D. to the eleventh century when romances reappear.[58] He is also a link with the tenth century's popular *Tragoudia*, or songs which produced in the eleventh century the famous romance of Digenes Akritas.[59]

The *Bibliotheca* also contains works of Western church writers. Photios reviews the works of Clement of Rome in two books, one under the title *Commandments of the Apostles by Clement*, and the other dedicated in the form of a letter to James, brother of Christ. In these two books the acts of the Apostles are told and enumerated; furthermore, the story of the recognition of Clement by his father and brothers, which in some copies is entitled *The Recognition of Clement of Rome*, is included. Concerning Clement, Photios writes: "According to some, Clement was the second pope of Rome after Peter, and according to others he was the fourth, as Linos and Anakletes were popes between Peter and Clement. He died in the third year of the reign of Trajan."[60]

Another work Photios read was by Irenaios, bishop of Lyons.[61] This was in five books under the title, *A Critique and Refutation of Faulty Knowledge*. Photios reports that it was said that Irenaios was a student of Polycarp, bishop of Smyrna and priest of Photinos before becoming bishop of Lyons. At that time the pope in Rome was Victor, to whom Irenaios addressed a number of reprimands and warnings regarding the expulsion of certain persons from the church because they had different customs in celebrating Easter.

The next author was Cassianos, whose small book contains two works. Photios likes his style and finds the books "useful to those who have chosen to become monks."[62] In this group is also included an extract from an anonymous biography of Pope Gregory the Great.[63]

Photios reviews lexica, or dictionaries, catalogued in sequence, in the *Bibliotheca.*[64] The lexicon of Helladios, alphabetically arranged, is according to Photios the best of its kind that he knows.[65] He likes the lexicon of Pollion on poetical terms.[66] Several other lexica are on the works of Plato and Attic words; only one concerns words of foreign extraction.[67]

Photios wrote and produced his own lexicon[68] of some seven to eight thousand words. According to Photios himself, he did not collect all the words in all their different meanings, which would have been an impossible task, but only the most current and most frequently employed. Many now archaic Attic words were thus preserved. He also collected a wealth of archaeological data and refers to historians, grammarians, and lexicographers whose works have been lost today. Thus, he forged an important link in the long chain of Greek lexicographers and gives testimony of his own literary and humanistic tastes as well as those of Byzantium in the ninth century.

Only a fragment of the *Lexicon* had been found until recently, when Professor Linos Politis of Thessalonike discovered a new manuscript in the monastery of Zagora, which dates back to the thirteenth century and contains the whole of the *Lexicon*. The study of this manuscript, when completed, will increase our knowledge of the number of classical and Hellenistic writers known in the time of Photios whose works no longer exist.

Thus, just as the *Lexicon* deserves to be placed among the great works of lexicography, the *Bibliotheca* deserves to be put in a special place in the great stylistic tradition of rhetoric. The influence of the terminology of the great critics of the past, such as Hermogenes, Dionysios of Halikarnassos, and Demetrios, can be seen clearly in Photios. But I agree with

Professor Kustas that Photios recaptured in his critical analysis that aesthetic appreciation of literature which had been stifled by the dry air of rhetorical excess and is in little evidence after the last of the great critics of antiquity, Cassius Longinus. [69]

Demosthenes and not Isocrates was considered the true teacher of the so-called Atticistic movement. The works of Hermogenes of Tarsos in the time of Hadrian should be studied, because he gives a clear idea and final definition of the ideas of prose literature as explained by Demothenes, whose definitions and categories, commented upon by so many after him, were intimately known and widely used by a good number of Byzantine men of letters, among them Photios.

While Photios was in exile, he wrote the *Amphilochia,* which he dedicated to his pupil Amphilochios, Archbishop of Kythera; it contains 300 chapters, in which he answers questions on dogma, ecclesiastical policies as well as questions pertaining to philosophical concepts. It is believed that he composed this work between the years 867-869. [70]

Photios wrote two polemical works, one of which is against the heresy of the Manichaeans [71] and the other the treatise upholding the procession of the Holy Spirit from the Father alone. [72]

A study of the *Bibliotheca* and of his other writings reveal how clearly the heritage of the ancient world was made useful to the Christians, and this without creating any disturbances in the Byzantine mind. On the contrary, we see in studying this period that the ninth-century Byzantines had achieved a well-balanced attitude in the study of the classical and Hellenistic inheritance and were adjusting it to their Christian environment. In that respect the Byzantines anticipated the Renaissance of the fifteenth century in the West, and Photios could very well be called the first Christian humanist. For Photios, with all his love and knowledge of the classics, was basically a Christian and used the Hellenic and

Hellenistic inheritance for the understanding of Christian ideas. In one letter he scolds the philosopher Leo for having criticized certain grammatical errors in the Bible and having called them barbaric.[73] Photios seemed aware of the danger into which an unbalanced estimate of the classical literary revival could lead some people. In his ninth homily, on the occasion of the Nativity of the Virgin, he denounces the absurdity of Greek mythology. He criticized those who were skeptical about Mary being born to a woman as old as St. Anna, but who at the same time gave credence to the absurdities in Greek mythology.[74]

Photios studied the Old and New Testaments and wrote extensively on the Gospels. Also his letters show ample evidence of his knowledge of the Bible. His commentary on the Gospel of Matthew has over one-hundred scholia by the patriarch.[75] His study of the letters of Saint Paul, his favorite apostle, and his commentaries on his work are quite extensive.[76]

Of the numerous sermons that were delivered by the patriarch from the ambon of Hagia Sophia or of Hagia Eirene on special occasions, only a few have survived today: three on Great Friday (1, 6, 14), two on Great Saturday (11, 17), two when the Rhos attacked Constantinople (3, 4), two on the Annunciation of the Virgin Mary (5, 7), one on her Nativity (9). Seven are on the question of icons, an issue which seemed to be still very much alive in the second part of the ninth century. Celebrating the Sunday of Orthodoxy, Photios delivered homilies praising Emperors Michael and Basil (10, 17, 18), one on the consecration of a new church (10), and two on heresies (15, 16). They were often delivered in the presence of the emperor and the imperial family.

The letters of Patriarch Photios, a translation and discussion of which constitute the main thrust of the present study, offer us perhaps the best opportunity to know the man and his times. The present translation of his letters should enhance other works already in process or completed on Photios and should provide scholars with a tool to aid in research on Photios and the period in which he lived.

CHAPTER TWO

1. The bibliography for Photios' *Bibliotheca* includes Hergenröther, *Photius*, vol. 3; J.H. Freese, *The Library of Photius*, vol. 1 (London, 1920); K. Ziegler, "Photius," *RE* 20 (1941): pp. 667-737; R. Henry, *La Bibliothèque de Photius* (Collection byzantine G. Budé), vols. 1-6 (Paris, 1959-1969), up to Codex 145. The only complete work is by I. Bekker, *Photii Bibliotheca* (Berlin, 1824-1825), 2 vols. This edition is reproduced in *PG* 103 and 104:9-356.

2. The date of the composition of the *Bibliotheca* is set by some Byzantinists from as early as 837 to as late as 878. Hélène Ahrweiler, "Sur la carrière de Photius avant son patriarcat," *BZ* 58:348ff., sets the date in 837. Warren Tredgold, "Photius on the Transmission of Texts" (Bibliotheca, Codex 187), *Greek Roman and Byzantine Studies,* 19 (Summer 1978):75, sets the date as between 844 and no later than 855.

3. Edgar Martini, *Textgeschichte der Bibliotheke des Patriarchen Photios von Konstantinopel*, 1st part; *Die Handschriften, Ausgaben und Unbertragungen* (Leipzig, 1911).

4. Audrey Diller, "Photios' Bibliotheca in Byzantine Literature," *DOP* XVI (1962), 289.

5. Stavros G. Kugeas, Ο ΚΑΙΣΑΡΙΑΣ ΑΡΕΘΑΣ ΚΑΙ ΤΟ ΕΡΓΟΝ ΑΥΤΟΥ (Athens, 1913).

6. *Excerptorum Constantini de nature animalum*, ed. Peter Lambros, vol. 1 (Leipzig, 1885), pp. 44-52.

7. Diller, p. 392.

8. *PG* 104:356.

9. Ahrweiler, "Sur la carriere," p. 53.

10. Ibid.

11. Henry, *Bibliothèque*, codex 67. Mango believes that Sergios was the father of Patriarch Photios, "The Liquidation of Iconoclasm," pp. 136-37.

12. Friedrich Fuchs, "Die Ekumenische Akademie von Konstantinopel in frühen Mittelalter," *Bayerische Blaetter für des gymnasialschulwesen* 49 (1923):177-92.

13. The author probably lived in the sixth century; see W. Ensslin, "Theodoros," *Philologische Woche*, 2nd ser., 5 (1934):1916.

14. Codex 8 (the numbered "codex" refers to the volume number of the *Bibliotheca*).

15. Codex 15.

16. Photios' extensive knowledge of church history is evident among other of his works in the long letter to Boris-Michael, the archon of Bulgaria. There, for the benefit of the neophyte Boris, the patriarch wrote a detailed account of the history of the seven ecumenical synods (Val. pp. 202-16).

17. Codex 143.

18. Codices 141, 144.

19. Codex 141.

20. Codex 6.

21. Codices 27, 31, 40, 41, 43, 46, 56, 203, 205, 273.

22. Codex 56.

23. Codex 60.

24. Codex 72.

25. Codex 213.

26. Codex 244.

27. Codex 83.

28. Codices 78-80.

29. Codex 245.

30. Codex 71.

31. In his doctoral thesis, "Photios' Idea of History" (Harvard Uni-

versity), Professor G. Kustas presents a good interpretive portrait of Photios; cf. also F. Dvornik, "Patriarch Photios, Scholar and Statesman," *Classical Folia*, 18 (1959), 2.

32. Codices 61, 100, 159, 259, 268.

33. Codices 74, 90. A good study is by G. Kustas, "Function and Evolution of Byzantine Rhetoric," *Viator* 1 (1970):55-73; also his "Studies in Byzantine Rhetoric," *Analekta Vlatadon* 17 (Thessalonike, 1973):45-59.

34. Codices 171, 242.

35. Codices 159-160.

36. Friedrich Fuchs, *Die Höheren Schulen von Konstantinopel im Mittelalter* (Leipzig-Berlin, 1926), p. 5.

37. Codex 40.

38. Codices 169 and 216.

39. On Oribasios, see H.O. Schroder, "Oribasius," *RE* (Stuttgart, 1940), 8:797-812.

40. Codex 217.

41. Ibid., p. 135. (The pages are quoted from Henry's edition.)

42. Ibid., p. 136.

43. Ibid., p. 138.

44. Codex 220.

45. Codex 221.

46. Codex 222.

47. Codex 163.

48. Codex 213.

49. Codex 128. On the Hellenistic influence there is a good study by Romily J.H. Jenkins, "The Hellenistic Origins of Byzantine Literature," *DOP*, 17 (1963):40-52.

50. Codex 73.

51. Socrates, *Ecclesiastical History from ca. 379-ca. 440 A.D.*, tr. E. Walford (Grand Rapids, Mich., 1952), pp. 5-22.

52. Codex 87.

53. *Palatine anthologie*, ed. F. Jacobs (Heidelberg, 1794-1817), 9: 203.

54. Codices 11, 34, 94.

55. Codex 127.

56. Codices 49, 73, 87, 94, 128, 129.

57. Codices 81, 112, 113.

58. K. Krumbacher, *Geschichte der byzantinische literatur* (New York, 1970), pp. 420-21.

59. H. Grégoire, "Digenes Akritas," *B* 4 (1929):45-90.

60. Codices 112, 113.

61. Codex 120.

62. Codex 93.

63. Codex 252.

64. Codices 145-157.

65. Codex 145.

66. Codex 146.

67. Codices 151-157.

68. The title of this work is ΦΩΤΙΟΥ ΤΟΥ ΠΑΤΡΙΑΡΧΟΥ ΚΩΝ-ΣΤΑΝΤΙΝΟΥΠΟΛΕΩΣ ΛΕΞΕΩΝ ΣΥΝΑΓΩΓΗ, ΑΙ ΜΑΛΛΟΝ ΤΩΝ ΑΛΛΩΝ ΡΗΤΟΡΣΙ ΚΑΙ ΛΟΓΟΓΡΑΦΟΥΣ ΑΝΗΚΟΥΣΙΝ ΕΙΣ ΧΡΕΙΑΝ.

69. G. L. Kustas, "The Literary Criticism of Photius," ΕΛΛΗΝΙΚΑ 17 (1962), 132.

70. *PG* 101:45-1160.

71. *PG* 101:16-264. See also H. Grégoire, "Les sources de l'histoire des Pauliciens," *(Bulletin de la Classe des Lettres de l'Académie Royale de Belgique*, 22 (1936), 95-114, and F. Scheidweiler, "Paulikianer-probleme," *BZ* 43 (1950):10-39. Also Nina Garsoian, *The Paulician Heresy* (The Hague, 1967).

72. *PG* 101:262-391. Also Ms. Vaticanus graecus 1923 of the 13th century, fols. 193-204v.

73. *PG* 101:45-1160.

74. Mango, *Homilies*, pp. 166-71.

75. J. Reuss, "Die Matthaeus-Erklärung des Photios von Konstantinopel," *Ostkirliche Studien*, I (1952), 1932-34.

76. Kurt Staab, *Pauluskommentare aus der griechischen Kirche aus Katenenhandschriften gesammelt* (Munich, 1933), 470-652.

CHAPTER THREE

THE LETTERS OF PHOTIOS

The entire scholarly work of Patriarch Photios expresses his love and thirst for learning and has bequeathed a legacy which is rich and manifold. He had amassed information and knowledge in many varied fields, much of it not to be found elsewhere, which raised him to the highest level among Byzantine scholars. Among his works, however, only his letters and his own correspondence give us a deeper view and more accurate knowledge of the real man, rather than the man who has survived in legend.

Photios was one of the most prolific writers of the ninth century. Today two-hundred and seventy-three of his letters have been collected and published. The study of these letters will enable us to discover the private side of this extraordinary man. The letters, in addition to dogmatic, legal, and political questions, include personal correspondence addressed to friends and relatives who are going through difficulties and trials in life. Photios writes to them answering their questions, sustaining and reinforcing their faith; trying to help them during personal losses or other calamities. The value and importance of the letters are evident from the several codices in which they were copied. They were included in one of the oldest codices of original letters, the *Codex Ambrosianus Graecus 81* of the second half of the tenth century, in the company of the best-known and best-loved letter writers of the early Christian era.[1] Early in the eleventh century an anthology of the letters of Patriarch Photios was created which has reached us through at least seven codices.[2]

Of all his works, Photios appears at best in his letters in the triple capacity as theologian, politician, and literary figure. It is impossible, however, to distinguish only one of these qualities at a time in the letters. He appears in all three capacities simultaneously, and this fusion is what makes him so interesting.

The content of his correspondence is, indeed, extraordinary. Most of his letters were written during his first exile: 867-878. In those letters the patriarch advises, reprimands, and tries to sustain the faith and fortitude of his friends who are suffering because of their support for, and belief in, the exiled patriarch. It is believed that the interpretive letters, which were included in the *Amphilochia*, were also written at this same period.[3]

It is obvious, from the references in the *Bibliotheca*, that Photios had studied epistolography, and he was aware of certain rules in letter writing. In reviewing the forty letters of Eunomios, the patriarch states that the writer "ignored the rules of epistolary style";[4] while in reading the canonical letters of Saint Basil, Photios finds his style "a model of epistolary writing."[5] Numerous references are also found in the letters of Photios: "the rules of letter writing," he points out in the letter addressed to his brother, Sergios, and again the same phrase appears, "the rules of letter writing," in the encyclical letter to the patriarchs of the East.[6] Also there is a similar reference in the letter to Pope Nicholas I.[7]

In several of his letters the patriarch is brief, occasionally laconic, to the degree that in one letter a single sentence constitutes the entire letter. Writing to Theodoros, Metropolitan of Laodicea, Photios' entire letter is:

> If the present life is a stadium and its conduct therefrom deserves rewards, do not wonder that some of the righteous contend here with distress, but admire rather that some consider the time and place of their struggles and conflicts as the day of their crowns and the platform of their acclamation.[8]

Several other letters to the same person are as brief. One of

Photios' best letters, in which he expresses his philosophy on education, is equally brief:

> The acquisition of education becomes for one who has grown old the strongest staff of life, and it transports without pain one in the bloom of youth to the beauty of virtue. Therefore, educate your children in wisdom and virtue in order that, not only when they are young, but also when they have grown old, they may not need the help of others.[9]

Photios can be brief especially when he chastises someone: "There is no side road for you to the gates of Paradise," he writes to Anastasios the Tax Collector, "because it is blocked by your love of money. Only love for the poor, proven by acts of charity, can remove the obstruction."[10] Two more very short letters are addressed to the same person.[11] Even more brief are two other letters that follow, both addressed to Helias Protospatharios: "Ask and it will be done. So thank God, the giver and cause of all good, that you will be delivered from the heaviest taxation";[12] and "The sufferings which we are going through become trials; if we remain calm, we will be the recipients of crowns and prizes."[13] Some forty letters written by the Patriarch are approximately four lines or shorter.

Photios does not forget this rule of brevity even when his letters become so lengthy as to be regarded as treatises. Such is the long letter addressed to Boris-Michael, Khagan of the Bulgars, who was the first to be baptized among his people. Patriarch Photios performed the ceremony, and afterwards he composed for his "spiritual son" a letter on the duties of a Christian ruler.[14] The letter is divided into two sections: the first gives the recipient a brief history of the seven Ecumenical Synods and thus a brief history of the Christian Church; the second part includes one hundred and fourteen axioms on the behavior and education of a Christian monarch. Although the letter is long, the ideas of Photios are brief and precise. The epistle opens:

Some gifts, most illustrious and beloved son, confer small and
fleeting advantages upon their subjects, but those that better the
soul, as they cleanse it from error and suffering and shine with the
radiance and glory of virtue and truth, are gifts in the truest of
senses. They confer great and eternal blessings upon an eternal and
godlike object, the soul, and gain for it imperishable, heavenly riches.
The most noble and supreme of gifts is the sure and saving introduction to divinity, if one has been granted the one and only instruction in the pure and blameless faith of us Christians and initiation
into it. [15]

The Patriarch then proceeds to give the historical summary
of the seven Ecumenical Synods, and in only two paragraphs
he manages to give an account of the First. In the first paragraph he mentions all the men present for the occasion, while
in the second he states the purpose and results of the Synod.
Only a man with great stylistic ability could produce such a
controlled but detailed account of a very complicated subject.
The second paragraph reads:

The sacred Synod, composed of such distinguished men, judged a
certain innovator, Arios by name, on charges of impiety and strengthened the divine and Apostolic message. This wretch had been born in
Alexandria, had been enrolled in the clergy of that Church, and risen
to the priesthood. First he assumed an overweening attitude against
his own shepherd and then extended his madness against the Shepherd and Lord of us all. He reduced the Son and the Word of God
(O, the daring of that tongue and mind!) to a creature and an object,
nor did he want to see something that is true of everything and is
self-evident: that every son is of the same nature as his begetter. In
placing the Son among creatures, he proclaimed that the Father, too,
is a creature. Since one knows that the Father's being is that of the
Creator and his nature eternal, he should admit that the Son's is the
same. Where would be the Son's legitimacy, if the Father's being
were of one kind, the Son's of another? How will the polytheism of
Greek error not reappear, if the Godhead is divided into greater and
lesser, with the one God as the first, the elder, the Creator, and the
other God as the second, the younger, and the servant? These are the
shoots of Arios' sowing. But since he had used these blasphemous

lips against the Creator, the holy Synod stripped him of his priesthood and placed his most impious and God-assaulting heresy under
an anathema. In their discussion of sacred matters, they declared
that the Son and the Word of God is of the same being, and of the
same co-eternity as the Father who begot Him, and of the same
power and majesty, in accord with the sacred scriptures and the
common belief of the pious. They knew well that, just as it is Jewish
and Christ-hating to confound the majesty and monarch of the
Trinity in one person, so it is Greek and polytheistic to divide the
simple Godhead, which exceeds being and nature, into unequal and
dissimilar beings. But these were the concerns of the First holy Ecumenical Synod. [16]

Photios continues in the same manner to give a unique historical account of all the Ecumenical Synods ending with the
Seventh.

At the completion of this task, he then gives the Ten Commandments in his own version:

That we should love and serve God absolutely and love and cherish
our fellow men. But our will does not always agree with our knowledge and so this understanding had to be embodied in an oral and
written law. From their very nature it is not difficult to see that our
absolute love of God and our perfect love for our neighbor embrace
all the commandments. Our Lord's words support this view: On
these two commands the whole law and the Prophets depend. The
man who has laid up the love of God in his heart and loves his neighbor as himself will love his mother and father exceedingly and judge
them worthy of honor second only to God. He will not only keep
his hands clean of the blood and death of his fellow man; he will be
as careful of his tongue and his thoughts. Nor would such a man
steal anything. No one would steal from a man whom he loves and
protects as himself. He will not disrupt another's marriage nor swear
a false oath. He will not bear false witness against his neighbor. He
will utterly refrain from injustice; he will neither strike nor abuse his
fellow man nor will he lawlessly covet his neighbor's goods. . . . So in
every way and with all our might we should observe these commandments within the context of our holy and spotless religion. [17]

Finishing with the catechism, Photios turns to matters pertaining to behavior, education, and politics. On personal appearance he advises "not to neglect what pertains to the body such as habits and appearance and movements, considering them as unimportant. For the acquisition and cultivation of such habits is no small proof of diligence. On speech he comments:

> For those who rule and especially the statesmen and government officials rapid speech makes them appear trivial and irresolute.... It is less dangerous, on the other hand, to be slow, indolent, disorderly and foolish, because when you err the effect will be less significant and damaging. [18]

On friendship:

> Do not be quick in making ties of friendship, but when you have made them try every device to keep them from being loosened; and share the burden of those near you, unless it endangers your own soul. For quarrels with friends corrupt our whole existence. For both, the one at fault, and the innocent too fall into suspicion. Make friends with those who kept their friendship towards others always honest, have never shown envy towards them while prospering, and have never neglected them while in difficulties.... Make friends among the best and not among the worst. For from one's friends one's character is judged. One is more at ease and secure among the best. [19]

The first and second letters addressed to Pope Nicholas are lengthy treatises. The first is the profession of faith of Photios as the new Patriarch of Constantinople — a masterpiece of analysis of the views of the Eastern Church. [20] The second mirrors the private life of the patriarch before his elevation, and at the same time is a testimony and source of educational customs of the ninth century. In this letter Photios assures the pope that he did not seek his appointment, revealing that his previous life was happier and preferable.

> I left a peaceful life, I left a calm filled with sweetness.... I left my favorite tranquility. When I stayed at home I was immersed in the sweetest of pleasures, seeing the diligence of those who were learning,

the seriousness of those who asked questions, and the enthusiasm of those who answered them.... And when I had to go to my duties at the imperial palace, they sent me off with their warm farewells and asked me not to be long.... And when I returned, this studious group was waiting for me in front of my door; ...and all these were done frankly and plainly without malice, without intrigue, without jealousy. And who, after having known such a life would tolerate seeing it overthrown and would not lament? It is all these that I have left, all these that I cry for, whose privation had made me shed streams of tears and has enveloped me in a fog of sadness.[21]

As was customary in Byzantium when a new patriarch was elected, he sent a letter of announcement to each of the other four bishops of Christendom: Rome, Antioch, Alexandria and Jerusalem. Immediately after his elevation, Patriarch Photios sent the above-mentioned letter to the pope and to each of the patriarchs in the East. Only the one sent to the Patriarch of Antioch, however, has survived. The text of all three was the same, as is evident from the title which is addressed to all:

"To the most God-loving, most holy fellow ministers, to the most pious Oikonomos and Synkellos of the Church of Theoupolis, Photios, Bishop of Constantinople, New Rome."[22]

The letter proceeds on a similar outline as the one addressed to the pope. First he announces his appointment, commenting on the prestige and the duties of high position. Then he asks for the prayers of the patriarch to help him in his difficult task. Proceeding, he talks about himself, his youth, his parents. Photios mentions here again that his father died in exile. The letter ends with the profession of faith of the new patriarch.

Another letter is the famous encyclical addressed to the Patriarch of Alexandria and also to the other patriarchs of the East, in which Photios condemns the 'Filioque' of the Latins. This letter is of the utmost importance to the Orthodox Church, as the patriarch sets down the true beliefs pertaining to the Trinity.[23] In this letter Photios also explains why the Eastern Church allows its lower clergy to be married, while the Western Church forbids it. The patriarch supports the Eastern practice by quoting the Gospels.[24] He concludes that once the priests are married no one can dissolve the marriage. Photios does mention in the letter that he could expand on his text, "but the rules of epistolography do not allow him."[25]

The long message in the form of an open letter sent to the Metropolitan of Aquileia contains for the first time an accurate account of the differences between the churches of East and West.[26] Photios calls it "the prototype of a letter."[27] In this category of long letters there are over seventy attributed to Photios. These are included in both the collection of his letters and in the *Amphilochia*. The former collection contains letters in which the recipient is named, and includes interpretations of Biblical quotations. This double entry of the same texts shows that the editors of the epistles knew of this double existence, and proves as well that the whole collection of the epistles is not just accidental but intentional. It also proves that while writing in the form of an epistle Photios had in mind that his letters were serving a wider purpose and were going to be preserved for posterity.[28]

The second rule of epistolography — exactness — is followed strictly by Photios. He uses the word 'explicitness' several times in his reviews in the *Bibliotheca*. About the letters of Saint Athanasios he comments that they are composed "with taste, brightness, and exactness."[29] He finds the seventeen letters of Saint John Chrysostom to Olympias good, because "he uses in these letters the accepted rules of letter writing; he is, therefore, clear and exact."[30] He notes that the letter of Polycarp to the Philippians is filled with advice stated with "exactness."[31] In reading the small book of Clement's letter to the Corinthians, Photios finds him "exact";[32] the same remark he makes in reviewing *The Song of Songs* of Athanasios the Great. He remarks that Athanasios is "exact here as in all his writings."[33] In reading the letter of Maximos to Gregorios the Commander, Photios again comments that he finds it to his approval because it has "its writing developed with exactness and also morality."[34] In the same review he repeats that its style is lucid and not without taste. While he praises clarity, Photios also expresses disapproval of its omission, as he does in reviewing another work by Maximos the Confessor, stating that even though he observed the rules of epistolography, "he lacks clarity."[35]

The next rule to be observed, according to Photios, is simplicity and grace. Several references are made to this topic in the *Bibliotheca*. He read the letters of Synesios which "were filled with grace and sweetness."[36] The letters of Polycarp mentioned previously embodied "clarity as well as simplicity."[37] The above letter to Clement was "pure in expression."[38] He comments on the letters of Ephraim Syros (ca. A.D. 306-73) as being written in "an uncomplex language."[39]

Turning to the letters of Patriarch Photios we can study how his knowledge of epistolography was applied to his own writings. The letters of Photios are as varied in form as they are in content. Their diversity mirrors his mood at the time of the writing, as well as his feelings toward the recipient. From their content the letters can be divided into three main categories: advisory, exegetical, and panegyrical. Usually the opening sentence sets the mood of the letter: "There is nothing more honest or holy than a real love as mentioned in the Holy Scriptures and accepted by all."[40] Consider also: "Thought is the mother of good works; impulse borders on sin."[41] The famous enthronistical letter addressed to Pope Nicholas begins: "When the importance of the position comes to my mind."[42] At this same time and for the same occasion the letter to the Patriarch of Antioch begins: "We have received the greatest gifts from above; we do not know why we are so blessed, nevertheless we are all very thankful."[43] The letter written in 867 concerning the procession of the Holy Spirit, addressed to the Patriarch of Alexandria, begins:

"There is not, as it seems, an end to the evil things or an end to evil plots."[44] The opening sentence of a letter of consolation to Eusebia, a nun and monastic superior, on the death of her sister sets a mood of reprimand. "If death began with us, and we were the first to experience it, then reasonably, as falling into something unexpected and new, we could be upset at what happened."[45] The letter to his brother Tarasios on the death of his daughter, on the other hand, sets a mood of tenderness and humiliation:

> Alas! Where is Elija now? And where is Elisha? And where is Peter, or Paul, or any of those who were considered holy and saintly men? Then I would not even need a letter, just to kneel at the feet of one of them and seize his feet because I am not worthy to touch his hands. I would not rise until the girl was restored to her parents. [46]

The letters in which the Patriarch advises, reprimands, or consoles his friends and relatives comprise the largest group among his correspondence. Often, however, Photios answers a certain question asked by a friend, or pupil. Usually the letter begins with a statement of the problem: "Whether mocking the ability of the apostles to speak many languages was noticed or not" was taken from the phrase in the New Testament "others mockingly said."[47] Writing to his brother Tarasios, Photios begins a letter: "As it is said in the Gospel, our Savior asks: 'Who is my mother? And who are my brothers?'"[48] To his brother, Constantine the Protospatharios, he states: "When John the Forerunner, while preaching, was asked a question he answered, 'He who is least in the kingdom of heaven is greater than me.'"[49] Addressing the Metropolitan Amphilochos of Kythera, Photios begins his letter: "Then Christ our God told Maria Magdelene, 'Stop clinging to me, for I have not yet gone up to my Father!' It appears that He is not visible; then why? It seems that He would have let her touch Him because He has been with the Father. What does that mean?"[50] To the same: "Your question is good, stating that if one pronounces the name of God how would he be

punished by death?"[51] To Metropolitan Georgios of Nicomedia, in one of the many letters addressed to this special
friend, Photios answers the question of Christ's circumcision:
"It is the deepest of divine providence that Christ our Lord in
the flesh underwent a circumcision."[52]

In his exegetical capacity, Photios appears as the great
teacher that he was. He is always able to handle a number of
difficult questions referring to the Scriptures. He shows deep
knowledge and understanding in analyzing passages from
both the New and the Old Testament. He is also very much at
home when questions turn to the realm of philosophy. While
in exile at Skepi, Photios wrote many letters of an exegetical
nature. Occasionally, he appears to be surprised, even vexed,
by the topics on which he is called to comment. In one letter
addressed to Theophanes, Diakonos and Protonotarios, who
had asked him to explain certain questions regarding the royal
order, Photios shouts: "Man of God, what happened to you?
What are you thinking and, after such a long time in which
we have been completely forgotten here, since our conviction
in silence, how do you suggest such questions can be answered."[53] To Gregorios, the Spathariocandidatos, on the
other hand, he writes: "The kiss from above, the immaculate
conception, labor free of suffering, these are the seals of virginity; the victory over pain."[54]

The long letter to Protospatharios Arsaber can be considered more than a letter — almost a treatise, because of its
length and content. Here Photios answers the question over
the perplexity of Arsaber about the nature of Christ, quoting
from the Gospel of John: "The Father in the Son and the
Son in the Father."[55] In a short letter to Leo the Logothetes
beginning: "Sell your belongings and give them to the poor,"
Photios is interpreting another passage from the Gospel.[56] In
this group are included some of the questions which are also
found in the *Amphilochia*, as well as five additional letters
without a title which pertain to the following canonical topics: eating forbidden foods during Lent, incorrect dismissal

of priests, a bishop ordaining a priest after he (the priest) commited adultery, and a priest performing a wedding ceremony against the will of the parents of the pair.[57]

The third category comprises the letters in which the sender is preoccupied by a certain problem and seeks to find an answer, to chastise a person or praise another. He begins with the famous letter to the bishops in exile: "I marvel how he, whoever he may be, has so quickly forgotten our relationship. For I should not wish even by name to bring a reproach against him, not even if he should still launch an attack against me rather insolently, since, in fact, I discern that most people are admonished more easily when reproached impersonally than bear advice when cited by name."[58] To his very good friend, Gregorios the Deacon, he announces: "I forbid you, oh friend among the best, to be called my friend anymore."[59] In his moving address to Emperor Basil I, the exiled Photios, who is sick, tired and depressed, opens with the phrase: "Hear, O most philanthropic king, I do not wish to remind you of our old friendship."[60] Addressing the Emperor Michael III, after the murder of Caesar Bardas, the letter commences: "The letter which we have received of Your Imperial Majesty, who is crowned by God and now has acquired sole authority, has filled us with both joy and astonishment."[61] A number of letters thus acknowledge receipt of correspondence: "I have received the letter of your eminence!" he replied to the pope;[62] and again: "You write us a letter!"[63] also: "You are not a coward and, even if you deny that, I was aware of it even before receiving your sweet letter," he states to Nikephoros, the Philosopher and Monk.[64]

In summarizing Photios' approach to his introductions ($\pi\rho o o i\mu\iota a$) to the letters, the student of Byzantine epistolography cannot help noticing the different well-known techniques which are utilized by the patriarch. At times, anticipating the objection of the receiver of his demands, he uses the form of $\pi\rho\delta\lambda\eta\psi\iota\varsigma$, as in the letter to Caesar Bardas asking a favor on behalf of Christodoulos, the Asecretis: "Even if I appear at the present time to be bothersome and excessive in the matter of clemency, still I will not abstain from exerting my efforts at least. Though perhaps I am beating against the air."[65] On other occasions, when he feels that he needs to inspire more pity, he uses the αὔξησις in the prooemion.[66] Again asking Bardas for a favor on behalf of a priest, Photios, to win sympathy, turns against himself:

> Knowing myself to be lacking experience and being undeserving of my high position and power, and for this reason when I was appointed I tried to turn away from them; I wished then that only death could have come to take me instead of force.[67]

In different circumstances he makes use of σύγκρισις, employing opposites to arrive at the desired goal: "Heavy the persecution, but sweet the blessings of the Lord. Difficult is the exile, but delightful the Kingdom of Heaven."[68] When he is requesting a favor such as in the letter addressed to the Emperor Basil I requesting permission to obtain some of his books, Photios uses the form of humiliation (ταπείνωσις). Occasionally, the prooemia to the letters will have a combination of a request with a praise of the achievements of the character of the recipient, as the above-mentioned letter to Emperor Michael III.

A number of letters, as we have noticed, begin by an attack (ἔφοδος), a device used by rhetors to offset the reservations and argument of the other person. Often, however, Photios uses none of the formal devices: he simply begins his letter in a direct and unceremonious way, as we have witnessed in many of the letters already considered. Letters written in rebuke and anger also have an abrupt prooemion. Similarly, when Photios writes to his friends complaining of his suffering while in exile, he begins abruptly. These type of letters follow more the rule of friendship (νόμος φιλίας) than that of necessity (χρεία).[69] We cannot, however, divide all the letters of Photios strictly according to the accepted rules of epistolography. Many of the different types are intermingled and are used to provide the desired effect.

In the appellation ($\pi\rho\sigma\sigma\phi\acute{\omega}\nu\eta\sigma\iota\varsigma$) of the letters certain stereotyped expressions are used according to the title and position of the recipient. Addressing the emperor of Byzantium, Photios uses appellations like these: "Michael Our Holy Emperor," [70] also "To Our Most Reverent and Great Emperor Basil";[71] and "To Our Great Emperor in Christ, Basil."[72] Regarding the *prosphonesis* of the first letter to Michael of Bulgaria we have at least five different versions.[73] In the *Codex Parisinus Graecus 1266*, which is the oldest codex with the original *prosphonesis*, the title reads: "To Our Most Illustrious and Most Admired and Our Beloved Spiritual Son, Michael, from God, Archon of Bulgaria."[74] In the two letters written to the pope, Photios uses the same type of *prosphonesis*: "To All-Holy and Saintly Brother and Priest Nicholas, Pope of Old Rome; Photios, the Bishop of Constantinople, New Rome."'[75] In addressing the patriarchs of the East, as we can conclude from the surviving letter to the Patriarch of Antioch, the appellation is: "To the Most God-loving and Most Holy Fellow Ministers, to the Most Pious Oikonomos and Synkellos of the Church of Theoupolis; Photios Bishop of Constantinople, New Rome."[76] The famous encyclical letter written in 867 and addressed to the Metropolitan of Kythera has no formal *prosphonesis.*[77] Another letter, however, also addressed to the Patriarch of Antioch, and which is believed to have been written in Photios' own hand without the help of a scribe, has the simple heading: "Eustathios, Patriarch of Antioch."[78]

Actually, except for the encyclical letters, this is the only surviving letter addressed to a patriarch. The letters destined for metropolitans simply state the name, the title, and the place: "Ignatios, Metropolitan of Claudioupolis";[79] "Amphilochios, Metropolitan of Kyzikos";[80] "Theodoros, Metropolitan of Laodicea,"[81] and so forth. Letters sent to metropolitans number twenty-nine.

Photios wrote a number of letters to high officials in the

government, who, as we can understand from the content, were personal friends of the patriarch or his pupils. The headings state the name and position of the receiver and occasionally his place of residence: "Ioannes Spatharios the Chresocheris";[82] to the same who by this time has been promoted: "Ioannes Protospatharios of the Drome";[83] Gregorios Spatharocandidatos";[84] "Alexander, Comes";[85] "Ioannes Patrikios and Strategos of Hellas";[86] etc. The number of these letters is seventy-three.

When the Patriarch writes to his brothers he addresses them simply by their name and title, or "brother." Occasionally, when he writes to Tarasios, he refers to him as "Dear brother," also "Tarasios, Patrikios, brother and beloved."[87] To the others he writes simply: "Sergios, Protospatharios, Brother";[88] "Theodoros, Brother";[89] and "Constantine, Protospatharios, Brother."[90] The number of letters surviving are seventeen; of these eight are addressed to Tarasios, one to Theodoros, two to Constantine, and six to Sergios.

In addressing the correspondents, the patriarch often uses an attributive adjective after the name: "Leo the Philosopher";[91] "Theodoros the Hegoumenos";[92] "Marcos the Sicilian and Monk";[93] "Paulos, the Monk and Apostate";[94] "Leo, the Spatharios known as the Drako";[95] "Constantine, the Spatharios of the Pure Turinians";[96] "Euthymios, the Monk and Sinner";[97] and others.

In his letters Photios also employs certain characteristic expressions which we find addressed only to persons who possessed special titles in church or state. In his letters to the pope, Photios uses the expressions "Your Reverence," and "Your Most Reverence," as well as "Your Holiness," and "Most Saintly Brother in Priesthood." In addressing the bishops of the three patriarchates of the East, he uses the expressions: "Your Reverence," "Your Holiness," and "Your Archiepiscopal and Hierarchical Reverence"; the Patriarch of Antioch in addition he calls "Hieratical Perfection," and "The Best among our Fathers and Brothers."[98] Other greetings for the Patriarchs include: "To Your Brotherhood in Christ," "To You My Brother," and "To Your Eminence."

Photios addresses the emperors of Byzantium in the following ways: "O Most Kindly Basileus,"[99] "in your most powerful rule,"[100] or simply "O Basileus."[101] To Emperor Michael, while he is on an expedition in Crete, Photios forwards a letter first giving his blessing, wishing him to excel over the enemy and then asking him to "hurry to me, O Most Illustrious of all Kings and their offspring."[102] When writing to Michael of Bulgaria, Photios uses certain unique phrases, not repeated in any other of his letters: "My Most Illustrious and Beloved Son," "Beloved in Christ and Our Spiritual Son"; also running out of adjectives: "You indeed, O what name could I give you that would match my love?"; also "My Noble and Real Prince."

Photios addresses the bishops and metropolitans as: "My most reverent son,"[103] "O, you the best,"[104] "In your priestly perfection,"[105] "My Son in Christ,"[106] and "To your perfection."[107] He calls the Metropolitan of Aquileia: "You Most Reverent among the Revered," and "To You Saintly and God's Most Reverent."[108]

The conclusions to the letters can be categorized in the same manner as the introductions. Two main influences seem to dominate Photios' formulae for ending his letters: first, the old form of the ancient private letter, and secondly, the traditional rhetorical form.[109] The former ends the letter with a greeting of a kiss ($\dot{\alpha}\sigma\pi\dot{\alpha}\zeta\epsilon\sigma\theta\alpha\iota$), or a wish for the health of the recipient or both. The latter consisted of a formal greeting of salutation, or a promise of spiritual rewards and followed the models set by Demetrios[110] and Pseudo-Libanios.[111]

Photios, in following the first formula, instead of the old stereotyped words prefers the word "farewell" ($\ddot{\epsilon}\rho\rho\omega\sigma\sigma$), which was adopted at the end of the first century of our era.[112] Often a prayer was added for the protection and preservation of the recipient, with the invocation of Christ, the saints, and the Virgin Mary. Approximately twenty-three letters end with the word "farewell."

Sometimes neither of the standard formulae is employed. Photios likes to end his letters with advice: "My son, do not limit yourself to only reading what I write; be eager to illustrate your understanding with deeds."[113] Also: "And when you see the bright and clear rays of heaven, do not use them only in theory, but adapt them to the practical side of life."[114] Discussing his favorite topic of silence, Photios advises Theodoros, the Hegoumenos, thus: "Do not trust words; even though the silent appears to lack forcefulness, he can silence the mouth of the long talked succinctly."[115] Advising Akakios, the monk and doctor, on suspicion and conceit, Photios strongly suggests that he should run away from conceit with all his force as, "it is a deep ditch where there is no hope of retrieval."[116] To Theophylaktos, Patrikios and Strategos of Armenia, after giving him advice on the three things which he, Photios, hates: deceit, lying and distraction of love, Photios concludes his letter with, "I have already advised you."[117] The letter addressed to Baanes, the Patrikios, is in its entirety an advisory letter in which Photios compares his friendship with Baanes to that of Joseph of Arimathea and Jesus, and concludes: "If friendship and good-will toward your friend did not come to you in this world, then everything was in vain, even the example of Joseph."[118] Consider the letter to Sabas, priest and monk: "I believe that in this letter I have sufficiently answered your question."[119] On the other hand, Photios often ended his letter with the conclusion he was interpreting. In the letter to Christophoros, Protospatharios and Asecretis, which interprets the biblical quotation: "But you, whenever you fast, anoint your head and wash your face,"[120] Photios concludes: "If you fast and use a superfluous amount of oil on your head, as if you were a king, only your face and body will be cleansed; your soul can be

cleansed of sin only through charity. This illustrates the use-
fulness of the Holy Scriptures."[121] To the same person the
conclusion of a rather lengthy letter states: "To you, who are
an eager learner and a faithful worshiper, I think that I have
answered your question even in these few words."[122] Letters,
such as the above, which concluded with a statement of advice, number approximately forty-five.

Several letters end with a prayer or a blessing calling on the
Holy Trinity, the Son, the Holy Spirit, or the Holy Theotokos.
Approximately ten letters end in the name of the Holy Trinity.
Most of them are addressed to high ecclesiastical officials.
The preoccupation of the patriarch with the sole procession
of the Holy Spirit is evident in the conclusion of a number of
his letters. The first letter addressed to Pope Nicholas, after
he has invoked the help of Christ, ends: "Oh, the Glory and
the Power with the Father and of the Holy Spirit, the life-
giver and of the same substance, now and forever, Amen."[123]
The first enthronistical to the bishops of the East ends with
the profession of faith by Photios: "I believe therefore in one
God, perfectly accomplished Father, the Son and the Holy
Spirit, the life giver, the consubstantial Trinity, now and forever, Amen."[124] In a letter addressed to his brother, Sergios,
he answers the question: "Why do we call the Father, God;
the Son, God; and the Holy Spirit, God?" Photios concludes:
"It is necessary to call all three God as they are the undivided
and unseparated divinity."[125] To the Metropolitan of Chalcedon, Zacharias, he concludes: "The grace of the Holy Spirit
will help him to see things clearly."[126] The entire letter to
John the Spatharios, which is less than five lines long, concerns the Holy Trinity and concludes: "According to the ecclesiastical rules, they are of one substance and are worshiped
as three persons, which comprises the Christian theology."[127]

Another way of ending is seen in the letter to Leo the
Logothetes of Madiam for whom Patriarch Photios interprets
the passage: "If you wilt be perfect, go and sell what thou
hast, and give to the poor, and thou shalt have treasures in

Heaven."[128] Photios ends the letter with the blessing: "Come,
I said, the blessed of my Father, for you have eternity."[129]

Numerous are the letters ending with a blessing in "the
name of Christ our true God." The letter to Ignatios, Metropolitan of Claudioupolis, after discussing the passage, "And
behold the curtain of the temple was torn in two from the
top to the bottom; and the earth shook and the rocks were
split,"[130] concludes: "And for this through his life-giving
death, he opened the Gates of Heaven to all men; who came
for this and our flesh received and suffered for us, our Christ
the true God."[131] One of the several letters addressed to
Euschemon, Archbishop of Caesarea in Cappadocia, ends:
"Truly and divinely did Christ speak when in Jerusalem, he
spoke to his disciples of leaving Galilee and going to Jerusalem."[132] Some ten letters have similar endings.[133]

Photios uses the name of the Virgin Mary only on very
special occasions and when writing to very special people.
Such is the letter to his brother, Tarasios, on the death of his
daughter, who was very dear to him, and whose death is a
personal grief to the patriarch. The letter concludes: "Even as
we have shared in His afflictions, so too, we shall enjoy his
happiness, glory and splendor, both now and into unending
ages by the intercessions of our supremely glorious Lady,
Mother of God and ever Virgin Mary, and of all the Saints,
Amen."[134] To Emperor Michael III, after the murder of Caesar Bardas, the letter concludes by calling on the Christ and
Mary: "We believe in Jesus Christ, our true God, who keeps
guard on your city and sends away the enemies, in the name
of our Holy Mother and all the Saints, Amen."[135]

Photios definitely and categorically avoids using the name
of God as such in the conclusions of his letters, Rarely, he
might express a prayer in concluding as in the letter to the
bishops in exile. Writing while he is also in exile, Photios states:

In action and by law he taught us to abide by the privileges which
are assigned to kings. That is why we in our sacred and solemn litur-
gies offer prayers for our kings. For to preserve and maintain these

privileges is right for our Christian kings, is dear to God, and is most suitable for us.[136]

Having examined the openings and closings of the letters, let us turn to the actual content. The letters are witnesses to the many interests and activities of Patriarch Photios. Through them he expresses his views and his immense knowledge becomes evident. In a number of them he discusses theological questions pertaining to the New Testament. The topics vary from "Regarding the Trinity,"[137] to "Christ's two natures."[138] He interprets the Gospel of Mark: "Look out, beware of the leaven of the Pharisees and of the leaven of Herod."[139] He interprets the meaning in Luke: "And being in agony He prayed more earnestly; and His sweat was as if great drops of blood were falling down to the ground."[140] Of the same: "And they understood none of these things: this saying was hid from them; neither knew they of the things which were spoken."[141] Of the same again: "John answered, saying unto them all, 'I indeed baptize you with water; but one mightier than I comes, the latchet of whose shoes I am not worthy to unloose. He shall baptize you with the Holy Ghost and with fire.'"[142] Also from St. John, Photios interprets the meaning of the following: "Jesus said unto her, 'Stop clinging to me, for I have not yet ascended to my Father.'"[143] From the same: "Ye have heard how I said unto you, I go away, and come again unto you. If you love me, you would rejoice, because I said, I go unto the Father; for my Father is greater than I."[144] From the same: "In my Father's house there are many mansions; if it were not so, I would have told you. I go to prepare a place for you."[145] This is compared with Matthew's: "But of that day and hour no man knows, not even the angels of heaven, nor the Son, but the Father only."[146]

Photios becomes even more alive when he discusses his favorite Apostle, Paul, in such topics as, "Which was the country of the marvelous Paul?"[147] In a letter to Euschemon, Archbishop of Caesarea of Cappadocia, Paul, concludes Photios, "was born in the small town of Gischala, and was of the tribe of Benjamin."[148]

The Patriarch comments on Saint Paul's own affirmations:

> I am verily a man who is a Jew, born in Tarsus, a city in Cilicia, yet brought up in this city at the feet of Gamaliel, and taught according to the perfect manner of the law of the Fathers, and was jealous toward God, as ye all are this day; and the chief captain answered 'with a great sum of money you can obtain your freedom.' And Paul said, 'But I was born free.'[149]

On another occasion Photios answered the question: "How is it possible for Paul not to be considered a liar when he calls himself Roman and sometimes Jew, and at times he claims as his place of birth Tarsus and other times Rome?" Photios begins his epistle stating that "whether he calls himself Jew or Roman, Paul, the student of truth, is not lying."[150] In a letter to John the Philosopher, Photios discusses what Paul told the Athenians about the epigrams on their altars.[151] Photios uses the speech of Paul again in *The Mystagogia of the Holy Spirit.*[152] He also discusses many topics from the letters of Paul.[153] In a series of letters to Georgios, Metropolitan of Nicodemia, Photios first discusses the statement of Paul "For I wish that myself were accursed from Christ for my brethren, my kinsmen according to the flesh."[154] The patriarch compares Paul to Moses, concluding that their souls are related, as both were ready to suffer the supreme sacrifice, that is to be banished from their people by God. According to Photios, however, "Paul excels."[155]

Another letter to Georgios discusses "Why Christ was circumcised."[156] A separate letter to Abbot Theodoros concerns the circumcision of Abraham.[157] Writing again to Georgios, Photios discusses Paul's phrase: "I want you to know, brethren, that I have often intended to come to you but I hitherto have been prevented, that I might have some fruit among you also."[158] Photios concludes how important it was for the apostle to see the fruits of his labors spread among all people alike.[159] In the next lengthy letter to Georgios, Photios discusses the depth of Paul's wisdom.[160] In the following letter to the same Metropolitan, Photios discusses various subjects from the letters of Paul.[161] To Zacharias, Metropolitan of Chalcedon, Photios again discusses Paul.[162]

Photios tries to find the meaning in Paul's words: "Wherefore, as through one man sin entered into the world, and through sin death, and so death spread to all men, because all men have sinned." The letter is written to his beloved brother, Tarasios.[163] In fact, there are a series of letters in which Photios discusses various subjects with his favorite brother. One letter regards God's love and providence. He advises his brother to follow the example of Christ and his love for humanity.[164] In the next letter, Photios speaks of the meaning of the Gospel of Matthew: "But he answered and said unto him, who is my mother? and who are my brethren?" In a lengthy discourse, Photios explains to his brother that Christ did not mean to hurt Mary for she knew that she had been selected as His mother by the Father.[165] "Paul said that all men sin," declared Photios in yet another letter, "because of Adam's sin; man will die — but not just as punishment in itself, for every man is going to sin while on this earth."[166]

When Paul talks about women, Photios adds: "That is why a woman ought to have a veil on her head because of the angels."[167] In a letter addressed to Eulambios, Archbishop and Skevophylax, he comments: "As for the head, the woman should have it covered because she does not cut her hair; neither does she shave as the man does. If she did, she could leave hers uncovered."[168] He had also other thoughts about women: "Woman is subservient to man according to Genesis, but woman is also the glory of man."[169] In another letter to Ioannes, Patrikios and Strategos of Hellas, Photios discusses Paul's comment: "Be not unequally yoked together with unbelievers; for what fellowship has righteousness with unrighteousness?"[170]

The Patriarch is equally at home when he discusses subjects

from the Old Testament. For example, in a letter to Proto-spatharios Constantine and his brother, he discusses the meaning of the old Hebrew law: "An eye for an eye and a tooth for a tooth." There is nothing more contrary, Photios comments, to the Christ's command: "When one strikes you on one cheek, turn the other," and concludes that only by understanding can one win over his enemies.[171] In the letter of Boris of Bulgaria, Photios goes even further: "Never be un-true even to your enemies."[172] What a far cry from the pic-ture of a Byzantine prevailing among literary circles even today.

In a letter to Theodoros, Spatharocandidatos of the Lala-kones, Photios discusses the third commandment: "Do not use the Lord's name in vain." The name of the Lord, Photios comments, should be mentioned only in the Divine Liturgy.[173] He goes further to quote Matthew: "But I tell you, not to swear at all, either by heaven, because it is the throne of God, or by the earth, because it is His footstool, or by Jerusalem because it is the city of the great king."[174]

As stated in the previous chapter, the end of the Icono-clastic controversy came with the edict of the Empress Theo-dora in 843 which ended the quarrel over icon worship and reinstated the icons in the churches. It is surprising, however, to find that in 861 the Emperor Michael III finds it necessary to condemn Iconoclasm again. In the 860's Patriarch Photios is also preoccupied with the problem. Photios' longest account of the Ecumenical Synods, in the letter to Michael, is that of the Seventh, which dealt with Iconoclasm. From a homily of Photios delivered on the occasion of the dedication of the icon of Our Lady Theotokos, in Hagia Sophia in 867 in the presence of the Emperors Michael and Basil, we are confronted with the astonishing discovery that this was the first icon to be dedicated by the Patriarch since the restoration. The synod, held by Patriarch Ignatios in 869-870, found it necessary to condemn the Iconoclasts again.

The preoccupation of Patriarch Photios with the question

of icons is evident from his letters. "Their idols are silver and gold — the work of men's hands," the patriarch is careful to point out in the letter to Stephen the Orthodox.[175] The Christian symbols of the icons and articles used for worship, Photios is very careful to mention, "are not just the gold or silver or wood, but what they stand for as venerated symbols."[176]

In a series of letters to Ioannes, the Spatharios, Chresocheris, Photios discusses repeatedly the icon of Christ and attacks the iconoclasts.[177] In a letter to the same John, who is now Protospatharios and Protonotarios, Photios refers again to the icon of Christ. To strengthen his argument, he quotes the Apostle Paul and John the Chrysostom.[178] In a letter to Theophanes the monk, Photios turns again to Paul for support.[179] Some of the same letters are included in the *Amphilochia*, which shows how troubled Photios was and how anxious he was to give a final answer to this prolonged problem.[180]

The Patriarch also delivered three sermons from the Ambon of Hagia Sophia on the subject of icons. The first two sermons seemed to be a part of a series of instruction in the early history of the Church, especially the story of Arios and his heresy, the story of the First Ecumenical Synod and that of the Second. Unfortunately, the first and last part of the series have been lost and we have only the two in between pertaining to the story of Arianism which is compared with Iconoclasm. In the first sermon, Photios compared the attitudes of the two patriarchs: that of Nikephoros toward the iconoclastic Patriarch John the Grammarian and that of the old Patriarch Alexander towards Arius. He concludes:

But then he [Arios] went astray and aspired to be proclaimed the leader of a heresy — just as neither the blessed Alexander nor God's Church shed a single drop of mercy on Arios' feigning repentance — so also the wondrous Nikephoros with a prophetic eye, barred the entrance of the church to John and his fellow-leaders of his heresy who had done similar violence to the faith asserting that, even if they should assume the mask of repentance their conversion would be unacceptable both to God and to the Church. But to what extent the heresies of image-breakers and Arian madmen resemble one another, will be expounded, with God's help in the proper time. [181]

In the second sermon Photios, comparing again the Iconoclasts with the Arians, concluded: "One may observe the Iconoclasts using this same device and base artifice as the Arians." [182] These two sermons probably date from Photios' first patriarchate. [183] The third homily was delivered on the occasion of the dedication of the icon of the Theotokos and Christ at the Church of Hagia Sophia, in the presence of the two Emperors, Michael and Basil. The entire homily is a refutation of the doctrines of the Iconoclasts who show their heretical attitude by

erecting trophies against beliefs hostile to Christ; piety lying low, stripped of her very last hopes; and the ungodly ideas of those half-barbarous and bastard clans, which have crept into the Roman throne — that hateful abomination being branded for all to see.

Attacking the iconoclastic emperors he continues:

They have stripped the Church, Christ's bride, of her own ornaments, and have wantonly inflicted bitter wounds on her, wherewith her face was scarred, and she was naked, as it were, and unsightly, and afflicted by those many wounds, seeking in their rage to submerge her in oblivion, in this too simulating Jewish folly. Still bearing on her body the scars of these wounds, in testimony of the Isaurian and godless purpose. [184]

In this memorable homily Photios expands on the views of the Orthodox Church regarding the reverence of icons:

Christ has come to us in the flesh and was born in the arms of His Mother: This is seen and confirmed and proclaimed in pictures, the teaching made clear through seeing it with our own eyes, and impelling the spectator to unhesitating assent. Does a man hate the teaching through pictures? Then how has he not previously rejected and hated the message of the Gospels? Just as speech is transmitted by hearing, so a form by the faculty of sight is imprinted upon the tablets of the soul, giving to those whose apprehension is not soiled by wicked doctrines, a representation of knowledge in accordance with piety.... The Virgin is holding the Creator in her arms as an infant. Who is it that upon seeing this or hearing it, will not be astonished by the magnitude of the mystery and will not rise up to laud the ineffable condescension which surpasses all words?.... Has the mind seen? Has it grasped? Has it visualized? Then it has easily transmitted the forms of the memory.[185]

In the encyclical letter to the patriarchs of the East in 867, after discussing and expanding on the single procession of the Holy Spirit and attacking the doctrines which the Frankish missionaries were trying to enforce in Bulgaria, Photios concludes with the request that the patriarchs send representatives to a council. Among the important things to be acted upon is the addition of the Second Synod of Nicaea to the six Ecumenical Synods; it was numbered as the Seventh: "We have heard," he writes, "that some of the churches under your Apostolic jurisdiction number up to the Sixth not counting the Seventh. But what this council has decided is very revered and important to the Church, and it should, therefore, be recognized as equal to the others."[186] The Synod of 867, because of the efforts of Patriarch Photios, added the Second Synod of Nicaea to the six Ecumenical Synods, and from that time on, the Eastern Orthodox Church counts it as the Seventh Ecumenical Synod. The importance of this fact was brought up again by the Ignatian Council of 869-870.[187] The Western Church, however, still continued to recognize only six Ecumenical Synods. It was not until the Photian Synod of 879-880, at the insistence of Photios, that the papal legate, Cardinal Paul, accepted the proposal that the Church should recognize in the future seven Ecumenical Synods.[188] Thus, as we have seen, more than one-hundred years after the summoning of the Second Synod of Nicaea by Empress Irene, and almost forty years after the edict of Empress Theodora and the triumph of Orthodoxy, the problem of Iconoclasm, it seems, was still alive in Byzantium. Patriarch Photios was aware of this problem throughout his life and he dealt with it through his homilies and his synods as well as through his letters.

We have already witnessed the extreme interest of Patriarch Photios in the question of the procession of the Holy Spirit and his indefatigable efforts to sustain the views of the Eastern Orthodox Church. He wrote his treatise on *The Mystagogia of the Holy Spirit* while in his second exile and after the elevation of Leo VI to the throne of Constantinople.[189] This interest is also evident in his letters. In the "Encyclical Letter to the Patriarchs of the East,"[190] among other problems and topics Photios discusses the question of the Holy Spirit and defends the position of the Eastern Orthodox Church on the single procession.

The letter to the Metropolitan of Aquileia is entirely dedicated to the topic of the single procession of the Holy Spirit. In this epistle, Patriarch Photios shows his broad knowledge of history, the Scriptures, and Western theology. He makes reference to the Scriptures to sustain his argument, to the Gospels, to Paul, as well as to the Western Fathers, Saint Ambrose, Saint Augustine and Saint Jerome. He also uses historical arguments through the Synods and the teachings of the Fathers in the East. The letter is a monument to Photios and to his extensive knowledge of Christian theology and beliefs.[191]

The Holy Spirit is the topic in a letter addressed to Eulampios, Archbishop and Skevophylax.[192] Photios comments on quotations from Matthew such as, "All sins and blasphemies are forgiven to men; but a blasphemy against the Holy Spirit is never forgiven."[193] Throughout the letter he quotes other passages from the Gospels as well as from Paul, in an effort to prove that the Patriarch is a firm supporter of the single procession of the Holy Spirit.

In numeroul letters, Photios quotes ancient proverbs taken from classical texts. It is not clear, however, if they were common knowledge and were used at this time in ninth-century Byzantium, or if they were special knowledge of the patriarch obtained through his extensive reading of the classical authors. The phrase, "the rivers flowing in reverse," used in a letter to Zacharias, Metropolitan of Chalcedon, is a quotation from Euripides' *Medea*. Still used in modern Greek today, it means the same thing that it did at the time of Euripides and Photios; that is, that things are confusing and difficult. [194] Consider also the proverbs with which he opens his letter to his brother, Theodoros: "There is a saying of those who suffered greatly, 'They sweat blood.'" [195] The proverb attributed to Chilon, "Do not in quantity seek quality," is the concluding sentence in a letter to Georgios the Deacon and Guest-Master. [196]

The entire letter to Ioannes the Patrikios and Strategos of Hellas is the parable of the story of Eunomios from Locros who was singing when one of the strings broke. It was replaced by a little cicada so that Eunomios was able to continue singing; "but you," Photios concludes, "do not depend on an insect for the continuation of your duties, for you are the Chief Priest of God." [197]

The opening sentence of the letter to Leo, who became Logothetes of Madiam, is a parapharase of Euripides' *Orestes.* The letter commences: "It is a great blessing to have friends when times are difficult and you need them." [198] Even in the letter to Pope Nicholas, Photios does not miss the opportunity to allude to the old proverb of the lonely oak tree — as he sees himself — while everybody else is deciding his future. [199]

The letter to Basil, before his acquisition of the throne, while he was still in the service of the Emperor Michael III, is addressed to him in the capacity of Patrikios and Eparchos of Constantinople. [200] In this letter Photios begins with the ancient proverb, "Say the truth, for lies make feathers fall, while the truth makes wings fly." The patriarch's courage and steadfast rule of righteousness are obvious here, as he is not afraid to criticize someone so close and so dear to the emperor.

Actually, Photios went even further after the slaying of Michael and the elevation of Basil to the throne, expelling the new emperor from the church and calling him a murderer. The enemies of the patriarch tried on many occasions to smear his name by accusing him of bending to and flattering the powerful; his letters, however, are witnesses to the contrary. Photios does not hesitate to criticize and reprimand a wrongdoer regardless of position or power.

In the letter to Michael of Bulgaria, most of the axioms on the behavior of the Christian prince are paraphrases from ancient sayings. In regard to control of tongue and speech: "Of all things, you should be careful not to fall victim to your own tongue."[201] "For words can, in a very short time, make a great difference and damage the lives and fortune of many."[202] "Have your ears open to those who have been wronged, and closed to the reasons and speeches of those who do wrong"[203] and others.

In a letter to Theodoros the Hegoumenos, Photios compares his situation with an episode from Homer.[204] Hunger fell on the Greek army which was besieging Troy. In need of wheat, Odysseus made a request to Anion, the son of Apollo and Creousa who was also the King and the oracle of Delos.

Another letter begins with a reference to Aesop, who in replying to the Lacedaemonian Chilon said, "The gods have the power to bring those who are up, down, and raise those who are down, up."[205] The letter to Zacharias, Metropolitan of Chalcedon, contains many references to the ancients, including Aesop, and the accusation of Socrates. Photios refers also to a proverb used by the ancients as well as by Paul: "beating the wind, or punishing the wind in vain."[206] Turning to the theatre, as he often does, Photios mentions laughter and Aristophanes, whom he considers the best in comedy; he concludes with a warning to Zacharias not to follow the example of Nikaias the Philistonian, who died from laughing.[207]

The letter to Georgios the Deacon[208] opens with a reference to Melanthos the actor, who regretted not having the long neck of a swan so that he might enjoy food longer. To Ioannes the Patrikios and Sakellarios,[209] Photios relates the way a viper comes into the world by eating its mother's stomach; he warns him, therefore, not to act as a viper. In this letter Photios' knowledge and interest in science are evident.

The letter to Leo the Protospatharios consists entirely of references to Hercules, to Hermes, and to the horn of Amalthia which, Photios reminds him, even the poets sometimes used for profit.[210] In another letter, Photios mentions the ventriloquists who delivered oracles. Although most of these were women, he says that there are also men who have that peculiarity and are called "enteromantes," a term meaning one who could make prophecies from the belly, or "egastrimantes." According to Photios, Sophocles, with his poetic talent of creating new words, called them "sternomantes," meaning prophet of the chest. Plato, on the other hand, calls them by the name of "Eureclea," which means one who is capable of lying and stealing.[211]

Photios certainly must have had a special interest in Alexander the Great, or for some reason admired him. He alludes to him in at least three letters. To Michael of Bulgaria he alludes to Alexander while he is discussing women: "After Alexander of Macedonia had conquered Asia, he used to say that the Persian women were darts in his eyes."[212] Writing to Alexander the Comes, Photios attributes to Alexander the Great the phrase, "I have not reigned today," used only if he were not able to help someone.[213] This phrase is usually attributed to Trajan and Titus, but Photios uses it only in reference to Alexander the Great. In the conclusion of the letter, Photios urges Alexander to do the same; but instead of using the phrase of Alexander of Macedonia, "Today I did not reign," he urges him to say, "Today I did not tyrannize." Another letter to the same Alexander begins: "If you feel affection for Alexander's example, then stay away from the bad curses of Alexander the blacksmith."[214] Another example of his knowledge of the ancients is a letter to Eustathios,

Patriarch of Antioch. Photios mentions that the fear of enemies makes him very laconic; then he continues using the word "skytale" (some kind of code to make the letter unintelligible), which the Lacedaemonians used when exchanging messages and which is described in detail by Plutarch in his *Life of Lysander.* [215]

Patriarch Photios of Constantinople was one of the most, if not the most, highly cultivated writers of the ninth century. His extensive knowledge in secular, as well as in theological literature, is evidenced by his numerous references to the various authors and sources of all ages. In his letters he also demonstrates his knowledge of rhetorical and epistolary rules, adding his practical and personal touch, which he acquired throughout his long and interesting life. He uses and mixes all of these ingredients with mastery and ease. His letters are not stereotyped formulae. While some follow the rules of epistolography, others have a varied form, enlivened by his personal touch, which has, indeed, produced some of the masterpieces of the world's literature.

NOTES

1. B. Laourdas, "The Codex Ambrosianus graecus 81 and Photius," *BZ* 44 (1951), 370-72.

2. *Codex Angelicus gr. 13* of the eleventh century; *Vossianus misc. gr. 12, Vallicellanus gr. 35, Matritensis gr. 4866* and *Barberinus gr. 181.*

3. Included in this group is a letter addressed to the Emperor Basil; see B. Laourdas, "Λανθάνουσα ἐπιστολή τοῦ Πατριάρχου Φωτίου πρός τόν αὐτοκράτορα Βασίλειον," ΟΡΘΟΔΟΞΙΑ 25 (1950), 472-74.

4. *Bibliotheca,* Codex 138.

5. Ibid., Codex 143.

6. Val. Ep. 9, p. 255.

7. Val. Ep. 3, p. 163.

8. Val. Ep. 86, p. 415. See below Letter 38.

9. Val. Ep. 126.

10. Val. Ep. 138. See below Letter 37.

11. Val. Ep. 139, 140.

12. Ep. 256. See below Letter 44.

13. Ep. 257. See below Letter 45.

14. Val. Ep. 6.

15. Valettas, p. 206.

16. Ibid., pp. 223-24.

17. Ibid., pp. 226-27.

18. Ibid., p. 227.

19. Ibid., p. 229.

20. Val. Ep. 1.

21. Val. Ep. 3.

22. Val. Ep. 2.

23. Val. Ep. 4.

24. Matt. 13:24-31, and 37-44.

25. Valettas, p. 175.

26. Val. Ep. 5.

27. Valettas, p. 182.

28. B. Laourdas, "Παρατηρήσεις ἐπί τοῦ χαρακτῆρος τῶν ἐπιστολῶν τοῦ Φωτίου," ΕΠΕΤΗΡΙΣ ΕΤΑΙΡΕΙΑΣ ΒΥΖΑΝΤΙΝΩΝ ΣΠΟΥΔΩΝ 21 (1951), 84.

29. *Bibliotheca*, Codex 32.

30. Codex 86.

31. Codex 126.

32. Ibid.

33. Codex 139.

34. Codex 192.

35. Codex 194.

36. Codex 26.

37. "with simplicity and explicity."

38. "be explicit with your sentence and to the point."

39. Codex 229.

40. Val. Ep. 3. The same in John 13:34-36.

41. Val. Ep. 91. See below Letter 39.

42. Val. Ep. 1.

43. Val. Ep. 2.

44. Val. Ep. 4.

45. Val. Ep. 144. See below Letter 3. Also by D. White, "Photios' Letter to Mother Superior Eusebia," *Classical Folia* 29 (June, 1975), 31-43.

46. Val. Ep. 142. See below Letter 1.

47. Val. Ep. 11; Acts 2:1-13.

48. Val. Ep. 13; Matt. 12:48.

49. Val. Ep. 16; Matt. 11:11 and Luke 7:28.

50. Val. Ep. 19; John 20:17.

51. Val. Ep. 21; Levit. 24:16.

52. Val. Ep. 25.

53. Val. Ep. 50.

54. Val. Ep. 61. From Matt. 1:25.

55. Val. Ep. 71. From John 14:20.

56. Val. Ep. 74. From Matt. 19:21 and 25:34-46.

57. Val. Ep. 80-84.

58. Val. Ep. 146. See below Letter 8.

59. Val. Ep. 155. See below Letter 5.

60. Val. Ep. 218. See below Letter 17.

61. Val. Ep. 221. See below Letter 7.

62. Val. Ep. 3.

63. Ibid., p. 146.

64. Val. Ep. 115.

65. Val. Ep. 158. See below Letter 33.

66. L. Spengel (ed.), *Rhetores Graeci*, 3 (Leipzig, 1854), 369.

67. Val. Ep. 159.

68. Val. Ep. 147. See below Letter 9.

69. Synesios in a letter to Diogenes reproaches him for omitting the accustomed greetings. (Ep. 23, in *PG* 66.)

70. Val. Ep. 221. See below Letter 7.

71. Val. Ep. 218. See below Letter 17.

72. *Amphilochia*, ed. Oekonomou, p. 130.

73. B. Laourdas, " Ἐπιγραφή τῆς πρός τόν Βασιλέα τῶν Βουλγάρων Μιχαήλ, Πρώτης Ἐπιστολῆς τοῦ Φωτίου," ΘΕΟΛΟΓΙΑ 23 (1952), 3-6.

74. Ibid., p. 4.

75. Val. Ep. 1, 3. See also Sister Lucille Dinneen, *Titles of Address in Christian Greek Epistolography* (Washington, D.C. 1929).

76. Val. Ep. 2.

77. Val. Ep. 5.

78. Val. Ep. 225.

79. Val. Ep. 18 and 163.

80. Val. Ep. 19-22, 232, 233.

81. Val. Ep. 23, 86-91, 166, 167.

82. Val. Ep. 52-60.

83. Val. Ep. 127.

84. Val. Ep. 61.

85. Val. Ep. 193 and 194.

86. Val. Ep. 72, 118, 200.

87. Val. Ep. 12-14, 142, 143, 220, 223, 224.

88. Val. Ep. 7-11, 85.

89. Val. Ep. 17.

90. Val. Ep. 15 and 16.

91. Val. Ep. 77.

92. Val. Ep. 43-45, 100, 101.

93. Val. Ep. 181.

94. Val. Ep. 175.

95. Val. Ep. 216.

96. Val. Ep. 133.

97. Val. Ep. 179.

98. Val. Ep. 3, "To Your Archieratical and Hieratical Beatitude." Ep. 225, "The best among our Fathers and Brothers."

99. Val. Ep. 218, "Hearken, O most benevolent Emperor."

100. Val. Ep. 219, "Your emperorship."

101. Val. Ep. 221, "O Basileas."

102. Val. Ep. 222, "Speed your return, O Ornament, in my opinion, of kings."

103. Val. Ep. 13, "Son of Ours most Saintly."

104. Val. Ep. 21, "O, among the best."

105. Val. Ep. 145, "in Your Archieratical Perfection."

106. Val. Ep. 92, "Our Son in Christ."

107. Val. Ep. 95, "O Your Perfection."

108. Val. Ep. 5, "Your Saintly and God-honored Eminence."

109. F. Ziemann, *De Epistolarum Graecorum Formulis Sollemnibus Quaestiones Selectae* (Halle, 1910), pp. 326-33; also F.X.J. Exler, *A Study in Greek Epistolography* (Washington, D.C., 1923), pp. 113-24. Ziemann attributes the gradual omission of the formal conclusion to literary letters to the copyists who omitted it because it was well known. Photios' literary letters usually end with a prayer whose origin can be traced to the apostolic letters, especially to Paul.

110. V. Weichart (ed.), *Demetri et Libanii,* ΤΥΠΟΙ ΕΠΙΣΤΟΛΙΚΟΙ *et* ΕΠΙΣΤΟΛΙΜΑΙΟΙ ΧΑΡΑΚΤΗΡΕΣ (Leipzig, 1910), pp. 3-4.

111. Ibid., p. 22.

112. Ziemann, p. 335.

113. Val. Ep. 10, "You then, my son, do not only read what I write to you with eagerness, but with your deeds, rather, show your eagerness."

114. Val. Ep. 28. In this long letter addressed to Georgios, Metropolitan of Nicomedia, Photios discusses twenty-seven topics from the letters of Paul.

115. Val. Ep. 100, "And thus, you should not be eloquent with words and silent with deeds."

116. Val. Ep. 107, "Avoid with all your might conceit."

117. Val. Ep. 119, "I, for my part, I advise you..."

118. Val. Ep. 122.

119. Val. Ep. 47.

120. Val. Ep. 65. From Matt. 6:17.

121. Val. Ep. 66.

122. Valettas, p. 370.

123. "With the power and the glory, with the Father and the Holy Spirit in the life-giving, of the same essence Trinity, now and forever, Amen."

124. Val. Ep. 3.

125. Val. Ep. 7.

126. Val. Ep. 30.

127. Val. Ep. 52.

128. Val. Ep. 74. From Matt. 19:21.

129. Valettas, pp. 399-400.

130. Matt. 27:51.

131. Val. Ep. 18.

132. Val. Ep. 40; in Matt. 26:32.

133. Val. Ep. 4, 12, 18, 40, 48, 53, 55, 130, 144.

134. Val. Ep. 42.

135. Val. Ep. 221. There are only three letters in all among the correspondence of Photios concluding with the name of Mary (Theotokos).

The third letter is addressed to the bishops also in exile (Val. Ep. 147).

136. Val. Ep. 134. See below Letter 8, p. 146.

137. Val. Ep. 52.

138. Val. Ep. 53 and 54.

139. Mark 8:15; Val. Ep. 36.

140. Luke 22:44; Val. Ep. 17.

141. Luke 18:31-34; Val. Ep. 37.

142. Luke 3:16; Val. Ep. 62.

143. John 20:17; Val. Ep. 19.

144. John 14:28; Val. Ep. 47.

145. John 14:2-3.

146. Matt. 24:36; Val. Ep. 71.

147. Val. Ep. 41 and 42.

148. Val. Ep. 41.

149. Val. Ep. 51.

150. "Neither when he called himself Jewish nor Roman, did the disciple of truth Paul lie."

151. Val. Ep. 78.

152. Hergenröther, *Photius,* 2, 73-74.

153. Val. Ep. 28.

154. Romans 9:3.

155. Val. Ep. 24, p. 293.

156. Val. Ep. 25.

157. Val. Ep. 45.

158. Val. Ep. 26; from Romans 1:13.

159. Valettas, p. 199.

160. Val. Ep. 27.

161. Val. Ep. 28.

162. Val. Ep. 30. Most of the introduction of this epistle is taken from the writings of Paul: 2 Cor. 12:3-5; 1 Cor. 15:33 and 6:3-6.

163. Romans 5:12; Val. Ep. 14.

164. Val. Ep. 12.

165. Matt. 12:48; Val. Ep. 13, p. 164.

166. Romans 5:12; Val. Ep. 14.

167. Val. Ep. 35. From Paul's 1 Cor. 11:10.

168. Valettas, p. 328: "woman needs a cover (κάλυμμα) on her head." From Paul's 1 Cor. 11:10.

169. Val. Ep. 35.

170. Val. Ep. 72; from 2 Cor. 6:14.

171. Val. Ep. 15; from Matt. 5:38-39.

172. Val. Ep. 6, pp. 237-38.

173. Val. Ep. 63.

174. Matt. 5:34-35. In a letter to Amphilochios, Patriarch Photios quotes an even more stern command: "He who blasphemes the name of the Lord shall be put to death." (Val. Ep. 21, from Levit. 24:16.)

175. Psalms 135:15.

176. Val. Ep. 76.

177. Val. Ep. 56, 58, 59.

178. Val. Ep. 60. Reference to Gal. 4:19: "My little children, with whom I am again in travail until Christ be formed in you."

179. Val. Ep. 76; also Ep. 43.

180. Val. Ep. 108; from Titus 1:15, 16 and 1 Cor. 11:19.

181. Dvornik, "The Patriarch Photius and Iconoclasm," p. 86.

182. Mango, p. 247.

183. Ibid., p. 264.

184. The 'Golden Age' of Byzantine iconography began during the time of Photios. When he was sent into exile, however, all priests and artists appointed by him were forbidden to paint icons in the churches. N. Kondakoff, *Histoire de l'art byzantin*, 2 (New York, 1970), 28 ff.; also see Constantine Kalokyris, *The Essence of Orthodox Iconography* (Brookline, Mass., 1971), pp. 76-87.

185. In the letter to Michael-Boris of Bulgaria, Patriarch Photios discussed extensively the background for the Seventh Ecumenical Synod. (Valettas, pp. 216-19.)

186. Val. Ep. 4.

187. Mansi, XVI, 181.

188. Ibid., XVIII, 493 ff.

189. Hergenrother, II, 714.

190. Val. Ep. 4.

191. Val. Ep. 5.

192. Val. Ep. 32.

193. Matt. 12:31-32.

194. Val. Ep. 30: " Ἄνω δέ ποταμῶν, ὡς ἡ παροιμία." In Euripides' *Medea*, 411, the Chorus sings: " Ἄνω ποταμῶν ἱερῶν χωροῦσι πηγαί, καί δίκα καί πάντα πάλιν στρέφεται."

195. Val. Ep. 17. Also in Luke 22:44.

196. Val. Ep. 110.

197. Val. Ep. 118. The same appears in Photius' *Bibliotheca*, Codex 186.

198. Val. Ep. 136: "Εὐτύχημα μέν καί τό φίλους ἔχειν, ἐν καιρῷ τῶν πειρασμῶν καί χρείας." In Euripides' *Orestes*, 658-81, the following is stated about friendship: "ἐν τοῖς κακοῖς χρή τοῖς φίλουσιν ὠφελεῖν ὅταν δ'ὁ δαίμων εὖ διδῷ τί δεῖ φίλων; ἀρκεῖ γάρ αὐτός ὁ Θεός ὠφαιλεῖν θέλων."

199. Val. Ep. 1: " Ἀλλά δρυός μέν ἅλις εὔκαιρον εἰπεῖν τήν παροιμίαν."

200. Val. Ep. 190: " Ἔρρει τά καλά." This saying is attributed to Hippocrates, the scribe of Mendar, in a letter written to the Lacaedemonians: " Ἔρρει τά καλά Μίνδαρος ἀπέσουα πεινῶντι τῶνδρες ἀπορέομες, τί χρή δρᾶν." (Xenophon, *Greek History*, I, 23.)

201. Val. Ep. 6, pp. 227-28. "Δι' ὅλου δέ, γλώσσης φυλάσσου παρολισθῆσαι." In Jesus of Sirach: " Ὀλίσθημα ἀπό ἐδάφους μᾶλλον ἤ ἀπό γλώσσης οὕτω πτῶσις κακων κατά σπουδήν ἤξει." (20:18)

202. The same in *Prometheus Bound*, by Aeschylus (I, 327): "Σύ δ᾽ ἡσύχαζε, μηδ᾽ ἄγαν λαβροστόμει ἤ οὐκ οἶσθ᾽ ἀκριβῶς, ὧν περισώφρων, ὅτι γλώσσῃ ματαία ζημία λέγων." Euripides in *Bacchae* (380) also says: "'Αχαλίνων στομάτων, ἀνόμου τ᾽ ἀφροσύνας, τό τέλος δυστυχία."

203. The same in Lucian, 31: "Χρή τοίνυν ἀποφράττειν τά ὦτα, καί ἀνέδην αὐτά ἀναπεταννύεω τοῖς πάθει προειλημμένοις."

204. The Patriarch quotes from Homer's *Iliad*, 3, 222, because Theodore was a Trojan: "ἔπεα νιφάξεσσιν ἐοικότα χειμερίῃ σι."

205. Val. Ep. 101: "Εἰς ὕψος τά ταπεινά κατάγει δέ εἰς ταπεινότητα τά ὑψηλά."

206. Val. Ep. 94: "Καί ὑπέρ μέν σεαυτοῦ εἰς ἀέρα δέρων ἐπυκτεύσας" (p. 419). Also in 1 Cor. 9:26. The proverb means doing things in vain. Other similar sayings: "write on the water," or "saw on rocks," or "saw on the water," etc.

207. Nikaias the Philistonian was a contemporary of Socrates. It is said that he died from laughing too hard, according to his epitaph (Valettas, Ep. 94, p. 420).

208. Val. Ep. 100.

209. Val. Ep. 120.

210. Val. Ep. 129.

211. Val. Ep. 64.

212. Valettas, p. 242. Herodotos, in *Persian Wars*, 5, 18, calls the Persian women "ἀλγηδόνες ὀφθαλμῶν." Photios refers to them as "βολίδες."

213. Val. Ep. 193.

214. Val. Ep. 194.

215. Val. Ep. 225.

CHAPTER FOUR

NOTES ON THE FIFTY-TWO LETTERS

In 1601 the first known collection of Photios' letters appeared, compiled by David Hoeschel. He published, with the *Bibliotheca*, thirty-five letters selected from a manuscript collection belonging to Maximos Margounios, Bishop of Kythra. Prior to this only the consolatory letter to the Abbess Eusebia on the death of her sister had been published by Conrad Ritterhaus in Nurenberg, with a Latin version in 1601. The largest collection, however, was that prepared in 1651 by Richard Montague, Bishop of Norwich , with a Latin version which was published in London after his death. Montague included two hundred and forty-eight letters, or according to Photios' biographer, Cardinal Hergenröther, two hundred and forty-nine, since the letter following number 38 has no number. These letters are addressed to the Eastern bishops, to certain monks, to the Emperors Michael III and Basil I, and to other persons in high places. The first letter in the Montague collection is addressed to Michael-Boris, Prince of the Bulgars. The second letter, also of considerable length, is the encyclical addressed to the Patriarchs of the East, discussing especially the procession of the Holy Spirit. Nevertheless, many important letters were missing from the Montague edition, especially two addressed to Pope Nicholas I, and another to the Archbishop of Aquieleia on the procession of the Holy Spirit, all of which Baronius had given a Latin version. A new edition, more complete, written by Dositheos, Patriarch of Jerusalem, and published by Anthimos, Bishop of Remnicus (Rimnik) in Wallachia, in 1705, included all the above letters. Also included was one written to the Armenian Patriarch Zacharias in the Armenian language, and

another to the Armenian Prince Afutios in support of the doctrine of the Synod of Chalcedon, in a Latin version done by
Cardinal Mai.

It was not until 1860 that the new publication of Abbé
Migne was completed, which included all the above mentioned
letters with the exception of three addressed to three Italian
bishops. The Migne edition has divided the letters into three
books. The first included the official and semi-official correspondence with the Court, and with other princes, patriarchs and officials and similar correspondence with persons
in spiritual positions: bishops, clerics and monks. The third
includes letters to laymen, especially those in high positions
in government. There was to be a fourth book with eighty
letters of literary and theological content. Most of these
letters, however, were included in the volume with the
Amphilochia and were left out. The first book of the collection
included twenty-four long letters, the second one hundred,
and the third sixty-seven, for a total of 193 letters. The addition of the eighty of the *Amphilochia* brings the total to
273 letters.

In 1864 a new edition was prepared by the Greek director
of the Syros school, Ioannes Valettas, Accordingly, Valettas
in this edition collected 260 letters of Photios which he
divided into five groups according to content. The first
eighty-four form a group of letters pertaining to dogmatic
questions and scriptural interpretations; the second fifty-
seven are called advisory; the third, fifteen in all, are the
letters of consolation; the fourth is a group of sixty-four
letters of reprimand; the fifth group is forty letters on
various subjects. The translations of the letters in this study
are based on the Valetta edition. In addition the following
manuscripts have been read thoroughly. MSS of Iviron 684
and 160 (both late sixteenth century). The MSS of Iviron and
the Montague edition are believed to have used the Baroccianus
gr. 217, a tenth-century manuscript, and bear great similarity;

MS Marcianus gr. 575 ff. 264-313 of the fifteenth century; MS Parisinus gr. 1335 of the fourteenth century; and MS Vaticanus gr. 2195 also of the fourteenth century.

The letters translated in this study are divided as follows: Letters 1-6 belong to the group of pure consolatory type. Most of the letters, 7 to 30 inclusive, were written by the Patriarch while he was in exile for the first time. They are addressed to friends, members of the clergy, as well as former friends who have forgotten their duties. Photios is concerned, compassionate, and a true friend in suffering. To others he sends letters of reprimand to remind them of their duties as men of the clergy or high officials including emperors. One letter (No. 7) is addressed to Emperor Michael III and two (Nos. 17 and 18) to the Emperor Basil I.

The next group of letters, Nos. 31 to 34, includes letters to high officials such as Ioannes Strategos, Caesar Bardas, and again to Emperor Michael III on behalf of some friend. The last group of letters, Nos. 35 to 52, show the many sides of Photios as humorist, intellectual, teacher, and a man of the world.

In the winter of 870 Photios was condemned and sent into exile to Stenos by imperial order. There he felt alone and tired. He would have been much happier if he had stayed as a teacher at the Magnaura School among his books and his disciples writing, teaching and reading; now after many tribulations he has time again to write. He takes his pen, in order to find his own consolation, and writes some of the most moving letters of his career.

His friends and partisans, the bishops he had ordained, had been sent into exile; the churches he had consecrated were destroyed. Whatever he had done as a cleric was nullified. He was heavily guarded in the prison and could not communicate with any person. Nevertheless, he finds a way to get his letters from prison to his friends. One letter is addressed to Ioannes, Metropolitan of Heraklia, who is also in exile, probable answering his complaints and giving his courage. He is very dis-

couraged and disillusioned in this letter. For this reason the
letter is written in consolatory form. Try to remember, he
reminds the Metropolitan, that the rewards are over there and
not in this world.

During this time, Photios also wrote the two letters (No. 8
and 9 of this study) addressed to the bishops in exile. Letter
No. 8 is a lengthy masterpiece of composition. It is an apology
for the reproaches of someone whom Photios does not name,
because, as he says, it is easier for him to receive advice in
anonymity. He refers sadly to his sufferings. His greatest com-
plaint is that he is not allowed to have at least some of his
books to read. His accuser is worse than a barbarian. His many
references to St. Paul verify his love and preference for this
disciple. He ends the letter recommending obedience to the
emperor and his laws. The Byzantine concept regarding the
relationship between patriarch and emperor is defined clearly
by Photios. In spite of the sufferings he undergoes, Photios
preaches obedience and respect to the authority of the emperor.

During his exile Photios composed at least ninety letters,
which is proof that in spite of his banishment and his heavily-
guarded position, he had many friends and was still the focal
point of the Church of Constantinople. Furthermore, the
bishops consecrated by him remained consistently faithful
to him.

Photios has been accused frequently by his critics of using
his friends; that he was not sincere in his expressions of concern and only used them to accomplish his aims. From these
letters of consolation, however, one receives a different pic-
ture. Most of the letters of consolation have been written to
other ecclesiastics, which proves the Patriarch's sense of duty
towards his suffering clergy.

In the letters of consolation, in particular, the tenderness
and gentleness of the nature of Photios become more evident.
These letters are addressed to persons very close to the Patriarch, such as his brothers or members of the clergy who were
special, close and dear friends. Thus, from all his writings,

including his other letters, this group of letters mirrors more clearly the real Photios. The main themes involved in these letters are: life on this earth is temporary and full of trials; the rewards are not to be found in this life but will be in the next; this life is to be compared to a stadium where all men are the athletes competing for the prizes; the crowns and the wreaths, however, are not to be rewarded here in this life but in the next; death is inevitable, lamentations to the dead are useless, even embarrasing. God is the timekeeper; Christ the bridegroom; life is a stage of a tragedy; man the actor. Job is cited often as the example of ultimate patience.

Photios has an extraordinary ability to create vivid imagery with his pen. The use of flowering branches, spring, light and brightness are always associated with the good, the pleasant and the virtuous; winter, empty branches, darkness and cold are the followers of sin, exile and difficult times. To Eusche-mon and Georgios, metropolitans, Photios writes: "I am not discouraged even when I see the winter of evil and tyranny stretching over us, because I hear that you are in springtime blossom..." Yet, Patriarch Photios does not repeat these themes as if he were moved by a machine or obligation. The way he applies the appropriate forms show genuine love, sympathy and compassion.

One of the most moving among the letters is the letter of consolation addressed to his favorite brother, Tarasios, who had just lost a young and lovely daughter of marriageable age. The letter was written circa 871. From a reference on the letter we understand that Tarasios had already lost another child still nursing. This letter is not the kind a brother would write today in consolation, even if that brother were the Patriarch. This type of letter, however, was not unusual in Byzantium. Patriarch Photios begins the letter sympathizing with his brother, the grief-stricken father of a young and beautiful bride-to-be. By mourning with him, Photios wins his brother's attention. Among all the calamities that have befallen the nation and the family, Photios tells Tarasios, he

considers the death of this young girl the worst calamity
of all. Actually Photios is following here the form of the old
ways according to Menander's rules, by beginning with a
lamentation and a eulogy which should occur in the beginning
of a funeral speech. At this time, Photios himself is in exile,
and deserted and alone himself, grieves with the father. Having
accomplished his aim; that is, to attract the attention of the
grieving person, he then changes his tone. "But," he continues, "did not their parents suffer greatly also? Did they not
bury some of their children, and under terrible conditions?
But does not all end in death by the nature of man? Then
why is his brother so grief-stricken?"

The tone changes again. Like the prophet from the Bible,
Photios points his finger at his brother and talks to him: "How
do you dare question the will of God; how do you dare
question his unfathomed grace and love for humanity? You
say that it is not time for her to go? But who knows best
when is the right time but God, the giver of life? You take it
upon yourself to be the time-keeper?" Photios reprimands
the lamenting father.

The brilliance of Photios' extensive vocabulary, his knowledge of mythology and especially the Scriptures are all evident in this interesting letter. Also in abundant evidence is
his use of imagery and references to nature, especially in the
moving passage where the departed girl talks to her father
trying to console him as she tells him how happy she is in
this "magnificient place called Paradise." Photios somehow
anticipates the romanticists of the nineteenth century in his
frequent references to nature.

The letter has a tenderness and a pathetic touch which is
not usual with the Patriarch and is useful in understanding
Photios the man. Neither his scholarship nor his patriarchate
obliterates his deep feelings for his brother. If he could help,
he tells his brother, he would fall on his knees and embrace
the feet of Peter or Paul or anyone who would restore the
girl to her parents. But it is of no use. The only thing that

remains is faith and obedience to God's will. The great example for us is Job, he adds. Patriarch Photios is first and always a Christian. To him the idea of death should be welcome. This life is only a short transitory state, a necessary tearful passage on the way to eternity. This is the stage where man comes in contact with sin; therefore, the less time one stays on this earth, the less he sins. The rewards are not here, but in heaven, and we have only to cross this necessary stage in order to arrive at the desirable end. The guarantee of our own immortality, the Resurrection, is given by Photios as the final argument for the rejection of all grief over the death of a loved one.

Another letter addressed to Eusebia, nun and monastic superior, was also written as consolation for the loss of her sister. In this letter, however, tenderness has left Photios. He does not suggest here, as in the previous letter, that he will fall on his knees and pray to the Apostles for the restoration of the deceased. Here the Patriarch is very impatient with the abbess. "Death," he says, "did not start with her loss." He calls her selfish and ungrateful for something she should consider as a favor to her sister. The idea of death should always be welcome; especially to a person as pure as her sister, for whom the Bridegroom of all, the pure-hearted Christ, is waiting. Here again, as in the letter to his brother, Photios includes many references to nature.

In the last group of letters the subjects have been chosen to show Photios' manifold interests; his views on food, his humor, his views on women, his comments on various people, his extensive knowledge of mythology, medicine, history, his play on words, etc. Every letter is unique in each kind.

In summary, the language of the letters is rich, intricate almost baroque, and at the same time revealing the profound scholarship of the author. There are a number of classical allusions and frequent echoes of ancient literature in the very words that Photios employs. He has obviously left the world of learning for the greater, nobler world of the Church, but he cannot escape his own education; his immersion in Greek literature. Beyond the words, the noble ideals of life with which he was familiar from his reading of Homer, Sophocles, Plato, and Aristotle, flow easily into the Christian concepts that occupy the center of the attention of the author of these letters.

CHAPTER FIVE

FIFTY-TWO LETTERS

Letter 1

TO TARASIOS, PATRIKIOS, BROTHER,
CONSOLATORY ON THE DEATH OF HIS DAUGHTER[1]
(ca. September 871)

O! Where is Elijah now?[2] Where is Elisha?[3] Where is
Peter,[4] or Paul,[5] or any of those who were in their times
holy and saintly men? Then I would not have needed a
letter, but, having taken hold of the feet of one of them
(since I do not have the favor of their hands), I would not
desist doing everything until they restored the young girl
alive to her parents. But what can be done now? Nay,
surely in view of such great misfortunes of our family even
the exile abroad imposed against me cannot be regarded
with aversion.[6] I do need to write a letter (alas!) which can
soothe the lamentation of a brother over a daughter lying
dead at the time when hopes for children had come and the
marriage would appear ill-omened if it did not make the
young girl a mother rather quickly. And so the young girl's
child is not leaping into the hands of its grandparents and
playing with them, prating about with its inarticulate
speech. But, while greater things were being hoped for, then
even what we had was on the verge of being snatched away.
Alas, for the deception of our ancient ancestors and their
transgression and punishment!

How did that wicked and sinuous serpent ever creep into
paradise![7] How did it mislead them! Or how thence forward
until the present day the bitter goad of death continues!
This blow has reached all the way to us, sharper than an
arrow, more formidable than a thunderbolt. And the girl
lies dead just at the time when she was in the bloom of
youth, a dreadful and sad sight to the eyes of her parents.
At the time when the flower of childbearing was growing,
then the plant itself began withering away along with its
roots. Her constitution was ready to propagate, and the
scythe of death, being plunged deep into her vitals, began
to reap fully the very substance of her life. What kind of
tear will suffice for this calamity? What groaning? What kind

115

of wailing? Her mouth is hushed with that long and unwanted silence, and her lips are shut and do not recount her dignity or express the decency of her character but are contracted for dissolution.

What about her eyes? Alas, for a calamity which conquers even silence and is beyond words! Her eyes (how should I say it?) having poured away every stream of life, wrap up the remains with their dead eyelids. Her cheeks, instead of redness and natural coloring, are spread over with the color of darkness and death, which utterly destroys the comeliness of every form. Her entire face, from such a circumstance, presents to those who behold it a shocking and terrible sight. What bewitchment, what attack hurls arrows of this sort against us? Our previous mourning has not yet passed and again another greater one has fallen upon us. The first checked a child that was on the breast; the other would have checked also a mother as well, but the evil arrived earlier.[8] Whence come so many such great blows? There are blows from men, blows from obscure causes of wrath. Horrors rise up from all quarters. The arrows were directed against us personally, against our children. We have become a scene of tragedy, and among us dance lamentation, sorrow, grief, dejection, and every Erinys of evils. A Klotho with her spindles[9] and unlucky threads gather together her chorus, as it seems, against us, interweaving our life with tragic events and supplying the materials for tragic songs that are to be sung by the cruel dancers.[10]

But what has happened to me? Where am I borne? When I begin to write a condolence, I myself do not know how I became carried away by my grief and, because my thoughts had not been able to hold out against the course of the evil, I was swept away to the opposite of what I had in mind. And, as I was embarking upon the argument of my consolation, I was mentally carried home to the tears of those who were mourning.

But let us get control of ourselves, and let us not let ourselves be submerged in the depth of sorrow. Grief has ruined many, not only by destroying the body, but also by injuring the vitals of the soul itself. Let us not gratify our

enemies, for dejection on the part of those who are spite-
fully treated greatly delights their enemies. Let us not commit insolence against our ancestors' patient struggles. They
have seen the deaths of their children, deaths such as are
not ours, and may they be not ours.[11] Fire, water, and the
pit took possession of their descendants; even the bitter
and heavy exile abroad was imposed upon them, and utter
privation of friends and relatives came to them. In a word,
everything that brings gratification was taken away from
them, and yet they accepted it with good grace, and they
glorified Him who governs the affirs of man in a way superior for humans to reckon.

Let us consider who we are. Whence were we born?
Was it not as mortals from mortals? Was it not from non-
existence and after a short while destined not to exist?
Where is my father? Where is my mother? Did they not
depart, after they had played a little with life, except in
the instances of those whom the crown of martyrdom and
patience adorned, as soon as they had left the theater?
Do not the kings and tyrants, who are immortal as regards
their wanton behavior and their conceit, sink into death
along with their acts of domination? Every class of mankind,
whether it be one exercising authority or one in private
station, old or young, men or women, is certainly cut off
from life, and will not at all escape death's scythe.

We have submitted to nothing new or strange or alien to
nature. She came forth as a mortal from a mortal womb,
and, having served the law of nature in the course of her
mortal life, she departed by the same law of nature to the
immortal state. She did not leave behind any children
bewailing their orphanhood; she did not depart, taking along
with herself her concern over her children, a sting more
bitter than death. She did not gain much experience with
miseries. She did not seek death, which many have often
longed for after they have been surrounded by inescapable
misfortunes. While she was still associating with her parents,
she departed from the storm of transient things; she left
while still being served by her mother's hands. In the hands
of her parents she laid aside her spirit; her body was taken

care of; it was committed to burial, escorted with proper obsequies, piety and sober-mindedness, and the prayers of many who have been given alms. She departed to a place from which every sorrow and sighing has been driven away. What more was needed? That which has been effected with reference to this blessed young daughter of yours has turned my grief to the opposite, and I deem her blessed for her departure, and I convert my lamentation to the glory of God, and my perplexity to thanksgiving, when I perceive that she has been freed from the circumstances of the present world so auspiciously and just as if one would wish it.

But she did not live for a long time. Why does it make any difference if more or less days differentiate our lives when both longevity and brevity transport us to the very gates of death? No one takes pleasure in the past; the future does not exist; the present, in which one might engage in pleasure, is quite brief. Consequently, either a long or a short period of life, since it confines the sensation of pleasurable things only to the present, brings together into the same and similar enjoyment both him who sinks deep into old age and him who flourishes in youth, leading astray the feeling of both by the pleasure of the moment and giving to neither of them a share in pleasure of the past or the future. Consequently, it is a matter of indifference living a long or short time; or rather there is a difference for if no human being is said to be clean from spiritual dirt, and this is seen being confirmed by the facts, even if his life consists of one day, then whoever has left behind this body of clay in a shorter lifetime departs with less amount, in fact, of bodily stains. Surely, then, whoever mourns the girl who departed because she departed rather quickly from the circumstances of the present world, because she shared less in the things that defile, makes this a subject for tears, and you consider as a calamity the fact that she is seen by the Bridegroom in Heaven as more pure. But she went before her time. May I not hear such a statement; the utterance of this statement is reckless and to think it is more reckless. Before her time! Now, how is it that when she

loosed her mother's pangs of childbirth she was not thought
to be loosing them before time? But, while she was born
by the consent of God and on time, yet in regards to her
departure to the Fashioner we appoint ourselves as time-
keepers. And, while the Creator brings us forth on time,
when He takes us back to Himself, then does He not know
the right time? He made her into flesh from a drop; He
molded her in the womb; He brought her forth into the
light; He preserved her from infancy up to childhood, up
to marriage, up to perfect maturity. None of these things
were done in improper time. When, however, He transmutes
her to immortal life, only then it is not the right time?
Let such a blasphemy be far from a tongue that practices
piety; let it be far from a sober-minded mind. This is a
matter for long lamentations, this is a matter for many tears,
that man should be overwhelmed with such greatly wicked
thoughts and should not exchange the corruptible for the
incorruptible. On the contrary, one should not mourn for
her who has gotten away from her mortal body, but for
him who has mortified the immortal mind. One should not
lament her whom a heavenly Bridegroom admits to the
bridal chamber, but he who has buried the soul in dead
hopes.

Yes, you will say, but she departed before her parents.
Why not? Would one wish her, worn out beforehand by
the death of her mother and father, to depart thus afflicted
with so many wounds? Such a person does not profess to
me the affections of a father but the disposition of a step-
mother, not the love of a father or a mother but rather of
one who is seeking his own pleasure rather than the favor
that has been granted to his daughter, and of one who,
under the guise of love for his child, is cleverly contrving
his own care.

What, then, is more distressing than to see the death of
loved ones? Surely, then, the young girl departed free from
this. But this is not a distressing thing. And so why are we
consuming ourselves with grief? If, however, the young
girl were present in person, having suddenly appeared to
you from Heaven, she would place her hand into your

hand, and with a cheerful and joyful face she would kiss you and would say to you:[12]

Why are you mourning for me as though I had departed to suffer evil? Paradise has been granted me to dwell in, a sight attractive to the eyes to behold, but it is more delightful to have enjoyment therein and experiencing it is beyond all belief. That celebrated Paradise is the first and marvelous fatherland of our race, where long ago the work of art of nature wrought by the Master's hand, our forefathers, before the serpent whispered softly, used to enjoy the truly happy and blessed life. But now that sinuous and wicked serpent cannot have any possibility of secretly creeping in or of insinuating slanderous words; yet among us there is no one whose knowledge is not superior to every contrivance and cunning of his, nor does any eye need to be opened or to enjoy any greater desire, for we are all made wise by the divine and heavenly wisdom, and live amid abundant and ineffable blessings. The totality of our life is actually a feast and a festivity. Living brightly radiant in incorruptible and most pure bodies, we see God as much as it is possible for a human being to see Him, and, delighting in His inexpressible and incomprehensible beauty, we continually rejoice, and there is no satiety of this. But the abundance of delightful living results in the culmination of loving, and the power of enjoyment that accompanies this love makes that joy and exultation an inexpressible and truly indescribable one. Even now as I am conversing with you thus, an awesome and irresistible desire so turns me around to those things that it does not permit me to relate even the smallest portion of them. You yourself, too, will come here one day, including my dear mother, and then you will accuse me very much for saying but little about things so great, and yourself very much for lamenting over such beautiful and good things as ours which you bewailed. But now, my dearest father, joyfully dismiss me, send me forth, and do not detain me any longer so that you may not cause me further loss and on that account be bitterly grieved.

If, indeed, that blessed young daughter should relate these and other things, would you not then be abashed, put aside your lamenting, and joyfully send her forth to depart? And so, if the young girl says these things, we will feel better and cast away our lamentations. But if our common Fashioner and Master proclaims, "Whoever believes in me, even if he dies, shall live,"[13] and when "He has prepared for those who love Him that which eye has not seen and ear has not heard and has not entered into the heart of man,"[14] will we not at all, as if we were disbelievers, be better convinced by Him but continue to lament? How, pray, is this good? How is it right? Where are the thoughts that suit propriety or advantage? Accordingly, you should not feel shame before my most decorous bride[15] when you descend to womanish tears and squander away your manliness. You should refrain from womanly weakness, because a compassion for her that is rational and useful dissipates one which is irrational and useless. For if men, from whom women recover their strength, mourn like women, what will be the case with respect to them? Whence will they get their comfort? Whom shall we exhort them to imitate in steadfastness? To whom to look up to? But, as for you at least, may you not experience anything unworthy of yourself or false and alien to our family, to say something more appropriate, indeed, to the occasion. Let us not indeed be carried away into cries of lamentations beyond what is fitting, and let us not behave like women because of our sorrow, we who have appeared as men on many grounds in many most difficult trials. The Fashioner has taken to Himself the thing that He fashioned, still He has given more sons and daughters than He has taken away, and may they at least live well for a longer time and gladden their parents. Does the past grieve you? Let those who are with us gladden us.

Let us give thanks on behalf of those whom He has taken away, in order that we may have a firm pleasure in enjoying and rejoicing in those whom He has given. It is a good thing in the course of life to have successors for our family; we have them. It is a good thing to offer first-fruits to our common Fashioner and Giver of all good things; we have offered them. Whereas before it was unclear which of the children would be credited as first-fruits to God,[16] and which for the purpose of family succession, now, however, if only we offer our first-fruits with good grace, no longer will we anchor our hopes amid uncertainties, but we will be firmly grounded in certainty.

He never takes away without granting more lavishly, and always the least exchange themselves with the greatest and unexpected. If, however, we insult the first-fruits with lamentations as if we are being wronged . . . but I will say nothing distressing since I expect you not to involve yourself at all henceforth in lamentations, griefs, and such emotions as are causative of distress. May I have the Divine Being, indeed, assisting both my judgment and my hope; yes, and it does indeed. He Himself grants me the freedom to speak freely, now that you, as I said, have recovered from despondency to the rendering of thanksgiving.

Many are the examples, both recent and ancient, of that which is contributory to consolation, or rather, to speak more truthfully, life as a whole is an example of this. It is easier for one who goes through life upon principles of reason to lay aside every bit of dejection. Shall I say that which is greater, or rather that which is full of holy awe "of whom it is characteristic to grieve about those who have departed"? Or rather not I myself will say but I shall summon the herald of the world to declare through His own voice the heavenly decree, "I do not wish you to be ignorant, brethren, about those who have fallen asleep in order that you, too, may not grieve, precisely as the rest who do not have hope."[17] Paul is the one who trumpets these words, he who compassed the whole world by his preaching. The mouth of Christ proclaims that grieving over those who die is characteristic of unbelievers who extinguished the hope of resurrection because they refuse to believe the power of Christ's mystery.

But let us lay aside grief lest we be manifestly guilty of such great evils as this and truly then forfeit the young girl.

For now the bosom of Abraham cherishes her, and after a short while we shall see her there enjoying herself and joyful. If, however, contrary to the Master's laws, I mourn the young girl, I drive myself away from that beautiful vision. Do you long to behold the young girl? Cast grief away from yourself; show yourself through your rendering of thanks worthy of joy from Heaven. But if we still acquiesce in lamentations, we deprive ourselves of the object of our longing. Joy in Heaven does not recognize lamentations as acceptable, nor does the bridal chamber of exultation and joy allow itself to become a place of mourners, nor is it wont to receive favorably those who lay in the grave escorted by tears, especially for those whom it has as inheritors of ineffable joy. The Fashioner has decided to refashion for immortality the thing that He has fashioned. Let us not envy the young girl for her happiness, nor let us grumble against the judgment which we ought to respect, nor let us distort the Master's benevolence as an occasion for ingratitude. The child of the great King David was once ill, and the illness indicated the grave. The King, taking the illness for a misfortune, lay prostrate, and with tears tried to appease the Divine Being, abstaining both from food itself and from any other care of his body. But when the child departed, he immediately lay aside at the same time also his grief. For hitherto he had prayed that that which was born of his flesh and blood remain alive. However, when he saw that the Fashioner had decided in favor of his child's departure, he did not dare to insult the Judge's decision by grief, but, after he had rendered himself superior to every bit of dejection, he proceeded to let loose cries expressing thanksgiving and resumed his cutomary mode of life.[18] We, too, ought to conduct ourselves thus.

Suppose a child is ill, or another relative, or any one of our friends, and the illness causes death. I beg God to grant that the illness pass away, to yield to those who desire it the object of their desire. Does He Himself consider death a better thing? It is fitting, then, to give thanks for what He has arranged, to accept what has been done, and not to insult the judgment of the Creator with lamentation and bewailings.

If, however, a demon is laying snares for us and again is asking for a Job, and God permits the malignant one to become a combatant with His servant and tests the latter's patience with a view to reproaching His adversary, and He opens the stadium for contests, on the one hand, to put His opponent to shame and, on the other, to reward the combatant with a crown; not even on this supposition ought one, nor indeed in any wise, to deem the proclamation of virtue as a ground for grief, or to render the time of trophies a time for lamentations or the day of the contest a day of tears. No, I swear by those who have been rewarded with a crown because of their perseverance and the unfading and radiant crowns themselves. Such things are not worthy of your noble soul or steadfast will or remaining excellence. [19]

Therefore, let us stand bravely; let us stand courageously, and as soldiers of the heavenly King let us attack the enemy, and let us not dishonor the witness of the Judge of the contest, nor let us strengthen the adversary's insolence by our bad bearing, nor let us weaken by our later actions whatever in the way of bravery we have accomplished earlier, nor let us, on the one hand, be brave at arousing the envy of the enemy but, on the other, be convicted in the end as reluctant to conquer him through perseverance. The enemy is inclined to fall whenever he sees one long-suffering bearing the temptations. More quickly he desists from his act of tempting whenever he sees a man established on firm perseverance. The Giver of the crown is near, welcoming the contestant with radiant crowns in return for his struggles. And no longer does He allow the enemy to attack, but drives him far off, all his wiles and plots and all, even if he is still determined to behave impudently. He replaces our griefs, too, many times over with true happiness and joy. And to all these things an unexceptionable witness is again, Job himself;[20] even as we have shared in his afflictions, so too we shall enjoy his happiness, glory, and splendor, both now and to the unending ages, by the interceding of our supremely glorious Lady, the Mother of God and ever-virgin Mary, and of all the Saints.[21] Amen.

Letter 2

TO TARASIOS, PATRIKIOS, BROTHER[1]
(June 873)

Our friend has died bodily, but not even you yourself can deny that he did not leave behind as an immortal monument his personal excellence throughout his lifetime. Shall we then call anyone[2] happy at all if we are minded to bewail him?[3]

Letter 3

TO EUSEBIA, NUN AND MONASTIC SUPERIOR, ON THE DEATH OF HER SISTER[1]
(June 875)

If death began with us, and we were the first in our race to experience it, then reasonably, as though having fallen into something unexpected and new, we could be upset by this occurrence. However, ever since men have been created, we share life and death and the penalty is ancestral, as there is no one who will live and who will not face death. Why do we consider our common debt a private loss and bewail loudly as though a new exaction has been demanded of us? In fact, it cannot be otherwise, nor does nature know any other law. Are we astounded beyond measure at it as something strange? And do we surrender ourselves without piety and not according to the laws of the Spirit, to be submerged in grief? And do we forget, whenever we loudly bewail the death of relatives, that we are aborning death for ourselves by our lamentation? And yet, if death is a harsh thing, why do we hasten it for ourselves and try to stop the condition set by the Shaper? If, however, it is good and salutary, and then according to the judgment of the Master, why do we grieve beyond measure for the departed?

My sister, you say, departed; my sole consolation after God, my comfort in my distresses, and the dissolution of my sorrows, the foundation of things that cheer me. And what of this! Both your father and mother have left you, as well as other relatives, and your family going as far back as Adam. You, in turn, are going to leave others, and you cannot find anyone who is not left by very many. Sister has left behind sister,[2] but she has found her parents who preceded her (in Heaven). She left her sister behind, but she departed to our common Master and Father, and she went to that state to which we are also journeying. Then you consider only that she left you. Do you, however, not think of those whom she has reached? Do you not think of them? You sigh because you cannot see the body, but do you not rejoice that the soul has found rather freer association with you? You complain that she has been liberated from the corruptible.[3] Do you not consider it a great thing that she is enjoying the incorruptible? How, indeed, did she depart?

If she had departed into non-existence, or if she had gone under another jurisdiction and dominion, then she would really have deserted us. But if she is guarded by the very hand of Him who fashioned her and we have the same Master who both rules and takes care of us, and the same habitation and dwelling is prepared for each of us, and if a life free of tumults now has her, and we, on the other hand, are still carried to and fro by the billowy sea, how did she leave us? If we, too, are not being steered toward the same port of rest, if we are traveling the same road, if the same end does not await us, then you should think of her as departed, then you should mourn for her as separated. If no matter what one plans and does, He is going to direct all to that destination, why do we grieve in vain? Why do we display anger against the laws of nature? Man, being mortal in nature, has served death, because he has spent the present life in the same and like manner as his father and mother and the rest of the human race. Then what? Should the course of nature be overturned because of us alone, and the laws of creation be disturbed? What, indeed, has ever emerged through birth that does not again sink through dissolution and death?

I leave out the flowers of plants and their beauty, which please not only the eye, but the other senses also. I pass over the beauty of plants and herds of all sorts of animals, all of which, in the course of time, have their birth as a prelude to their dissolution. But recall with me the well-ordered chorus of stars; how they not only embellish the firmament, adorning the heavens with rather brilliant colors, but also how they illuminate the night, driving away its gloominess and providing the viewers with a sight that is griefless. Look, again, at the moon how, borrowing its light from the sun, it lights up the air freely and bestows its gift and strives to make another day before day. But all these things look to their end and know their debt, and hasten to make repayment. Is not the sun itself bright to look upon, but also wonderful for its beauty? Now, what else, indeed, can I say but that it, like a happy giant from one end of the sky to the other end of the sky,[5] unraveling that immense and well-regulated course in the midst of the universe itself, makes a spectacle and also shows off, striking everything with its rays, on the one hand giving life; on the other hand warming and containing the world by the Word and Law of the Creator. And it does not grow old, although it continuously does this for such long periods of time, nor does its beauty undergo a change, nor does it slacken its course, nor is there any act through which its dissolution will be demanded! But even it, which is so great and so old, cannot escape its end but succumbs to the laws of nature, and nothing which has been invested with existence through generation seeks to find out about the immortal before death.

What then? See these things are transformed and changed and do not complain against the law of creation, but with ready obedience bear the will of the Artificer. Shall we, however, by lamenting uselessly, not fear the divine wrath against us? And since we have so many examples before our eyes, shall we not come to our senses from any of them, and shall we surrender ourselves to all such things as suffering and the Evil One prescribe? The Shaper has taken the thing which He has fashioned unto Himself, and you do not bear the fact that He frees it from toils and cares which certainly crop up in the course of life? And you are displeased at the fact that He will raise it up? And you lament over such a favor? He personally immortalizes it. And you, as though she no longer exists, fall into lamentations? And how is this worthy of your virtue?

But let us take hold of ourselves; let us know our nature; let us know the Shaper; let us comprehend the depths of the Master's clemency. He gave death as a punishment, but through His own death he transformed it as a gate to immortality. It was a resolution of anger and displeasure, but it announces the consummate goodness of the Judge. The thought surpasses methods of reason. For though He dissolves such nature as was destroyed through original sin, the dissolution becomes a prelude to recreation. He separates the soul from the body, and the separation is the beginning of a union that is both rather brilliant and holy. "A physical body is sown, but it is raised as a spiritual body; it is sown in dishonor, but it is raised in glory."[6] The Creator takes back the work of art of his own hands, and He draws it to Himself; He removes it from human eyes, but He places it under the protection of the flashes and the brilliances of the angels. How could you mourn over this? How could you cry? Is not mourning very far from them? Thinking of all this and giving it your attention, and most of all remembering the fact that from infancy you have devoted yourself to God, and you have been united to the incorruptible and immortal bridegroom, Christ, having denied your parents and brothers and every relation, promising Him alone your whole manner of living and life, do not disgrace the agreement with lamentations, and do not becloud that grace with mourning, and do not now exchange that joy of the angels with your present sullenness. For, if the angels are now rejoicing in the reception of this soul that is virginal and superior to sufferings to fill up the number of demons that have fallen away, and you make this a cause for sorrow, beware lest you are bitterly insulting the former by the latter.

No one who abounds in love for the bridegroom abandons his love and falls into mourning and forgets that he has Him and speculates on, and is much concerned with deaths, and is afflicted with pain over the latter; overwhelming his love with his emotion and giving up his joy as a prisoner to grief. If, therefore, the departed woman, or rather she who has preceded us, happened to be one of those who had lived carelessly and impiously, perhaps tears and groans would be pardoned. And yet at least our Lord and Savior, the fountain of love toward man, has laid down a law to those who choose to follow Him and to reflect on such things. For He said: "Let the dead bury their own dead, you follow me."[7] Since, however, that virginal and blessed vessel happened to be one of those who had lived piously and in God-loving manner and had kept their faith in God pure, how can we not importune the Master's voice? How do we not find it in the dissolution of all our rejection? "He who believes in me, even though he dies, shall live."[8] Through death she has obtained immortal life; through dissolution she has inherited that dwelling which is indestructible. Again, the common Savior of men and the bridegroom of those who are saved said: "The sons of the bridal chamber cannot mourn so long as the bridegroom is with them."[9] Do you hear what He says? Do not condemn yourself to separation from such a bridegroom because of your mourning. Do not deliver that sentence against yourself, which, even if someone else cared to do so, you yourself would not bear that insult, but you would have denounced him as an enemy, a foe, and altogether wicked. Do not, in grieving for her who is enjoying glory, prove yourself guilty of lamentations. "Those who are with Christ cannot mourn." What is more wonderful than this utterance, or rather the Master's statement? You mourn? You have departed from the bridegroom. You cry? You insult the bridal chamber. Are you doing what is characteristic of the majority of human beings? You are deserting the bridal chamber. But let us no longer mourn for her who lives with God as though she were dead; nor let us, in thinking that with our lamentations we are demonstrating our love for her, insult her personally. Lamentation is an insult against those who dwell in the heavenly bridal chamber, and tears belong to those who speak ill of the blessed, who question their happiness, who doubt (not to call them disbelievers) the resurrection.

Having thought of all these and having considered with sober judgment, discard your mourning, lay aside your sorrow, sighs, and your tears. Cherish this advice and other comments which I made earlier, and if you separate yourself from all the other things and keep completely for yourself only the blessed and indestructible love of the pure and immaculate bridegroom Christ, you will never cease turning to and looking at Him.[10]

Letter 4

TO GEORGIOS, METROPOLITAN OF NICOMEDIA, ON THE DEATH OF A PRIEST IN EXILE, AFTER HIS ORDINATION[1]
(871)

I wanted immediately upon receiving the sad news (how I wish that it had not reached my ears), to try to soothe your pain with words of consolation, and to try to remove your grief with whatever comfort I could provide. But, since I myself was being racked with the same sorrows (I could, indeed, not say greater, not because I was afraid of the truth, but because I would not believe) and I grieved in my soul; I became somewhat spiritless to attempt to relieve the sorrows of others when I could not find consolation myself. Finally, and with difficulty, I collected my thoughts and remembered foremost that that archepiscopal and saintly hand is still with us and may it, at least, remain with us for a longer time than it has already, that hand which molds and fashions for us such servants for our sacred office; yet more I got control of myself and I rose up over my distress and thereafter I made bold to draw your perfection over to the same disposition as myself. And, I reflected, what is so strange or unusual about what has happened to us?

A member has been taken away; yes, but he has been dedicated to God; the first-fruit of those beautiful things which therefrom we have been enriched had to be given to Him. An ancient law is this: to offer to the Giver and our common Master the first-fruits of such as are precious. A well-flowering branch, bearing beautiful fruit, has been removed, but the root remains; it will flourish again, not less luxuriantly. And if that which has been removed causes rather great grief, let the root produce even more branches, in order that there might not be grief again whenever the gardener takes unto himself one of the branches; but we should forget the consciousness of that which has been removed in the enjoyment of those that are left behind.

The lovely and wonderful image of virtue is gone, but the painter again sets his hand in motion and He will surely produce not one but even many more, because He is a lover of bearty. For me this is a remedy for my despondency. I think, however, that everyone of those who are pious would gladly adopt this. The body of the Church over which we have been called, even you yourself would deem right to be a solace even for your archepiscopal sympathy.

What then? He died before his time? Who, pray, is more precise in maintaining times and judging than the One who arranged all things with reason and sequence? But in the bloom of youth such men bear their struggles nobly; but continuing on into old age often becomes a hindrance to much of their nobility. He ran parallel with us to attain virtue; we should not take it ill that He completed His race first. Now, he was a consolation for afflictions, but he did not take with him his words of consolation. He will be such, even more now, both in regard to his prayers to the Divinity, since he is, indeed, closer to It and draws the more from Its decisive influence for assistance and advocacy. His lips are silent but his deeds shout aloud. His tongue has just been stilled but his reproaches against the violators of the laws perpetually whip the thoughts of those very individuals, let me say.

What then? He left this life in the midst of persecutions,

afflictions, and hardships.[2]   You are giving me the greatest
of all consolation. For one seeking the Kingdom of Heaven
and pursuing his inheritance,   there should not follow a
life of luxury. The athlete should not be at rest, nor should
the contestant recline and rest under the shade of trees and
in gardens, but he should be tested in the midst of struggles;
amid tribulations themselves; in the midst of the bloodthirstiness of his pursuers. It is good for him to appear before the judge of the contest still dripping with the sweat
of his labors. Blessed is the man who is seen panting from
the races and labors. This, I say, is more blessed than the
crowns, for the latter is given by the judge of the contest,
while the former is the result of the zeal and the distinction
of the athlete. In the midst of the height of the persecutions
he sped off to the giver of crowns.

What then? Did you want the contestant to toil endlessly
and not receive more quickly that for which he endured to
the end and suffered? Are you expressing to me the wish of
an enemy, but not the care of friends, not grief, not compassion? He has departed from the eyes of all, this commonly
shared child of the Church, this man of God who was dear to
me. But he has gone to Heaven, to our common Master, to
dance with the angels and to sing the divine praises as a priest.
Oh! How much consolation I have found in this. For he had,
yes, he had to be offered to God, this priest, as the first offering for us who are persecuted for sacred glory and the sacred
laws. He was a priest who, with his rather great frankness,
blocked up the mouths of the profane and bridled tongues
which were skillful in pursuing vanities; a priest even though
the impious did not think him so.

What else? All sorts of virtue bloomed in him. It is for
this reason, indeed, that he departed rather quickly for the
imperishable state of paradise, so that none of his accomplishments might wither away. For, if no one is free from stain,
even if his life consists of one day, he who more quickly
executes the course of his life is most able to escape from
stain. He was the common support of the pious. He left behind for them a beautiful canon of behavior and model,
having left his life in the course of his toils on behalf of

piety. He did not see the restitution of the Church for which he struggled. For this reason he is receiving the wages for his labors in full in Heaven. For the attainment of happiness here in return for one's struggles shuts off the reward of blessedness there. He did not see the restitution with sentient eyes, but he sees it now with intellectual ones. But perhaps because he is rather close to God he will hasten it for those who are still alive, if it be to advantage. The grave has his body, but the mansions of Heaven have his soul. The earth has his dust, but the bosom of Abraham has his spirit. He has been deprived of his friends but he has found better ones. He will, however, shortly meet also those whom he has left, if they remain in actuality friends of God. He has escaped the plots of his physical and intellectual enemies, plots that are clandestine, from without; from within, straightforwardly, and in ambush. He saw, even though as in a mirror (for I for my part see this in my God-sent dreams), what he desired and what he constantly strove after, towards which in soul he had flown up, and towards which, even though he was burdened by his earthly tent, he was elevated. He saw the King calling him and the radiant angels serving the call; he saw that sacred chorus untouched by the profane and unseen, in which he was being escorted; he saw that indescribable and unending glory and pleasure.

Oh, enjoyment of sweet visions, even before the enjoyment. Oh, blessed departure, which is worthy of being marveled at but not provoking tears; of being envied but not being mourned. With spendid obsequies he went up to the gates of Heaven, with a brilliant lamp, not only glistening with oil but also watered with sweat from his struggles; adorned not only by virginity but also glorified by the office of the priesthood. Not only with these but also with other virtues through which the shedding of light is abundantly and everlastingly enriched.

All these have become for me a comfort, a consolation, or rather after they began with consolation they have transported me to spiritual joy and exultation. May these thoughts become also a comfort to your archepiscopal perfection as well, and a foundation for joy and delight; all the more, in fact, because the accomplishments of the deceased depended upon your instruction and care.

Letter 5

TO GEORGIOS, DEACON AND CHAMBERLAIN[1]
(870/877)

I forbid you, best of friends, to be called any longer a friend of ours.[2] For I perceive myself to be the most miserable of all men with regard to the possession of most faithful friends. Our good and faithful Oikonomos, our mutual friend (alas, I say this and write because he is silent) has left us, his temporal friends, and in place of us, as it seems, has taken in exchange eternal friends as though he could not allow such great virtue to dwell in times such as these. Now, whereas that celebrated Timon of old, having perhaps fallen in with unusual instances of wickedness, decided to do a wise thing, namely, both to be and to be called a misanthrope instead of a philanthrope, I should manifestly be acting, I believe, much more rightly if I am minded to become a misophile.[3] For, when I am beginning to enjoy extraordinarily marvelous virtue in the case of friends, no sooner do I rejoice in such an enjoyment than I am exceedingly and bitterly grieved and driven away from it; as though only in order to cause grief and to release the unbearable sense of pain, for this reason alone is either the envy or some other motive of him, whoever he is, who hurled against us such a great missile let us taste of such a pleasure. I am, indeed, carried away by this grief, and I do not know what I should say except that he did not pity us either for our exile or for our imprisonment or for the other difficulties with which we are completely drowned in the course of our life. Since he was not abashed by any of these things, he suddenly seized and tore away from us our friend and departed, having fixed the bitter and inexorable point in the very center of our heart. But perhaps it will not be a long time before he will have completely put an end to this heart of mine (for this is the only thing which refreshed us among such great misfortunes) and will drive me away to Him whom I long for.

You, then, who are my life's remaining hope, farewell! And continue to love me. Also, perform memorial rites for him, in our place, in a manner befitting your virtue and his friendship. And appoint yourself, in our place, a protector and guardian of his relatives and family and of yourself, and try to alleviate the greater part of their grief. For there is nothing else, I believe, that one can do for the deceased. Even if I wanted to write anything more, a very strong flow of tears has hindered my writing.[4]

Letter 6

TO LEO, WHO HAD BEEN A LOGOTHETES AND BECAME A MONK, TROUBLED BY ONE WHO SEEMED TO BE A FRIEND[1]
(870/877)

A man who is dull of character, soft as regards toil, unstable in judgment, who succumbs to gain, and is a slave to pleasure could neither do a nobly good thing and yet could commit a great evil. All those, however, who are sharp by nature and marvelously strong to hold up against all things, and disdainers of both money and pleasures, and not to be diverted to reject their judgment, these, then, whenever in fact power from some source or other has been conferred upon them, either could accomplish by virtue of their influence very great things for good, or, whenever they incline toward evil, become both intolerable and inexorable to both friends and family as well as all men. We must not, therefore, be vexed that we are not enjoying the best from one who was formerly a noble friend, but we must be thankful that not only have we received nothing distressful; but because we do not experience from him those annoyances that reach the point of excess. If, however, he ever reforms and should return to his cognate virtues along with his friendship, perhaps he will efface by his gladdening goodness even all the saddening things that earlier occupied us.

Letter 7

TO MICHAEL, THE GOD-CROWNED EMPEROR[1]
(April or May 866)

As we read through the letter of your God-crowned and truly imperial Majesty, we became filled with joy and at the same time with amazement. Joy, on the one hand, because through it we were given the good news that your Majesty was protected by God beyond the reach of every plot, and was mightier than every insurrection; loftier than the machinations of all your enemies; and removed from every other mishap and infirmity. This has filled us with inexpressible joy and exultation.

On the other hand, we became seized with amazement and were reduced to tears, loudly bewailing human vanity and particularly how some men who, while being deemed worthy of many graces and much glory and becoming possessed of much wealth, when they ought to be contented with such things as they enjoy and to be fully conscious of their own limitations, to celebrate their benefactors with every praise and respect; yet, by showing their desire as insatiable and by having contentiously striven to expand themselves toward everything, dare to snort at both their own head and that of their benefactors and to bring forth into fulfillment the myth of Salmoneus. As a result of this, they not only fail the hopes of which they dream and on which they were being borne, but even foolishly drive themselves away from those very things of which they were possessed by a just and given power.

Some such thing, of course, we have learned through letters (how I wish that I had not). Such was the case also with that base man (for I do not know how otherwise I should call him, calling to mind human wretchedness), for, having been elevated by your bountiful and munificent right hand to approximately the sceptre itself of sovereignty, and having had a share in the imperial dignity, though not the name but the power, he could not bear, as they, the greatness of this benefaction, nor was he content with what he had been deemed worthy, nor did he render thanksgiving for what he had enjoyed. However, moving his foot beyond boundaries, and having extended hands of insolence against the head of his benefactor, he has departed, leaving behind his very life, his haughty hopes, and his vain conceits piteously, alas, and pitiably.

I did, however, feel sorrowful, O my benevolent and wholly gentle imperial Majesty, when I learned that that man had been handed over to untimely death, but, in addition to this, especially because he had death exacted from him, paying, in fact, the penalty for tyranny. Certainly, the virtue and clemency of your imperial Majesty do not permit us to suspect that your letter was forged, and that the circumstances concerning his coronation and the subsequent lamentation of others, had happened in any other way than it indicated. Therefore, I bear with grief particularly his mortal blow. Taking in mind, besides other things, the fact that the man was carried off in the very act of working wickedness without either having washed away with his tears both the pollutions and filths of his life which are accustomed to be rubbed upon our wretched nature, or having exhibited repentance for those things with which perhaps he had unjustly harmed others, or in some other way having succeeded in propitiating the heavenly judge. Thus, with these very burdens, he was sent on to the heavenly tribunal.

But, while he, as the mysteriousness of the judgments of God decreed, so also brought his life to an end, having been to many an object of terror, to many chastisement, to many an object of pity, and to a greater number perplexity, do yourself, O ornament of emperors, exaltation of our fatherland, fortress of our government, and much-loved pride of all over whom the news of Christ has been invoked, come to us as quickly as possible.   Bestow upon those who have a desire the object of their desire.

First, deliver us from the captivity which we have undergone, deprived of you.   Refresh us from the hardship with which we are being troubled because your consolation is not present. First, grant this greatest favor to your city and to your citizens; namely, with completely free hands and tongues to address you with the acclamation that has been due you, that is the name "emperor." Second, respect the antiquity of the venerable and sacred senate. Third, respect the request of every person—men, women, children—for all with one mind and one voice request the presence of your imperial Majesty.

If, however, the High Priest, too, has ever been held by you in account and thought (and I know that he has been so held), continue to consider that He is at your side and, having taken hold of your hand with His hand, is taking you to your city and the temple of God, in which you sustain your hopes, and to the imperial palace. Yes, we all beseech you, do not put our hopes and our request to shame. For we believe that with the help of Christ Jesus, our true God, when your imperial Majesty returns to the imperial city, you will both free government from the gloom of despondency and, still more, will humble the arrogance of your military and personal enemies, assuming mastery over them by deliberation, understanding, and military pursuits, by the intercession of the supremely holy Mother of God and of all the Saints. Amen.

Letter 8

FROM EXILE TO THE BISHOPS[1]
(870)

I marvel how he,[2] whoever in the world that person is, so quickly forgot our relationship. For I should not wish even by name to bring a reproach against him, not even if he should still launch an attack against me rather insolently since, in fact, I discern that most people are admonished more easily when reproached impersonally than bear advice when cited by name.

But how has he so quickly abandoned us beyond remembrance so as to accuse us not only of such great thoughtlessness but also of neglect of divine laws? Whence does he rise up so strongly against our humbleness, or rather who has exalted him all at once to such a great height that, even though we say nothing, still he hears and, even though we have not reached such a thought, He, as though from a watch tower, his own imagination looking at our hearts and entering them,[3] understands and comprehends those things of which some had not even been conscious? And did he think that he knew the affairs of men more than the Spirit which dwells in them? Even Paul did not expect that there would be a large crop of such men, nor did he bequeath the same knowledge to others.[4]

But, pray, whence is such great thoughtlessness, as well as the betrayal of the whole Church and the contempt for the established laws, shed against us? What did we do? What did we cogitate? What did we say and against whom? Let him by no means even think and may he not reckon that, because he has not couched his insult with the same words,[5] he has uttered against us something better than anyone of those who rail such things against us;[6] for it is not the words which give weight to the thoughts but it is rather the bitterness of the intention which renders the words harsh and hard to bear. When, however, in fact, words are in harmony with the thoughts, and the harshness of the intention coincides with the harshness of the language, how does uttering the same words or presenting the same thought through equivalent ones make the difference?

But if, looking at the storm of misfortunes which has been heaped upon us and at the burden of difficulties which has encompassed and constricts us from all sides, he really thought that we had fallen into derangement, he certainly thought and contemplated that which is human (Why, what else could one actually say on his behalf?), for the excesses of afflictions generally produce in those who are distressed perversion and change.

If he resolved that the evil one should receive even greater authority against us than against the divine Job by his customary means, even though surely he (the evil one) did not receive authority over his (Job's) soul, he[7] who is against us has entrusted to him (the evil one) mastery even over our soul. For, as a result of the fact that he heaps upon us the charge of untempered thoughtlessness along with the charge of acting contrary to the laws, he clearly shows himself as having both thought and confirmed this. But, even if he was seduced to this suspicion about us, still he finds this also as as means for the plausibility of his other abuse. Let me for the moment[8] set aside the subtlety and refinement of his defense—he ought not to have attacked us nor to have made my suffering even more grievous by the addition of personal insults, but rather to have soothed my pain by some consolation and words of gratification and to have attempted in every possible way to devise encouragement.[9] To exasperate, however, and to attack, and to reproach my calamities is characteristic of one who delights in the misfortunes of his neighbor and not of one who shares the pain nor of one who undergoes the same suffering, and is not characteristic of one who performs the function of a friend but works wickedness as enemies would do.

They[10] have emptied against us the dregs of every wickedness of theirs by having deprived us of friends, by having cut us off from relatives, dissevering beforehand from you yourselves (the most bitter of my sufferings) and having kept us separated, by having desolated us of attendants and servants, by having imprisoned us, by having placed about us guards and jailers (in order that it might not even be possible for us, if we so wished, to weep and to mourn over our personal calamities, and that even mercy might not secretly slip in to us from any source either by word or by deed), by having suspended us over countless dangers of death, by having imposed against us (alas!) the starvation of divine utterances and of every other thing. And, while simultaneously completely surrounding us with many evils that do not cease, having both torn apart all our senses and having marshalled themselves against all of them, they have contrived novel devices against each one[11] (for keen as regards evil is alienation from God and humaneness).

In fact, while they have blocked up our eyes (Why, what can one surely say when one can neither see anyone at all nor yet consort with books, and especially in the case of those whose great and primary consolation is reading?[12] For, in fact, even this sentence against us they issued with all their decrees.),[13] they have shut up our hearing altogether, for they permit us to hear neither the voice of those who love us reading, nor even of our enemies. (What, indeed, can I say?), but, so far, at least, as it depends upon their effort, we do not hear men singing to God or even offering thanks to Him with hymns. For they have not even left behind anyone, even for a short while, even of those who are mediocre with respect to singing to be with us (O cruelty surpassing even the minds of the barbarians!),[14] but instead of clergymen, instead of monastics, instead of chanters, instead of readers and scribes, instead of friends and intimates (by whose company the weight of oppressions generally is wont to be relieved), instead of all these, in a word, we have been handed over to garrisons of soldiers and military companies. But why should I recount these things one by one and lacerate my wounds by mentioning them?

[Not only did they do these things] but they also assaulted all our senses by contrivances of countless evils; not even our soul itself (to such an extent, in fact, had their actions gone) did they allow to be unharmed (a deed most foul and most cruel of all that God has loathed), destroying houses of God, expelling the poor, the maimed and the mutilated, whom we had supported as a propitiation for our sins, from their own hearth and resting place,[15] and distributing their possessions as though these were spoils of the enemy;[16] and they smote the flesh of our servants with lashes so that throughout their entire body they produced wounds thereupon by the frequent swing of their lashes[17] in order that they might inform them of the gold and silver which we had stored away, which those wretches had not seen even in a dream, although the torturers themselves knew more clearly than all the rest that we had always been slandered with references to money, and that we are not as fond of money as they (those avaricious persons). Our disdain for it never accustomed us to keep committing an irrationality for the sake of it (much less to store up treasure), but that very thing which the sun saw whenever rising (the violence on the part of those who were acting despitefully frequently caused even the teacher of virtue, Paul, to embark[18] upon words of this sort), the time of the day and especially of the night not only betrayed but also unloaded.

Though they knew these things no less than anyone else, they kept butchering, they kept whipping, not in order to find any of those things which they pretended to be seeking (unless in this, too, they have become yet further demented, [namely,] seeking to find those things which they know do not exist), but in order to grieve us even therefrom and to omit no manner of maltreatment which they could inflict against us.

But I would not deny that Satan (or I do not know what, in fact, I should say) asked[19] for these things and for more things than the above-mentioned against us, and that we are completely exhausted by these things. With regard, however, to the fact that such great wickedness has driven us out of our senses and has rendered us disdainful of the divine commandments and has made us as common traitors, I do not know why anyone who accuses us of such things should not agree to rage against us more violently than our obvious enemies do. If one, however, when hearing these things, blushes and shrinks back and denies both that he ever would have said such a thing against us, or that he even would have taken it into his mind (for a sin, whenever it is revealed by the reproaches of just words, is disposed to nature to be clearly

seen as more unseemly than previously, so that not even
to his very parent would he seem genuine but as a bastard
and an object of aversion, especially by the sting of the conscience, which the Fashioner all-wisely has placed in our nature, being aroused for the purpose of clearly seeing the
deeds that are to be done); if, then, accordingly, he should
earnestly maintain that none of those things even entered
his mind, but, as is fitting, he relegates even those who ever
dared such things to remote regions and with terrible execra-
tions, ask him in the name of our friendship itself: how does
what he has said about us differ from saying that we are in
the number of enemies and that we do make a distinction
between friends and enemies? And whose friends does he
mean? (Oh, for the abuse against us!)—the friends of Christ
or the enemies of Christ? For this is the end result of wanting
to enroll in the lot of those who suffer on behalf of Christ
and those who wage war against us and Christ, who, having
considered the blood of His covenant an ordinary thing[20]
(let me for the moment pass over the other matters), have
defiled the sanctuaries of the Lord and have derided the
sacred chrism, or rather the Holy Spirit, through whose
agency the chrism is prepared.[21]

Ask them, therefore, I again implore you: How does the
latter differ from the former except in respect to excess
of wickedness? And if he really can show that the latter is
slighter than the former, consider that I am truly talking
nonsense[22] and deem him worthy of countless praises. And
yet, of course, he was sophistically arguing not that he had
insulted us more lightly than the others, nor that, in fact, he
had given the opportunity to the others to heap an excess
of insults upon us, but that he had openly said nothing
which led to our reproach. Even if he shows his arguments
too mean to be praised, do not excommunicate him. If, on
the other hand, he proves nothing, as, of course, he will
not be able to prove anything, do chasten him to keep silent, but do consider that my misfortunes stem also from
him because, in truth, revolts and slanders on the part of
friends support the treacheries of our enemies. For how
does anyone who says or thinks such things as that good

friend has imagined that we said and thought not reach the ultimate of thoughtlessness, and is he not a common traitor of the whole Church and a disdainer and an insulter even of the tradition of the Fathers? Furthermore, countless other sins are included therein: [namely,] falsehood, deceit, impious and faithless thoughts, mutual quarrels, and an endless multitude of wickedness. Did not that good painter delineate our image with beautiful colors, he who maintains that he has said nothing bad about us? But if these things really proceed from the simplicity of character, let us comply with the injunction of the Lord who proclaims, "Be cunning as the serpents and innocent as the doves!"[23] If, however, from wickedness, let us change our minds, since He again proclaims, "Unless you are converted and become as children, you will not enter into the kingdom of the heavens,"[24] especially since we know perfectly well what sort of punishment lies in store for one who gives offense even to one of the least of the brethren.[25] If, however, he who gives offense to a single person inevitably has punishment exacted from him, I leave that very person who shakes and disturbs the whole church to reflect what great evils he is making himself responsible for, of which no one may be guilty since Christ holds His hand over us all.

But how shall I bear that unfeelingly and without tears? If he should accept those whom (he says) he ought not to accept, why should we not be in their numbers? If, on the other hand, he should not accept them, we should maintain, however unwillingly, our present piety because of the fear of future punishment.

What about God, my good friend? What about faith? What about the judgments in the other world? What about conscience? But what about truth? What about steadfast resolution? Have you no concern about these things? Has Charybdis taken everything and engulfed it in oblivion?[26] I, however, would have expected him not only to think but also to say the opposite; so that, if really he were to accept those whom he ought not to accept, we should all shout together loudly and piercingly, nor would there be any sparing of anything, either of paternal love in which we take pride, or of the befitting piety which we have been taught always to extend to our fathers, or any other respect which we have maintained towards him, but, having banished all these things far from ourselves,as I said, we would loudly shout, "What are these things that you are doing, brethren? Where are you going? Why do you not perceive that you are putting yourselves into the hands of your enemies? Why have you reduced our struggles to nonsense? Why do you disgrace the company of those who are pious? Why do you exalt the presumption of the enemy?" I, for my part, would rather expect him to take such things seriously if he felt that I were making a mistake in any way, and not doing such things as he is now doing, imitating the judgments of those who are mocking us. I would expect this, too, [namely,] that if ever anyone of our enemies had dared to utter one of these statements of his before him, striking him with countless stones, he would have driven him away, giving him a dressing with such reproaches as "deceiver" and "liar."

For, though it has been commanded that we tolerate those who otherwise despise us because we are disciples of Him Who is gentle and peaceful, still no one can tolerate those who commit violence against the faith; since even He Himself, though He gently bore other things and did not retaliate, not only those who had become so desperate as to make His Father's house a house of commerce did He drive away therefrom with a vehement censure,[27] but also, having threatened with a double punishment[28] those who were sharpening their tongues against the Holy Spirit, He made their city, men and all, a work of fire and sword and famine in this world and assured them, through the fact that He had disclosed their present punishment with much anger, that they should not escape their future judgment as well.

But with such great expectations, I was feeding myself into starvation. Who in the world, then, lodged information with him against us after we had entered upon the archepiscopal throne and had been entrusted with the authority over every action and deliberation? For such foul rumors and controversies are distressing (and yet[29] it is necessary that such be directed, generally speaking, against some persons) to

those who have already gloriously and conspicuously under-
taken the reins of rule and are presiding upon the common
throne, although some, having sinned, are on their knees and
are not only wetting the ground with many tears but are
also earnestly pleading for mercy, whereas others, having
toiled up to the end on behalf of virtue and truth, adorned
with glittering crowns, are sitting along with them and are
having the rank of judges allotted to them;[30] while others,
furthermore, because of the forbearance of those who are
of the same nature, are being caused to fall, whereas others
set nothing before themselves in preference to fairness and
canonical authority but, like the eyes of justice, make all
things fit into the nature of the good. At that very time,
if it is ever meet and proper, questions of this sort can
be directed to those who have attained that lot, but not
now, nor to those who are struggling in hunger and thirst
and imprisonments and countless hardships and are engaged
in the struggle over life, for to the former is reserved the
question about judgment and condemnation and forgiveness,
as well as that time, but not the present.

But, my fine and good man, if they ought not to be accepted, how is it that you are not ashamed to be associated
with them, and, though it is in your power to appear crowned,
to be included among their prisoners, and to dream of kind-
heartedness on the part of the others, having made yourself
devoid of the heavenly nobility and freedom, and a traitor?[31]
If, however, you do not consider association with them dis-
graceful,[32] know that in spirit you are in the company of
those of whose action you are a denier and that you honor
that flock at the head of which you say are wolves instead
of shepherds.[33]   But, if you will, you treat it with greater
respect than even some who are in it.   If, in fact, some of
them, though they are associated with them in body, their
conscience causing them to be at variance with their judgments, nevertheless crouch down. You, however, even before
becoming associated with them in body, are eager to asso-
ciate with them in their thoughts and judgment. At any rate,
your falling short of association with them signifies timidity,
not piety; shame, not deliberate choice. What sort of person,

then, is he who accepts them? Is it one who not even in a dream has accepted such a thing, or one who has assigned to fear the reason that until now he has not inclined towards them and considers being disgraced along with the enemy, provided he will not be punished later, better than being altogether admired along with his own people? If they ought not to be accepted, who, having accepted those whom he sought not to accept, instead of considering them differently, would not, in truth, destroy himself along with them? For words do not ameliorate deeds, but it is through deeds that words doubtless are confirmed.[34]

Then, supposing that one, though he sees that robbers or betrayers of their states are loathed by all and are loathsome to all, then, though he himself hitherto is unspotted by such crimes, conceives vain fancies and says to him who has custody over the laws: "If you allow such men as ought to be executed to go unpunished, why should I not sooner practice robbery and become a traitor in order that I may obtain forgiveness? If, however, you demand of them punishment, in fear of the latter, I will not imitate them." If one, then, should come forward and say such things, is there anyone, then, who would not condemn his derangement and feebleness of judgment and countless other things? What then? Everyone among those who have sense surely will condemn him. If one, however, should bring forth into our midst betrayers of the faith instead of betrayers of the state and predators of the divine laws instead of predators of bodies, then utters the above-mentioned words, will we not suppose that such a person should fully receive the same, or even greater, sentence from those who at least are of sound mind? Apart from what has already been said, if they are really guiding their actions on the basis of the ordinances of the church, why do you need your untimely discussions and to wrestle and to be choked with thoughts and rather not quickly become one of their faction and ask for much forgiveness because of your tardiness? However, if you know that they are underlings of unlawful deeds, why are you unduly concerned as to whether they will be punished in this material world or not? For, if

they are punished [here], they will be better off, being
cleansed of their sin by their punishment; if, however, they
are not punished [here], this renders them more wretched
because the judgment which they will encounter in the other
world will be harsher. Consequently, if a choice between the
two alternatives were set before one, the latter plainly would
choose the lesser evil and look after his own advantage. It
is not he who avoids being punished in this material world,
but he who is plainly punished in the present world and now,
that has soothed the judgment in the other world. For, even
as regards one who is sick, it is not he whom the physician's
hands, cuttings, and cauteries relieve from his suffering,
but he whom we see not accepting the procedures of the
art of medicine we forthwith absolutely acknowledge and
know[35] as being found in extreme misfortune.

But why should one count over the consequences of his
thoughts?   It is these that will prepare us to be more un-
wearied[36] with regard to things that happen to us. These we
will have as a means of consolation. With these, O friend and
brother, you have exerted every effort to win us over. For
I do not retire from the rather august words, nor do I surrender everything to that which has been contemplated, but, because hitherto it has not been executed, and in consequence
of my hope for your correction, I take a share in these ap-
peals. "If the salt becomes insipid," says the Lord, "with
what will it be made salty again?"[37] If such is the case with
my friends, my brothers, my children, my members, my
viscera, with absolutely all who are most precious to me, on
whose account, furthermore, being present in the flesh is
judged preferable to having departed and being with Christ,[38]
on whose account I mourn and I am pulled to pieces and my
tears become bread for me;[39] if, then, such is the case with
them, of what sort ought one to expect the case of the others
to be? But nothing is a matter of astonishment, for I know
that even the divine Paul was left behind in chains alone.
"At my defense," he says, "no one came to my aid" and
"Luke alone is with me."[40] For perseverance and patience
are not characteristic of all men. For this reason even the

Lord, when He spoke of the afflictions and trials in which those who have believed in Him were destined to struggle, introduced the statement, "Whoever has endured to the end, he shall be saved."[41] I know that even before Him the prophet David bitterly lamented his desertion by the many and offered this as a supplication to God: "Save [us], Lord, because the godly has disappeared, because truths have been neglected by the sons of men."[42] But why should I cite the latter or the former? I know that my Master and God, when He had been arrested and was being led to prison, was left alone. "And all left Him," say [the Scriptures,] "and fled."[43] What wonder, then, is it if now, too, one has taken thought to abandon us, men who are pitiable and righteous, men who are not permitted even to breathe in free air, men who inhabit a prison, daily expecting countless dangers of death, and with every fair hope taken away? But would that they had only abandoned us, however unbearable, of course, that is. For such men do not abandon us, but in our designation of the truth and of the ecclesiastical and correct thought, on behalf of which until now they have chosen to suffer immensely, they both cut themselves off and excommunicate themselves. What precisely strikes and exhausts the heart most of all is to see the members of Christ, our head, with which we are united and are joint sharers, being both torn asunder and utterly destroyed.[44] But still, however intolerable the evil is, it would be tolerable through the examples that I have mentioned. How could one, however, even if one had acquired training to endure all things, be able to endure the cunning contriving of ascribing to us also the charge of abandonment, an example of which until now cannot even be found to have existed?

Beautiful, indeed (since I am receiving in full the rewards for my sacred and paternal love towards you and for those spiritual and extraordinary and awesome travails by which you were endangered in the mystical portico of the Church as a luminary in the world to offer the word of life[45]), are these things which I am made to endure through your admirable and divine understanding towards him who, until very lately, bestowed upon us receptions, and excessive receptions at that,[46] and attempted to receive our arbitration for his own motive as, forsooth, an escape and retirement from shame and sins, even though the opposite to what he was doing has happened to him. For the transference of an accusation to another, if the artifice of a moral lapse does not certainly find its proper place, turns around into a rather harsh con- demnation of the conscience, producing from within a re- proach that is both clear and inescapable. Why, indeed, were you seeking an alliance from elsewhere and cunningly con- triving an appearance of defense for yourself unless you had your conscience within as a bitter accuser of your intention? Why do you not do by yourself those things which you strive to do from another source? And if the law had not hindered me from letters, and the scribe's hand (and then a smuggled in one at that) were not standing in my way, I would have explained more precisely and more extensively both our grief and the ways in which that person has outraged us.

But how is it that his own brilliant confessions of faith, which he had publicly made in the presence of God and an- gels, in the presence of all men—emperors, officials, and sub- jects—did not lead him to great shame? How is it that the pride of the Church,[47] which it had been able to bear down through all time and rule, was not respected? And may it, of course, the heavenly Palm strengthening it, unceasingly keep boasting and enduring. How did the adversary (the Devil) de- termine through himself and himself alone to beguile the souls of the living and, by his own fall deliberately choose to cripple the common and admirable state of the Church? The resourceful serpent rashly undertook to present to the world something new and unreasonable, but the Fashioner of our nature and Creator established truly a newer and more glor- ious and divine work.[48] For, whereas the former (the Devil) secretly got into men who were thrice-sinful, men held of no account, long since stripped of their sacerdotal office and banished from their ecclesiastical congregations, for reasons which it is not even right and meet for us to say, who have died twice, uprooted in accordance with the apostolic tradition about them, "blots and blemishes,"[49] venturous, self-willed men, and put them forward as a workshop of his own wickedness and through them insolently sought to destroy and to lay hold of the entire Church, the Latter (God), since manifestly He alone works wonders and relieves from care those who call upon Him in affliction and shows the ineffability and wisdom of His providence especially at that time when difficulty and dread surround them from all quarters, showed that it (the Church) has been so constituted and perfected and truly founded in Himself that the evil one not only received a blow counterbalancing his wickedness but is getting for himself a much harsher and more painful one. For how is the blow inflicted upon the Devil not very great and incurable, as is proved by the fact that in such a strong storm and such a great confusion and change no small man, no great man, no chief priest of an obscure city or of one that possesses prominence, no individual held in esteem, no one armed on both sides, that is, one who has fluency of tongue accompanying sharpness of mind, no one illustrious in life, no one conspicuous for preciseness of doctrine, nay, not even one of them at all was reproved for having let himself be altered in any way along with the crisis or even yielded to the force of advantage? All, in a word, who have become members of the assembly of piety (who admitted this before it had been achieved by an obedience of long standing, much less a new hope?) proved to be superior to every trap of the evil one and every plot and every artifice and violence of his.

It is a pleasant thing for me to go through these matters in detail, and especially with you who effected a great part of such a great miracle; since, in fact, there is nothing more pleasant for fellow soldiers, even if they are at all events in situations of grief, than to discuss with one another their acts of bravery in wars. But, as I was saying, whereas the evil one was becoming puffed up and was rashly seeking to swallow down all with a single gulp and to prove the accomplishment of his wickedness, the holy complement of the Church so greatly mocked and also derided his wiles and designs, being both led under the generalship of Christ, their Head, and being guided by Him, that they captured some from him (the Devil) and led them to the truth rather than anyone of them gave way to become a deserter from their noble state. Consequently, if one gave the Devil his choice as to whether he wished to find such vessels as he had now fallen in with which are able to contain all his activity, then the Church which struggles so bravely and steadfastly to oppose him smashes them, craftsmen and all, as if vessels of a potter. To experience neither of these, he would have set at a great price neither to be fortunate for such vessels and dream of delight over them, nor to see the Church becoming strong and flourishing and inflicting through the midst of his viscera a blow that is so mortal and bitter, setting up a glorious trophy against his entire domination. For this very reason, if for no other one, he, too, who now (for I do not know how I should state it more inoffensively) has been clandestinely shaken, ought to be importuned and not well nigh to try to remove the crowns of victory from his own forehead. No doubt, even if he has not done what he had planned, still he has wasted away his flourishing grace by his hesitations. In fact, while his contemplation has convicted his intent, divine grace has shown now, too, the providence which it has for us by not having permitted his deliberation to become actualized.

But let nothing henceforward, nothing of this sort,[50] my child, be diligently practiced by you. For I have now all but dismissed the reproaches over which[51] until now I had manifestly been striking and wounding my viscera[52] and which I had been bearing with distress;[53] for, even if medicines and surgeries are necessary, still the sympathetic affection for griefs and pains prevails over the laws of medical treatment and education.[54]   For this reason, no longer bearing the tyranny of being sympathetically affected, having abandoned all those things and having embraced you as if you were present, my child,[55] my member of pure birth-pangs, what is this I recall? Where is my boast in you? Where are my expectations, or rather the deeds along with these expectations? Do you see my sad countenance, my dejection, if you will, also my tears? My concern for you is the cause of these things. My distress over you touches my very life. But if you are not at all concerned about my life (not yet, however, does any reason convince me that you are not concerned), let nothing of this sort or even anything resembling it any longer penetrate either into your will or contemplation. For blessed is a man, not one who has not hastened to adopt the deeds of the lawless but one who has not even walked in their counsel.[56] Nor let us plume ourselves because we understand that there are some who are worse than we, but let us be ashamed if we are proved worse than some; since, in fact, one excels in valor not when one is caught as a deserter, nor is one respected and admired when one is seen not worse than the fugitives, but when one plainly appears superior to one's fellow soldiers in wars[57] and prevails over the enemy, then, in fact, one has a right to receive the crowns of victory. Yes, I beseech and I beg you, show the end worthy of the beginning, worthy of the struggles.

Oh, how many sighs, how many tears! to sail calmly in the sea in the midst of winds and storm[58] but to capsize in the port itself, and as regards wars to prevail over the enemy but to give up to them all claim to the trophies, and to bear the struggle in the stadium brilliantly but to face the crowns of victory like a weakling![59]

You, then, O lovers of virtue and heralds of piety and defenders of truth, as in all other things, so also in the face of the present sorrow, I was destined to find as a consolation. Not only because that which grieves, whenever revealed to friends, is inclined by nature to be dissolved somehow by words and to evaporate, as it were, along with them, but, much more, in fact, because I have high hopes that through your wise and noble charms and admonitions the man will rather regain strength. Having completely turned away from the whispering of the serpent, he will no longer be content with a counsel which throws correct thoughts into confusion and shifts to doubt, which is a cause for fall, but, having hastened back to his earlier perfection, will be preserved throughout his entire life unshaken and unmoved upon the firm and unbreakable rock of confession to Christ and the principles of His words. But so much for this.

"If, however, there is any exhortation in Christ (along with the divine Paul, let us proclaim to you and through you to all); if there is any solace afforded by love; if there is any fellowship with the [Holy] Spirit; if there is any affection and sympathy, fulfill my joy,"[60] in order that, just as up to now, so also continually, you may be in agreement, with one spirit and one mind struggling together for the proclamation of truth and not being intimidated in any way by your opponents. "This is a sign of destruction for them and of your salvation, and this is from God, because it has been granted to you for the sake of Christ not only to believe in Him but also to suffer on His behalf."[61] And I write these things, not because you need my words, but because I am in debt to you and, in fact, also because I desire to participate with you, whenever the occasion requires, in deeds themselves and struggles and on other occasions with my words. "For, in fact, you (speaking as the theologian does) have an anointing from the Holy Spirit, and the anointment which you received from It abides in you, and you know all things, and you do not have need of anyone to teach you, but, just as that same anointing teaches you concerning all things, and, as it has taught you, abide in it in order that, when the Son of God shall make His appearance, we may have confidence and not shrink from Him in shame at His coming."[62] The dispenser and sovereign of peace, the cause and upholder of our life, "in whom we live and move and exist,"[63] by Whose indissoluble bonds of love we have been joined together, the first and great High Priest, Christ our true God, "He who has made us from a non-people His own people by His own blood, and not simply people but even beloved and a consecrated nation and a royal priesthood" (oh, for His ineffable love towards mankind) and has adopted us as sons and heirs, and in fact, fellow-heirs with Himself, "with whom there is no variation or shadow of variation,"[64] He will preserve us blameless up to the end, binding us in the bond of peace and love, confirming us in Himself and among ourselves and in an unshakable and steadfast feeling of piety, all having one and the same thought, saying the same thing, looking to the same thing, hastening towards the reward of the heavenly calling, where the church of the first-born is,[65] where the choirs of martyrs are, where the tents of the patriarchs are, among whom there is no falsehood being honored before truth, no strife, no tyranny, no desperation, among whom there is deep tranquility, as well as infinitely great beauty of truth obscured by no artifice, among whom there is total peace and concord, and the vision and participation and enjoyment of those blessed and indescribable sights. Finally, the perfection of sonship, no longer being hoped for but already being gloriously shared in, for the sake of which we are at present suffering persecutions and imprisonments, and on account of which we thankfully and joyously bear our countless horrors and our daily dangers of death.

While before us the divine Paul exhorts us to pray for sovereigns,[66] so does Peter, too, the chief of the apostles, saying, "Be submissive to every human institution for the Lord's sake whether it be to the emperor as supreme,"[67] and again, "Honor the emperor."[68]   But still, even before them, our common Master and Teacher and Creator Himself from His incalculably great treasure, by paying tribute to Caesar,[69] taught us by deed and custom to observe the privileges which have been assigned to emperors.   For this reason, indeed, in our mystical and awesome services we offer up prayers on behalf of sovereigns. It is, accordingly, both right and pleasing to God, as well as most appropriate for us, to maintain these privileges and to join also our Christ-loving emperors in preserving them.

Letter 9

FROM EXILE TO THE BISHOPS ALSO IN EXILE[1]
(870)

The persecution is heavy, but the promise of blessedness by the Master is sweet. Banishment is painful, but the Kingdom of Heaven is delightful.[2] "Blessed are those who are persecuted for the sake of righteousness, because the Kingdom of Heaven belongs to them."[3] Many are the oppressions and they surpass every difficulty, but the joy and exultation there not only know how to relieve their harshness but to transform it even into cheerfulness for those who live in conformity with the expectations of Heaven. Let us, therefore, cling to our struggles in order to gain the rewards. May we, too, shout along with Paul: "I have fought the good fight, I have finished the race, I have preserved the faith; therefore is reserved for me the crown of uprightness."[4] What is sweeter and more graceful than this triumphal exclamation? What has greater power to put to shame the common enemy of the human race?

"I have finished the race, I have preserved the faith; therefore, there is reserved for me the crown of uprightness." O voice which lulls to sleep the storm of every sorrow, or rather grants the grace of every spiritual joy, which in turn renders the persecutors stunned but crowns the persecuted, strengthens afresh the feeble and restores the fallen. If my deeds echo my words, may I, too, along with you, my good companions in the struggle in the Lord, be deemed worthy to call out loud that exclamation, by the intercessions of our supremely holy Lady, the Mother of God, and of all the Saints. Amen.

Letter 10

TO IOANNES, METROPOLITAN OF HERAKLIA[1]
(870)

You loudly bewail your condition because you are ignorant of ours. If, however, you knew what we are suffering and how many struggles we endure every day, I believe that you would stop enumerating and bewailing your own misfortunes.

Even when the crashing sounds of thunder become very loud we can get used to hearing them, and we do not get as disturbed after a while as we did at first.

What, then, are we to do? Nothing, but patiently bear up bravely under those things that fall upon us, because we know precisely, in accordance with what the divine and sacred utterances affirm solemnly, that the present life is not one of luxury and prizes, but one of struggles and toils and conflicts.

It is fitting for us to seek after rewards and crowns and enjoyment there where (unless it is an extraordinary thing to say) by God's mercy we will encounter them.

Letter 11

IOANNES, METROPOLITAN OF HERAKLIA[1]
(870)

It seems to me, indeed, that Christ, who is also our God, the Sovereign and Lord of the universe, for reasons that are not only beyond understanding but many other inexplicable ones as well, fully effected salvation for the whole world rather through His willing passion and not by despotic and absolute power.

Nonetheless, exactly for this reason I believe that he has left an especially great and clear consolation to those who endure hardships in life and suffer the worst in the example of His personal sufferings and His own shameful death.

Having these things in mind, you, too, should rather rejoice in the fact that you, the servant, happen to be imitating the Master. But do not be concerned over the question of crowns as though you have been educated by the enemies of truth, and the unwilling.

Letter 12

TO EUSCHEMON AND GEORGIOS, METROPOLITANS[1]
(870)

I am not discouraged at seeing the storm of ills and tyranny being intensified. For I hear that, because of your hopes in God and your piety, you are in bloom and like spring. I rejoice all the more that the impudence of those who were eager to dishonor and discredit you has rendered you both more beautiful and more noble.

But, my friends, sons, and brothers, if there is anything more befitting than the love of one's natural relatives, let us preserve until the end the same affection and love for God. And, as the noble Job through that marvelous patience and bravery of his triumphed over the defeat of him who exercised authority over him,[2] so let us, too, both the holy people of Christ and the priesthood of royal rank, just as we have up to now, continue to show these present-day genuine and consummate disciples of Him as lamenting and helpless. For, in fact, as you too know well, the rewards and the crowns belong to those who strive to the end.

Letter 13

TO MICHAEL, METROPOLITAN OF MYTILENE[1]
(858)

While someone else might say that your sufferings at the hands of your persecutors are too great to be consoled, I would say, if you will, that they are too great to be praised. It is time, then, for you to decide whether you should choose to be one of those who is very pitiful or one of those who is deemed very blessed. For if you bear them with good grace (I know that you bear them so), I long to partake of your crowns and, furthermore, your sufferings. But if (which I do not pray for) . . .but I will not say it, for I am convinced that I will be babbling. Wherefore, once more, may both your struggles and rewards be shared by me.

Farewell.

Letter 14

TO MICHAEL, METROPOLITAN OF MYTILENE[1]
(858)

Though someone might wish to obtain your crowns, without having gone though your sufferings, and your struggles on behalf of piety, your sufferings confer honor upon me even if no one is yet stretching out his hand and is bestowing crowns upon my head. You should not, therefore, be disheartened, because so enviable and blessed is that man who has become so illustrious and conspicuous in respect of his personal dangers and sufferings as well. For even if absolutely all the mouths, be they of lawmakers, be they of prophets, be they of pious kings, be they, furthermore, of men who love truth, should keep silent regarding the present affairs, while they declaim tragically the vanity therein, still you see that in their continuous flow and change things do not remain fixed since they undergo change.

But all glory, riches, fortunes, and splendors move to and fro, and there is nothing in the present world which would entice a sober mind and surreptitiously charm it. Since, however, things in the other world, on the other hand, are beyond description and because of their changelessness and imperishability offer the enjoyment of blessings to those who are worthy, who, when he has his hopes fixed towards things in the other world and his eyes open, will fall in the things of the present world, which like dreams cause grief, and who will be disheartened by those sufferings through which it is possible to be distinguished?

It is better, therefore, I believe, and beyond any argument, for one to have the worst in dreams and to possess an unending enjoyment of things that are in actuality good and ineffable than to be led astray by dreams and play with things that are of brief duration and transient and to experience perpetual troubles.

Letter 15

TO EUSCHEMON, ARCHBISHOP OF CAESAREA[1]
(870)

Wickedness (and nothing should seem less strange to you, for experience in the course of life is the sure teacher of such things), unless it puts on the guise of virtue, very quickly perishes.

Do not, then, be disheartened seeing her, as the saying goes, brazen with uncovered head, and with a face past blushing behaving licentiously against all.[2] Short will be her time and you will see her ending in destruction with a great sound. You have also the Prophet agreeing with me: "I saw the impious man raising himself on high and exalting himself as the cedars of Lebanon. And I passed by, and lo! he was no more; and I sought him, but his place was not found."[3]

Letter 16

TO METROPHANES, MONK AND HESYCHAST FROM SICILY[1]
(866)

Though great is the pain for the churches of God, for evil has been poured into the world, greater is the joy, for in the whole world your accomplishments and your virtue are admired, and from every mouth issues, instead of anything else, [news of] your brilliant struggles and your trophies and that celebrated promise of blessedness which you deserve for your sufferings on behalf of Christ.[2]

Letter 17

TO THE MOST PIOUS AND GREAT EMPEROR BASIL[1]
(June 870)

Hearken, O most benevolent Emperor. I am not trying to appeal at this time to our old friendship, or to your awesome oaths or agreements, or to your unction and coronation as emperor; or to the fact that you used to approach my hands and partake of the awesome and undefiled sacraments; or to the bond with which the adoption of your good son has bound us together.[2] I wish to speak of none of these things. I call your attention only to the common rights of mankind. For all of both the barbarians and the Greeks remove from life those whom they condemn to death, but those whom they permit to live they do not compel to die from starvation or countless evils. As for us, we are leading a life more bitter than death; we have been made a prisoner; we have been deprived of everything—relatives, servants, friends, and, in a word, of all human consolation. And yet, the godly Paul at least, while he was being led about as a prisoner, was not deprived of the routine of his acquaintances and friends; but, even while he was being led away for execution, he found human kindness even on the part of the Christ-hating pagans.

But perhaps time in its length reveals that even if not the high priests of God, still at least some criminals have suffered such punishments.

But the fact that we have been deprived even of our books, is novel and unexpected and a new punishment contrived against us. For what reason? In order that we may not hear even the word of God. May the fulfillment of this curse not occur during your reign; namely, "In those days there will be a famine of bread and a famine of hearing the word of the Lord."[3]

Why, then, have books been taken away from us? For, if we have done any wrong, more books should have been given us and, in fact, even teachers, in order that by reading we may be benefitted more, and by being proved wrong we may correct ourselves. If, however, we have done no wrong, why are we being wronged?

No one of the orthodox has suffered such a thing even at the hands of the heterodox. Athanasios,[4] who suffered much, had often been driven from his see both by heretics and by pagans, but no one passed a judgment that he be deprived of his books. Eustathios,[5] the admirable, endured the same treachery at the hands of the Arianizers, but his books were not, as in our case, taken away from him, nor from

Paulos, the confessor;[6] John, the golden-mouthed;[7] Flavianos,
the inspired;[8] and countless others. Why, pray, should I
enumerate those whom the Book of Heaven has enrolled?
And why should I mention the orthodox and holy Patriarchs?
The great Constantine[9] exiled Eusebios,[10] Theogonos, and
along with them other heretical men for their impiety and
the fickleness of their views. But he neither deprived them
of their belongings nor punished them in the matter of their
books. For he was ashamed to hinder from reasoning those
whom he used to exile because they acted contrary to reason.
The impious Nestorios was exiled;[11] in turn, Dioskoros,[12]
the wretched Petros,[13] Severos,[14] and many others. But
none of them suffered captivity of books.

Why should I keep talking about days of old? Many even
of those who still survive know that the impious Leo[15] dis-
played the nature of a beast rather than that of a human
being. But, when he drove the great and well named Nikephoros[16] from his see and exiled him, not only did he not
exile him from his books, certainly he did not even starve
him to death, as we are being weakened by hunger. And
yet, he no less desired that this champion should die than
that his reign should by all means be protracted over a length
of years, throughout which he acted impiously but still he
guarded against getting the reputation of bloodthirstiness.
He did not weary the flesh of those who served him in the
way that he did that of bandits and traitors, although, as a
matter of fact, he was impious and breathed forth cruelty.
He did not deprive them of the company of their relatives;
he did not inflict upon them loss of their possessions. For,
since he professed Christianity, he was ashamed to behave
more cruelly than the pagans. For the latter, whenever they
arrested the martyrs, they did not bar them from the service
of their servants; nor did they deprive them of their legal
right to their possessions. Nor again did he [Leo] prohibit
the singing of hymns, but he even granted the right for many
monks to dwell together as a consolation. He did not destroy
the houses of God and churches consecrated by Nikephoros.
For, though he offended man, he was afraid, as it seems,

to inflict indignities against the works dedicated to God. But against us, alas, all measures that are novel and beyond the point of tragedy are adopted. Made a prisoner, deprived of all our friends, deprived of our relatives and servants, deprived of chanters and monks, and instead of friends, instead of monks, instead of chanters; in a word, instead of anyone else, we have been given over to military persons and military troops. Houses of God have been destroyed, and the mutilated bodies of the poor have departed and their possessions have been confiscated as though they were the booty of the enemy. For what reason? In order that we might be distressed. We have been distressed very bitterly, for both the houses of God and their servants had been consecrated to us to serve God as a propitiation for our sins. But one ought to have pondered as to whether God, too, who is suffering loss, would along with us be more grieved if, as it is the fact, He claims the goods of the poor as His own.

The laws of the Romans devised bodily torments for those convicted and condemned for villainy for the purpose of cleansing the soul, but until now we have not received from even oral tradition torments and plots against the soul as being practiced among some men, if even now we have learned by experience. For it is clear that both the removal of books and the destruction and abolition of the redemption of sins do this. The former extinguishes and destroys the eye of contemplation itself, while the latter exacts punishment and dissolves the most beautiful of deeds. Who, since the long space of time, has heard of wars being contrived by men against the souls of men? For bodily punishments, exile, captivity, hunger, imprisonment and a constantly impending death are not sufficient to deflate utter anger. Death spares a living being only to the extent that it does not simultaneously destroy the sensation of pains. This is the most grievous sting of death, namely, the unbearable agony that we suffer also the pains of dying, and these pains are not dissipated also along with death. This is the sole consolation for the dying, as it would be for us in our plight.

Reflect, O Emperor, on these matters within yourself.

Now if your conscience finds you innocent, inflict also other sufferings upon us if perhaps any has been omitted; but if it condemns you, do not wait for the condemnation of the next world when repentance will be useless. I ask of you a somewhat novel request but one that is brought on because of most unusual circumstances. Halt, O Emperor, these evils in whatever way you choose. Either remove us from this life rather quickly, and not with the present great and unspeakable preservation, or cut short the extraordinary degree of our vexations.

Remember that you are a human being, even though you are Emperor. Remember that we are clothed with the same flesh, whether we are kings or private persons, and that we share the same nature. Remember that we have a common Master and Fashioner and a common Judge.

Why are you convicting your gentleness by your acts of ill-treatment against us? Why are you bringing into discredit your goodness by your abuses against us? Why are you depreciating your kindness into a simulation and pretense of gentleness by your anger and severity against us?

We are not asking for honor, or glory, or happiness, or ease, but we are asking for those things which are granted even to prisoners, which not even captives fail to gain, which even barbarians humanely grant to those bound in chains. For my circumstances have so completely reversed that I make this request of an emperor, nay of a most benevolent race, the Romans.

What, then, do I request? Either to live a life that is not harsher than death or rather swiftly to be released from the body. Respect nature, revere the common laws of mankind, revere the common rights of the Roman Empire. Do not allow an unheard of story to be told of your life: namely, once an emperor who professed goodness and kindness, having made a high priest a friend and co-parent, under whose hands both he himself and his empress were anointed with the chrism of emperorship and put on this office, by whom he was exceedingly loved and to whom he had given pledges and awesome assurances, whom he showed to all that he loved exceedingly and cherished; him he gave up to exile and bitter hunger, wore down with countless other ills, while he was praying on his behalf, and sent on to his death.

Letter 18

TO THE MOST PIOUS AND GREAT EMPEROR BASIL[1]
(after 873)

I used to believe that while your emperorship was exercising your sovereignty I would be offering you many expressions of gratitude for your beneficence towards me on behalf of friends, on behalf of relatives, on behalf of acquaintances, on behalf, in a word, of all the things which, in service to us, you would graciously grant without satiety.

For we were led to this belief both by our genuine and sincere disposition towards you and by the steadfastness of the countless oaths and promises which, though we did not want you to do so, nevertheless, you yourself did not cease from making before all.

Now, however, our expectations have so completely reversed that, even though late, still we offer thanksgiving to your emperorship. For what and why? Because you have endeavored to make more moderate the punishments of robbers and criminals, with which we were laboring and were being consumed.

But consider, my beloved (even if you do not choose to be) Emperor, that to attempt to persuade men not only contributes nothing towards persuading God, but even produces the opposite effect; in fact, the judge of what is being done without restraint in this world is, in truth, the all-seeing Justice in the other world.

Letter 19

TO MICHAEL, METROPOLITAN OF MYTILENE[1]
(870)

Just as the Christ-hating Sanhedrin of the Jews, by expelling the Master's disciples from the synagogue, brought
them closer to their Teacher and Master and completely
excluded themselves from initiation into the sacred mysteries and the Kingdom of Heaven, so now, too, these imitators of the Jews, by expelling us, the zealous followers of
the apostles, from the Church, have both linked and united
us more with those godly eye-witnesses of the Word. For our
sharing in their sufferings makes our connection with their
life and faith more precise.

But they have pitiably and wretchedly cut themselves off
from the teaching of the apostles and from our orthodoxy.
By having completely separated their own party from both
the name and polity of the Christians, by being carried away
into warring against Christ and the bloodthirstiness of the
Jews, whom they have perversely emulated, they have lapsed.

Letter 20

TO TARASIOS, BROTHER[1]
(870/877)

Suffering is at its height and wickedness is increasing
in intensity, but without God and hopes dependent upon
Him there is no consolation. Plots, threats, and fears render
the experiencing of them lighter by those who have previously incurred them. Who will halt these things? But perhaps death, the birth-pangs of which they are producing
against us, will remove either them from taking vengeance
and inflicting punishment on us or from our oppressors.

Letter 21

TO BAANES, PRAIPOSITOS AND PATRIKIOS[1]
(873)

At one time Joseph was a secret friend of my Master and God, but later he broke off the chains of timidity and became more fervent and more confident than those who loved Him openly. And he took down from the Cross the Master's body, which was hanging there ignominiously, and did not neglect every possible care that he could give it.

How long, then, will it be before you, who yourself also have loved us by night but have not become a son of light and day, let loose a voice worthy of the frankness of Joseph and take down from a cross not, of course, a person's body, but rescue it from countless trials, oppressions, hardship, and a bitter and daily death? If, however, your love of the world and sympathetic affection for it do not permit you [to do so], in vain has Joseph been thought of and is adduced by you as your refuge and model.

Letter 22

TO IGNATIOS, METROPOLITAN OF CLAUDIOUPOLIS[1]
(April 870)

The anathema was once a thing to be dreaded and to be avoided because it was pronounced by the heralds of piety against those who were guilty of impiety. However, from the time that the wicked in their rash and shameless madness, contrary to every law, both divine and human, and contrary to all reason, both Greek and barbarian, have insolently turned their own anathema against the champions of Ortho-doxy and have contended to make their barbarous madness an ecclesiastical privilege of theirs, instantly even that for-midable and final consummation of every penalty has lapsed into fables and playthings, or rather it has become for the

pious even an object of desire. For, in fact, the wholly auda-
cious mind of the enemies of truth does not make the penalties formidable, and especially the ecclesiastical ones, but
rather the sense of guilt does, felt by those who suffer them,
just as the sense of innocence, indeed, not only converts
their punishments even into an object of ridicule, but also
reverses the sentence of condemnation against those who
issue it and produces for him who is being punished by them
unfading crowns and undying glory. Therefore, anyone
who is pious and holy prefers numberless times to be treated
contumeliously by those who are alienated from Christ and
to be anathematized rather than with brilliant acclaim to
share in their un-Christian and God-loathed villainies.

Letter 23

TO PAULOS, FORMER ARCHBISHOP OF CAESAREA
AND APOSTATE[1]
(861)

"You ask me for great things," an author of proverbs
would say, and quite reasonably. I, however, will not give
you abusive or blunt talk, but whatever truth likes.

You have become worthless to your friends and a traitor
to the divine dogma and an enemy to your own profession
[of faith]. Then you ask why in the world the pious avoid
you as polluted and do not deem you worthy even of an ordinary salutation?

Oh, why should I really and truly address you? They believe that even to share in your wicked deeds by greeting
you is a terrible thing.

Letter 24

TO MANUEL THE PATRIKIOS[1]
(870)

You will not be able to escape, even if you should try to escape, the inescapable eye of God, you who are doing and trumping up those things by which you might remove me forcibly from life. For he who drives men from life in a way that is different from the death that has been determined by nature, even if he should not hold the knife in his own hand and dip it in the slaughter, still he is a murderer even if he does not provide the executioner. Even if, however, you have avoided this, you render the tribunal of the other world rather harsh.

How long will you not remove yourself from those things which you send on to the other world lamenting loudly and in vain so bitterly bewailing that "I would not wish nor would I any longer plot against him"?

Letter 25

TO THEOPHILOS, PROTOSPATHARIOS AND SAKELLARIOS[1]
(861)

To demand justice of one who has done wrong is human, while not to retaliate shows forbearance and to requite even with benefactions is then acturaly divine and renders the earthborn imitators of our Father in Heaven.

To initiate, however, an unjust assault, when it has no place in the above-mentioned instances, no doubt manifests an act that is characteristic of wild beasts or of demons, even though the perpetrator is clothed in human form.

Since there are, therefore,[2] four characteristic marks that are observed in acts, when with respect to your own case you have adapted the form which is suitable to your present action, then look at it; you will yourself see, even though another does not point it out to you—alas for the most hideous sight!—what sort of image you have cherished out for yourself by your deeds.

Letter 26

TO GREGORIOS, DEACON AND KEEPER OF THE ARCHIVES[1]
(870)

For many years every heretical synod and every council of iconoclasts have anathematized us; not only us, however, but also our father and uncles,[2] men who were confessors of Christ and the pride of bishops. But though they had anathematized them, they elevated us to the archepiscopal throne, though we did not wish it. Now, too, then, let those who, similarly to their predecessors, have paid no regard to the Master's commandments, and have opened the gate of every lawlessness broad and wide, continue to anathematize us in order that they themselves, too, may cause us, hesitant though we are, to ascend from the earth[3] to the heavenly kingdom.

Letter 27

TO GREGORIOS, DEACON AND KEEPER OF THE ARCHIVES[1]
(shortly after October 870)

If there is any doxology, if there is any prayer of gratitude, I offer it to God with all my heart that during days such as those He did not permit me to rule men or with my own eyes to behold that inconsolable calamity when the City of Constantine became a tomb instead of a city, and lamentation instead of singing of hymns gripped not only the homes but also the churches. The sight of some, totally reduced to the ground, and of others, to a very great extent cast down, they say, is piteous and too unbelievable to describe.

Not even one proved stronger than the quake. But not only did the earth itself by the unbearable tossing motion and agitation split open in many places but also made all that the city had suffered since the beginning seem obscure [in comparison to] the magnitude of these calamities.

Now, whereas at the present time I look only to my own circumstances and matters of my own concern and agony are being directed towards the latter, formerly it was necessary for me not only to tremble by reason of the sins of others and to lament rather bitterly over their calamities, but also lest I myself, too, who was held to be at their head, because of common association with their unrighteous deeds might be condemned to bear along with them the punishment that was common to the multitude. God, however, by His own grace and kindness has rescued me from all of these things since human conspiracies had adopted them.

Letter 28

TO GREGORIOS, DEACON AND KEEPER OF THE ARCHIVES[1]
(shortly after October 870)

Though I would not say that the city, being punished for its wrongs against us, became instead of a city a common burial place, I do exhort your holiness not to think of such a thing. For who are we, although we have endured indescribable sufferings, that we should call forth so great an anger on the part of God?

At any rate, however, at that time we, too, were suffering, but we suffer more now by the common law of sympathy and nature over those things which they had done to us. If, however, they have shorn the glory of the churches throughout the Roman Empire, and have dishonored the mysteries of the Christians, and have driven away the bishops and priests of God from their sees and churches by every contrivance and every form of violence, and in an age of Christianity have let the practices of the pagans enjoy unbridled freedom, by deep silence or rather by complete subversion, having betrayed the divine theological doctrines and the awesome sacred rites; if, therefore, on account of these things they are having punishments exacted from them for their audacity, with regard to this I could not be able to affirm confidently until the heavenly tribunal should prove them as having committed some other more serious than this great audacity of theirs.

Letter 29

TO IOANNES, PATRIKIOS AND SAKELLARIOS[1]
(861)

A proverb which used to be said in days of old states exceedingly well and sagaciously, it seems to me at least, that, though many already have ascended that tree which is called tyranny, none of them, however, descended it, but absolutely all fell down.

If this is the case, why are you yourself prancing and leaping when you are foolishly letting yourself be borne, not on that tree's branches but on the leaves of its foliage, and that because you are oppressive, violent, and inflamed.

Letter 30

TO METROPHANES, MONK WHO HAD APOSTASIZED[1]
(866)

David fell but he arose. He arose, however, by the prayer of the prophet, and tears, and bitter reproaches brought on by reason of the deed which he had done. Yes, indeed, [it was] by deeds and repentance and every other virtue [that he], though he had been weighed down by his fall, was uncomplainingly disposed to censure.

You yourself, too, have fallen, but I do not see a prophet, nor David's humility and repentance. It is, therefore, your responsibility to reflect and to consider how you will raise yourself from your fall, unless suffering punishment, and that [punishment] one in the other world at the [appointed] time, is for you more preferable than to escape it.

Letter 31

TO IOANNES, PATRIKIOS AND STRATEGOS OF HELLAS[2]
(ca. December 865)

If you show affection, you are weak; but, if you do not show affection, you are unjust. If, however, showing affection and not being weak you neglect your friends who suffer so unjustly, I do, indeed, pray that you neither fall into such great calamities nor, having fallen and having felt need, get such affection and help as you grant to your friends. But you, at least, must nevertheless remember the Master's oracular response, clearly proclaiming, "the measure you give will be the measure you get."

Letter 32

TO BARDAS, INTERCESSION ON BEHALF OF CHRISTODOULOS, ASECRETIS, WHO INCURRED DANGER[1]
(ca. March 858)

Even if I appear at the present time to be bothersome and excessive in the matter of clemency, still I will not abstain from exerting my effort at least.

Though perhaps I am beating against the air and toiling in vain (this, in fact, has accustomed me to take into account the fact that I have frequently failed in obtaining my expectation), yet, as far as it depends upon my strength, I am fulfilling my duty. The poor man jestingly did what was customary for him. For he made fun, even though it was with those with whom he ought not and like a comic poet said such things as he ought not. He was the apex of drunkenness, falling into which things men frequently go wrong. He paid the penalties for his unbridled tongue, having undergone bitter punishment, [namely,] severe bodily tortures.

Let the matter of his punishment stop here. The temple of God is sacred and an asylum to all the pious, into which he has taken refuge. The priest of the temple intercedes on his behalf. The matter of sin is easy but, if you please, so is also "forgive and you shall be forgiven," and "the measure you give will be the measure you will get."[2]

Letter 33

TO CAESAR BARDAS[1]
(ca. April 858)

I knew well even before the experience that I was unworthy of the archepiscopal rank and of the pastoral function. It was for this reason, in fact, that, when I was being carried off and dragged to it, I was greatly vexed.

Would that death had snatched me away at that time before my promotion or rather, my intolerable compulsion. For the waves of so many and such great sufferings would not be deluging and immersing my wretched soul every day; their prospect and expectation (since the nature of men is skillful at comprehending future difficulties especially if the difficulty is direct to it) at that time totally disturbed and distressed me.

Being agitated and bitterly vexed by these things, I constantly wept, I insistently begged to be excused, I would rather have done anything than consent with those who were voting for and compelling me, loudly imploring that the chalice of many and manifold cares and trials be turned aside from me. Now, however, the circumstances themselves teach me more correctly and prove my unworthiness; and no longer do I have the fear of expectation but pain connected with the timely circumstances and sighing and helplessness because of what has already come to me. For, whenever I see priests, whoever they might in fact be, who are all alike affected by one offense, being beaten, being tortured, being disparaged, having their tongue cut out (be merciful, Lord, unto our sins), how shall I not deem more blessed than myself those who have died? How shall I not reckon the burden which has been placed upon me as a proof of my sins?

A helpless unprotected man, one who does not have an untroubled mind (a thing which arouses pity, not indignation), has suffered at the same time so many misfortunes; he was betrayed, he was beaten, he was imprisoned; what is inconsolable is the fact that he had his tongue cut out, and that since he was invested with the priesthood, on whose behalf I frequently interceded, on whose behalf I frequently appealed, on whose behalf I was powerless and received words of apathy, and those who have seen him understand. Although they have forgotten him, the Divinity has not forgotten.

What hope, then, is there in things that are invisible when in the case of things that are visible and lie under our view I thus fail and am ridiculed? How shall I intercede and make atonement for sins, both yours and of the people, when, having interceded on behalf of one person, I have so failed, when I have been thrust aside thus?

I have written these things with the blood of tears. It remains for you to receive this letter of mine either as the first or the last. For I say in the presence of the Lord that if it is your objective to reject or dismiss me thus, my requests and entreaties are reasonable, and if consolation and comfort cannot come in any possible way to that wretched man, I will neither write nor will I bother you in any other way, but I will remain quiet, looking to myself and bewailing my own circumstances. For, if along with the daily trials and circumstances which are being blown up against me from the outside, I further lose also my wretched soul, I would be the most wretched of all men.

Letter 34

TO EMPEROR MICHAEL[1]
(866)

You have departed from us, and we are away from you. And we live without living, and we move without moving. If, however, the Master's promise consented to be near our humble prayer, either we would have transported Crete to Byzantium or we would have joined Byzantium along with us to Crete. But how can I write when dead, and how can I speak when silent? After I have said one thing, I will remain silent. Speed your return, O ornament, in my opinion, of Kings and your children, either carrying off the Cretans as captives, or liberating the Byzantines from their captivity, since they are cursed with captivity in the absence of your countenance.

Letter 35

TO GEORGIOS, DEACON AND GUEST-MASTER[1]
(ca. April 875)

Melanthos, the tragedian actor, they say, was such a slave to the eating of delicacies that he was even despondent because he did not have the neck of a swan in order that he might enjoy for as long a time as possible the food that flowed through his neck and the pleasure therefrom.

If, however, he had been a participant in your dinners, I believe that he not only would have found a great remedy for his despondency, but also would wish that the neck had not continued in its ancient length in order that he might not be spending a long time putting up with your table and your foods. What, then, ought one to do? It is absolutely the best thing to constantly accept the sentiment "Do nothing in excess."

Letter 36

TO MICHAEL, PROTOSPATHARIOS[1]
(865)

The acquisition of education becomes for one who has grown old the strongest staff of life, and it transports without pain one who is in the bloom of youth to the beauty of virtue.

Therefore, educate your children in wisdom and virtue in order that not only when they are young they may possess a beautiful conduct of life, but also when they have grown old they may not need the help of others.

Letter 37

TO ANASTASIOS, THE TAX COLLECTOR[1]
(ca. October 858)

There is no entrance for you to the gate of the Kingdom of God because the love of money has blocked this for you. If, however, you break down the barrier through love of the poor, living by almsgiving will more quickly make you acceptable.

Letter 38

TO THEODOROS, METROPOLITAN OF LAODICEA[1]
(ca. November 869)

If the present life is a stadium, and its conduct therefrom deserves rewards, do not wonder that some of the righteous contend here with distress, but admire rather that some consider the time and place of their struggles and conflicts as the day of their crowns and the platform of their acclamation.

Letter 39

TO THEODOROS, METROPOLITAN OF LAODICEA[1]
(869)

Meditation is the mother of good conduct, while thoughtless impulse borders on sin. One ought not, therefore, to neglect the process of deliberating and to run after the latter, through which, along with accomplishing those things which we are eager [to accomplish], we are caught giving proof of our lack of understanding.

Letter 40

THEOKTISTOS, HEGOUMENOS[1]
(ca. January 860)

Admire the virtues; do not, however, praise your pupils in their presence for pursuing them. For the first is an invitation and appeal to do good deeds, whereas the second is akin to flattery, which gives false notions of self-worth to those who have been praised, or lowers the value of the virtues by cheapening them. Through such flattery, the sweetness of toils in accordance with the will of God is inclined to diminish and the pleasures of the flesh are rekindled.

Letter 41

TO AMPHILOCHIOS, METROPOLITAN OF KYZIKOS[1]
(ca. December 863)

While some of Plato's dialogues are by nature guides to the theory of government, except if he has been negligent somewhat in some places with regard to the selection of names, his epistles are bequeathed to posterity as a fair measure of his eloquence and of the epistolary form.

Those, however, of Aristotle, indeed, are somewhat more endowed with the command of language than, of course, his other writings, but they are not equal to those of Plato.

Whereas the other works of Demosthenes fill with praises the mouths of both orators and literary critics, you will find his epistles not at all better than those of Plato.

To what epistles, then, ought we direct our attention and the practice of which epistles should we pick out for ourselves, applying the style that has been recognized by us because of their artistic form? Though there is also another countless multitude, you have, I believe, in order that the stage of exercise may not be long for you, the epistles that are ascribed to that famous Phalaris, the tyrant of Acragas, and those upon which is inscribed the name of Brutus, the general of the Romans, and the philosopher among emperors, and the rhetorician Libanios among the very many [epistles]. If, however, you wish along with their style to receive benefit from many other great men, the dear Basil[2] will suffice for you, as well as Gregorios,[3] the producer of beauty, if anyone else is, and furthermore, the complex muse of our talented

Isidoros, who is deserving of being called a canon as of words so also of both the sacerdotal and ascetic state, and any other person with the similar disposition who was invigorated to embody their form in his own epistles.

Letter 42

TO ANTONIOS, ARCHBISHOP OF THE BOSPOROS[1]
(ca. March 864)

The Scythian Sea was once *Axine* ("inhospitable"), for it used to make food (a horrible thing to hear!) out of those of the foreigners who sailed thereon. The Milesians, however, by their humane feeling and civilized government tamed that brutal and also barbaric character and converted it into *Euxine* ("hospitable").

Now then because of you and your struggles and toils on behalf of virtue and your other service for the Divinity it is also called, along with being so, not only *Euxine* but furthermore *Pious.*

You cannot imagine with how much joy and good cheer I am filled, not only as I reflect upon, but also as I write these words. If, however, furthermore, having captivated the Jews who live there unto obedience to Christ, you shall have removed them from the shadow of the letter to grace, as you have written, I am receiving in full and I abound with regard to the seasonable fruits of the noble hopes which I continually nourished for you.

Letter 43

TO METROPHANES, MONK WHO HAD APOSTASIZED[1]
(861)

No man, even one who is perfect, is free from pollution; and no man, even the basest, is completely without a share of virtue.

Do not by your own example undo an old belief, which even up to the present is preserved both by the judgments and by the deeds of absolutely all men, by tending to exhibit yourself devoid of every virtue and a new tale to be told by men.

Letter 44

TO ELIAS, PROTOSPATHARIOS[1]
(ca. March 879)

You asked; we agreed; it has been done. Therefore, thank God, the giver and cause of all good, that you have been delivered from the heaviest taxation.

Letter 45

TO THE SAME ELIAS[1]
(879)

The temptations of those being tempted become trials; but, if they are not tried, they do not become recipients of crowns and prizes.

Letter 46

TO AKAKIOS, MONK AND PHYSICIAN[1]
(874)

Conceit is a great evil. It makes man senseless, and it does not permit him to be set free from his passion or to learn better that which will be good for him. It misleads him to view as enemies those who undertake to draw him away from his error and to help him, and it renders more intimate those who inflame the disease by flatteries and make it incurable. Avoid conceit with all your might; it is a deep precipice which causes the ascent to salvation to be taken away.

Letter 47

TO GEORGIOS, METROPOLITAN OF NICOMEDIA[1]
(ca. June 871)

Would that my deeds were a match for your words of praise, not in order that Galen and Hippocrates, who are the object of glory among the sons of the healer (Asklepios),[2] might give up to me all claim to their rights of supremacy, as you yourself write extolling me, nor in order that the great name of the sons of Asklepios might be buried in obscurity by my name, but in order that I might be, even if not for anything else, but in this turn of mine at least, a small help to my friends and companions in the struggle against their bodily sufferings.

Letter 48

TO THEODOROS, HEGOUMENOS[1]
(ca. October 864)

Not he who produces in abundance the flow of words on his tongue is forthwith also effective with respect to his hand, just as he who is superior in action does not have also the persuasiveness of words pompously lying on his lips. Now, though I can cite to others many examples of all sorts, since I am writing to you who admire Homer I think that if I point out one example it suffices.

Famine was afflicting the soldiery who were encamped around your Troy beseiging it. And so Odysseus was dispatched to Anios[2] to request grain, for the Achaeans had confidence in the art of his tongue. However, because after his arrival he had rained down very many "words like snowflakes in winter-time"[3] and with these had deluged the man, not only did he not accomplish any of those things which he had expected to accomplish, but also, because he had seemed to be a nuisance, he returned empty-handed and rendered difficult the life of those who were all agape in expectation of him.

The famed Palamedes (you know how much more silent

the man was than Odysseus) ventured to undertake the embassy after "that clear-voiced speaker,"[4] and, when he had come upon Anios working, he said nothing but threw aside his coat and proceeded to join in the work. When after their toil he invited him to dinner, he ate with the man and then he uttered a brief statement that he had come to request grain for his beloved and starving army, and, when he had gained his request, he departed joyfully and brought help to his compatriots instead of words.

You, too, should not entrust everything to words, for a small deed on the part of one who maintains silence in conjunction with sagacity often silences long speeches and shows that mere sounds and meaningless voices do not at all have the advantage.

Letter 49

TO THEODOROS, BROTHER[1]
(ca. June 872)

A proverb is told with reference to those who are extremely distressed and in agony "he sweated blood," just as also with reference to those who mourn bitterly "he cries blood." If one, then, should consider also the statement in God-inspired Luke (for the man was not ignorant of such matters of learning) "His perspiration occurred like clots of blood"[2] to have been parodied after the above-mentioned manner, you have the object of your inquiry.

If, however, this shall seem to you to have been conceived rather curiously, still of itself it admits of an easy comprehension, because, when he said "like clots of blood," he did not declare that He had sweated clots of blood (for he could not have meant that the drops of sweat had resembled clots of blood, for it is manifest that the expression "like clots" clearly proves this), but, desiring rather to show that the Master's body was perspiring not with some light moisture and one that appeared for the sake of display, as it were, but that truly it totally dripped all over with large drops of sweat after the manner of large drops, he employed the "drops of blood" as a likeness of that which had occurred.

He showed, therefore, as by His prolonged prayer and His great agony, so also by the thickness of His drops of sweat, that the Savior not only was a human being in nature and reality and not in appearance and illusion, but also submitted to the natural and irreproachable passions of men. For the Master, in fact, demonstrated this very thing by His actions and that not in His divine nature but in that of a human being He sustained His suffering and prayed and agonized and perspired those drops of sweat that were thick and about as large as drops of blood.

Refrain, therefore, from thinking any longer that it is plausible that this passage should be excised from the Gospel (even if some of the Syrians, as you said, think that it should). But now that you have recognized well that nothing is contained therein that is feeble but rather, in fact, quite consistent, place it in the same category as the other divine scriptural statements and read it with an unwavering mind.

Letter 50

TO IOANNES, PATRIKIOS AND SAKELLARIOS
AMONG THE ANGURIANS[1]
(850)

The learned men among the pagans trace back a person such as you to Attis, whom they call *Gallos,* and the worldly-wise both know and call a person such as you *androgynos* and confine him to the women's quarters. Whence, then, did you cross the boundaries on both sides and slip into the mysteries of the Church of God, turning them upside down, and are you wont to practice in the Church of Christ which is very favorable to generation and encourages many children that which is both fruitless and useless in your corrupted nature?

But know well that, though you have placarded yourself as more shameless than Hades and its gates through what you are doing and you are even weaker, we and along with us the populous and holy congregation of Christ will expose you even if we will grieve you.

If then Christ, the Truth, has rendered that architect of villainies along with his pillars (of which you yourself happen perhaps to be one since you have concealed to him entirely your mouth and tongue and voice) and his entire battle-formation powerless and ineffective against His Church, still how long will it be before you give up behaving shamelessly and discharging against Heaven with much insensibility the offensive weapons of your madness? With these you are not only stirring up an occasion of laughter for the demons who are cooperating with you but you are also causing the saints grief over your loss and you are making your race more now than formerly hated and defamed for depravity.

Letter 51

TO ALEXANDER, COMES[1]
(ca. 860)

Alexander the Macedonian, the one who lifted the kingdom of the Macedonians to its heights, believed that he would cease to rule on the day on which he could not show that he had, in some way, helped someone. This only happened very rarely, because he was extremely solicitous. And whenever it did occasionally happen, he would say, quite disappointed, "Today I was not a king."[2] He was a pagan, a Greek, and ruled over Greeks. He was a man who liked pleasure, luxury and success, and so created gods of the same type to be the guardians of his state.

You, however, are a believer [in Christ] and you rule over Christians. You have been appointed to rule by law, and you have received wave after wave of the hardships of life. Yet, in the middle of the priests and their flocks, you still hold as values self-control and virtue. As a matter of fact, you are unable to reject the true God as the overseer of your actions.

But, what then? I even hesitate to mention it, for fear that I might see one of those under your rule who instead of recounting your gracious favor or benevolence, he rather laments his severe punishment and inexcusable injury. Or again to see another, who because of a deed by your very hand, exits in tears at the spectacle of a tragic scene. And while Alexander in disappointment used to say, "Today I was not a king," you will, it seems, not miss a day on which you can honestly say, "Today I was not a tyrant."

Letter 52

TO ANASTASIOS, PRESBYTER AND LIBRARIAN AT ROME[1]
(ca. May 867)

Though your struggle is hanging from the sacred line, as the proverbial statement says, it is late in the course of your need, and yet I do not complain of your decision, but I see that Opportunity has gone by.

In fact, the riddler who presents the latter as long-haired in front but close clipped in the back seems to me to have described him not inelegantly. For, whenever one goes in quest of Time, even though one pursues after him with countless tricks, it is not possible to grasp him.

But good for you, your sympathetic disposition, though it has come belatedly! For it is characteristic of friends not to deal out favors on the basis of need, but to judge affection on the basis of intention.

NOTES

Letter 1

1. Val. Ep. 142; PG 102.969; Montague, Ep. 234; MS Iviron 160, fols. 265-73; MS Marcianus No. 849, fols. 287-91; Jager, *Histoire de Photius,* pp. 417-27; D. White, "Photios' Letter to his Brother Tarasios on the Death of his Daughter," *GOTR* 18 (1973), 47-58.

2. The one who raised the widow's son from the dead (I Kings 17:17-24).

3. He raised the dead child of the Shunammite woman (II Kings 4:32-37.

4. In Joppa Peter raised a disciple named Tabitha from the dead (Acts 9:36-43).

5. Paul raised a young man named Eutychios from the dead in Troas (Acts 20:7-12).

6. It is clear from this reference that Photios was in exile at that time.

7. Patriarch Photios makes frequent reference to the serpent, whom he always associates with the devil or sin, in his letters.

8. MS Iviron reads: "Τό μέν εἶχεν ὑπομάξιον παῖδα, τοῦτο δέ καί μητέρα ἐπί ἄν. Θᾶττον τό κακόν ἀπέστη." The texts of the MS are correct. Valettas has incorrectly amended to καί μητέρα, εἰ μή. Ἐπί here is used adverbially (as well) with ellipsis of the verb εἶχεν, which is omitted because it can be easily understood since it occurs in the immediately preceding phrase; ἄν is to be taken with the implied εἶχεν. Photios is referring here to two tragedies: (1) the death of a child that had died while still nursing, and (2) the present one, that of a young daughter who was fully grown and ready for marriage and child-bearing but died before such a marriage took place.

9. The word ἄτρακτοι used here is correct. Montague changed it to Atrops, the second fate of the three, the one who cuts the thread of life.

10. Photios' theme, that life is a theatre or a stadium and man is the actor or the athlete, recurs throughout his letters.

11. Photios' parents were martyred during the iconoclastic upheavals

of the first part of the ninth century. Probably some other members of his family had died during these upheavals, unable to withstand the hardships.

12. In the Montague, Valettas, and Migne editions, the sentence reads as follows: "Εἰ δ᾿αὕτη σου παρῆς ἐκεῖθεν ἡ παῖς ἐπιστάσα καί χειρί χεῖρα ἐμβάλουσα, ἱλαρῷ δέ καί χαίροντι προσώπῳ κατεφίλει τε καί προσεφθέγγετο." In the *Codex Baroccianus graecus 217*, in a marginal note, a whole phrase has been inserted. It reads: "Εἰ δ᾿αὕτη σοι παρῆν ἐκεῖθεν ἡπαῖς ἐπιστᾶσα, οἶδεν δέ ἄρα ψυχή φιλοσοφεῖν καί μετά θάνατον μάλιστα ὀνείρων τε ὄψεσεν ἐπιφαί-νεται καί βαθύν ἀφοσιωμένη πόθον ταῖς φαντασίαις ἐφίσταται καί λόγῳ φύσιν εὐλαβουμένη πάντα μετά τοῦ εἰκότοι τῷ γράφοντι γί-νεται, ἀλλ᾿εἰ παρῶν καί χειρί χεῖραν ἐμβαλοῦσα, ἱλαρῷ." The same phrase appears also in the *Codex Parisinus graecus 1335* (four-teenth century), *Parisinus graecus 2671* (fifteenth century), and *Mar-cianus graecus 575* (fifteenth century).

13. John 2:25.

14. I Corinthians 2:9.

15. "Bride" refers to the young girl.

16. The idea of the first offspring, the best of offerings, appears also in the letter to Georgios, Metropolitan of Nicomedia.

17. I Thessalonians 4:13.

18. 2 Samuel 12:15-23.

19. Demosthenian speech: "Οὐκ ἔστιν, οὐκ ἔστιν ὅπως ἡμαρ-τήκατε, Ὦ ἄνδρες Ἀθηναῖοι." (περί στεφ. Ξ᾿.)

20. In the *clausula* Patriarch Photios makes reference again to Job. The names of Job and David were frequently quoted in Byzan-tine letters.

21. The letter ends with the special invocation to Panagia Theo-tokos, which the Patriarch uses only three times in all his surviving epistolary output.

Letter 2

1. Val. Ep. 143; PG 102.956; Montague, Ep. 131. MS Iviron 684, f. 90.

2. Migne reads τινά which appears preferable to τίνα read by Valettas.

3. Photios is very laconic but very much to the point. The frequent theme that lament brings shame to the departed is used here as well as in the letters to Tarasios and to the Nun Eusebia.

Letter 3

1. In Val. Ep. 144; PG 102.917; Mont. Ep. 245; also in Hoeschel's edition of the *Myriobiblon*, p. 916. The Greek title of the letter is: "Εὐσεβία μοναζούση καί Ἡγουμένη παραμυθητική ἐπί ἀδελφῇ τελευτησάση." MS Iviron 160, fols. 285-91; MS *Marcianus gr.* 575, fols. 285-87. The letter has appeared in English translation by D. White, "Letter to Eusebia," *Classical Folia* (June, 1975), pp. 32-43.

2. The letter to Mother Eusebia is the only surviving letter written by Patriarch Photios addressed to a woman. Even though Photios had a vast knowledge of philosophy and antiquity, the depth of his Christian thinking is evident in this letter. To him the idea of death should always be welcome. This life is only a short stage—a tearful passage on the way to eternity. Therefore, the less time one spends on this earth, the less he sins. The guarantee of our own immortality, the Resurrection, is given by the Patriarch as the final argument for the rejection of all grief over the death of a loved one. He quotes the Bible: "He who believes in me, even if he dies, shall live" (John 11:25). The language at time becomes almost poetic. He makes many references to nature. There is a lovely passage about the beauties of nature and the universe, as he describes the Heavens with "the orderly dance of the stars, as they enrich the Heavens with the most brilliant colors bedecking the skies." At other times the language becomes intricate, almost baroque. He does not make direct classical allusions in this letter, as in many others, but he cannot escape his own education, his immersion in Greek literature and philosophy. The neoplatonic concept of the real existence of the soul in contrast to bodily things is evident throughout the letter.

3. The body.

4. The soul.

5. Ps. 19:5-6.

6. I Cor. 15:43-44.

7. Matt. 8:22.

8. Jn. 11:25.

9. Matt. 9:15.

10. The *clausula* of this letter is unique among the letters of Photios. After using the already familiar theme that tears and lamentations are an insult to the blessed ones who are in Paradise, Photios promises Eusebia—a nun, a bride of Christ—that she will see the bridegroom if she stops lamenting.

Letter 4

1. PG 105.845; Mont. Ep. 201; Val. Ep. 145; MS Iviron 684, fol. 223. Among the surviving letters of Photios, eleven are addressed to Georgios, Metropolitan of Nicomedia. Five letters are exegetical in nature and refer to passages from the letters of Apostle Paul. A sixth is a short letter of advisory nature. The seventh and eighth are the two letters of consolation, and the last three are on various topics. In the letters of consolation, Photios uses his favorite allegory of the time-keeper. In other places, he becomes prophetic; he admits that he has God-sent dreams, visions, and that he is sure the departed had also had similar experiences: "He saw the King calling him and the radiant angels serving the call." In concluding, Photios admits that now he is rejoicing for the departed and he hopes that Georgios will feel the same way, as the "accomplishments of the deceased depended upon your instruction and care."

2. Photios is referring to the internal strife in the Church of Constantinople among the followers of Ignatios and his own, most of whom were in exile.

Letter 5

1. Val. Ep. 155; PG 102.876; Mont. Ep. 104; MS Iviron 160, f. 106.

2. The beginning of the letter is a perfect example of *ephodos*: "I forbid you, you who are among the best of our friends, to be called a friend of ours anymore." This stern command by the Patriarch should surprise his friend the deacon.

3. In the main part of the letter Photios explains the reasons for his decision. The loss of the friend of Georgios was also a loss for the Patriarch. It is difficult and painful to lose a friend, he remarks. For this reason, he has decided to become a misophile, "a hater of friends,"

as Timon of old was a misanthrope, "a hater of men." Photios uses the word "μισόφιλος."

4. The letter ends with a request by Photios that Georgios remain faithful to the memory of the departed, observe his memorial services, and take care of the bereaved family.

Letter 6

1. Val. Ep. 156; PG 102.945; Mont. Ep. 81; MS Iviron 160, f. 91.

Letter 7

1. Val. Ep. 221; PG 102.717; Mont. Ep. 18; Jager, *Histoire de Photius,* pp. 125-27; MS Iviron 160, fols. 58-59. Patriarch Photios wrote this letter after he learned of the murder of Caesar Bardas.

Letter 8

1. Val. Ep. 146; PG 102.741; Mont. Ep. 174; MS Iviron 160, fols. 180-94. D. White, "Patriarch Photios' Letter to the Bishops in Exile," *GOTR* 19 (1974), 113-29.

2. Patriarch Photios refers to this anonymous friend who is the cause of his many tribulations as "he" in many places throughout the letter. In this respect, the present letter reminds one of a So-cratic dialogue.

3. Valettas' correction αὐτούς is correct because ἐμβατεύσεν takes the accusative when it means "explore, penetrate."

4. I Cor. 2:11.

5. Αὐτοῖς is correct.

6. Λογίζοιτο is correct; an optative can occur coordinately with an indicative, subjunctive, or imperative.

7. The anonymous "friend."

8. Νῦν is correct. Valettas has τοίνυν.

9. Making his point, he ends what we might call the prologue of the letter, a characteristic of the Photian style.

10. The μετέωρος ὀνομαστική is being used here. The phrase be-

gins ἐγώ and the verb in reference appears about forty lines later: οὐκ ἀρνηθείην (Valettas, p. 474, line 18).

11. Αἰσθήσεις.

12. In two other letters Patriarch Photios makes reference to the sad fact that he is not even allowed to have some of his books with him. In a letter addressed to Spatharios Michael: "στερήσεις καί αὐτῶν τῶν ἀναγκαίων, ἁρπαγαί βιβλίων." (Val. Ep. 211.) In the second letter, to the Emperor Basil, the Patriarch asks: "Why were the books taken away from me?" (Val. Ep. 218, see below Letter 17.)

13. Ψήφοις.

14. Photios as the acclaimed orator is evident in this passage. This epistle as it progresses gives the feeling of liturgy in progression, which at the end climaxes to a Doxology.

15. The beggars were considered sacred in Constantinople (Justinian, Novel 7 in *Novels,* ed. R. Schoell and G. Kroll, *Corpus Juris Civilis,* Vol. III (Berlin, 1928); a good study by Demetrios Constantelos, *Byzantine Philanthropy* (New Brunswick, 1968); also by the same author, "Philanthropia in the Age of Justinian," *GOTR* 6 (1960-61), 206-26. Emperor Basil I is known to have built in Constantinople and in the provinces numerous hospitals, xenonas and other institutions for the poor (*Theoph. Cont.,* pp. 220 and 339-40).

16. The relative clause οὕς ἡμοῖς ἱλαστήριον τῶν ἡμετέρων ἁμαρτημάτων προστησάμεθα must not be transposed (as in Valettas) but remain where it is in Photios' text. The antecedent of οὕς is πτωχούς, ἀναπήρους καί λελωβημένους not οἴκους θεοῦ. Photios is saying that he supported (i.e., maintained or kept) the poor, maimed, and wounded as a proprietor to good for his sins, not that he established churches for such a purpose.

17. Χαράδρας.

18. Ἐξεβίβαζετο is correct. Valettas has ἐξεβιάζετο.

19. Ἐξῃτήσατο is correct. Valettas has ἐξηστύσατο.

20. Hebrews 10:29.

21. Patriarch Photios, while in exile, was informed that the churches he had consecrated had been torn down by order of the Emperor Basil I. Photios wrote to the Emperor a letter in which he reminded him that even the impious Emperor Leo X, when he exiled Patriarch Nikephoros,

did not destroy the churches dedicated by him (Val. Ep. 218, see below Letter 17).   Other letters of Photios on the same subject: to *Arsenion Monachon,* Val. Ep. 105; *Emmanuel Patrikion,* Val. Ep. 205; and *Konstantinon Notarion,* Val. Ep. 197.

22. II Cor. 11:21.

23. Matt. 10:16.

24. Matt. 18:3.

25. Matt. 18:6.

26.   There are often references to mythology and mythical creatures in Photian letters.

27. Matt. 21:12.

28. Mark 3:29.

29. Εἰ need not be absolutely necessary before καί.

30.   Crowns and rewards for the athlete which will be expected only in the next life to come, is a frequent theme of Photios.

31. Col. 3:1-2.

32. Ἡγεῖτο can be corrected to ἠγεῖ as well as ἠγῇ τό.

33. John 10:12.

34.   Photios in this passage makes allusions to a small number of bishops who have gone to the side of the enemy for fear of punishment.

35.   Ἀναγινώσκομεν is correct as in Montague. Valettas has ἀπο-γινώσωμεν.

36.   The addition of φέρειν (as in Valettas) is unnecessary because τά συμβαίνοντα is an accusative of respect.

37. Matt. 5:13.

38. Phil. 1:22-23.

39. Ps. 42:3.

40. II Tim. 4:16 and 11.

41. Matt. 10:22.

42. Ps. 12:1.

43. Matt. 26:56 and Mark 14:50.

44. I Cor. 12:12-27.

45. Apparently he is referring figuratively to the pains of childbirth in "giving birth" to these new priest-bishops. The "full recompense" will be his joy at seeing them mature. I Cor. 4:17. Also Philemon 10.

46. Ὑπερδοχάς ("excessive receptions") is undoubtedly correct, even though it is not recorded in any lexica. The context of the sentence makes this clear.

47. Rom. 1:20-22.

48. God created the priesthood.

49. II Peter 2:13.

50. The correction of Valettas, μηδέν τοιοῦτον, does not stand here. Μηδέ τοιοῦτον is correct.

51. Ἄδη ἴδια should be transcribed ἅ δή ἴδια.

52. Σπλάχνα.

53. The addition of δηλώσω (as in Valettas) is unnecessary.

54. Photios among his other accomplishments had studied medicine. See below Letter 47.

55. One of the addressed bishops.

56. Ps. 1:1.

57. Πόλεμον is correct (as in Valettas) because it is an accusative of respect.

58. A touch of poetry.

59. The imagery of the stadium, the arena and the athlete competing for the crown is repeatedly present in Photian letters.

60. Phil. 2:2-3:9.

61. Phil. 1:28-29.

62. I John 2:27-28.

63. Acts 17:28.

64. In a dramatic conclusion, like a great doxologia, the Photian doctrine of the relationship of church and state is stated clearly: the heads of state and church are the emperor and the patriarch, respectively. Those two leaders of the Universe have a task to work together in close and peaceful harmony for the good of mankind. The Patriarch's duty is to care for the souls of his flock, while the

emperor looks after their bodies. In the conclusion of this epistle, Photios simply and clearly defines the relationship of the Byzantine Church toward the emperor. The priesthood in Byzantium is supposed to follow Christ's example and leave Caesar's things to Caesar, because their realm is not of this world. This doctrine is explicitly stated in the *Epanagoge* commissioned by Basil I, whose author is suspected to have been Photios. (J. Schraft, "Photius and the Epanagoge," *BZ* 49 [1956], 358-400.) The theory of the dual control is not new in Byzantium. Earlier, in the sixth century, Emperor Justinian in the *Sixth Novel* had stated explicitly the distinction between the *sacerdotium* and the *imperium,* as two completely separated authorities coming from God to mankind. The great Photios is simply reminding his bishops of this fact.

65. Again the theme of reward, but only in Heaven.

66. I Tim. 2:2.

67. I Peter 2:13.

68. I Peter 2:17.

69. Matt. 17:24-27.

Letter 9

1. Val. Ep. 147; PG 102.764; Mont. Ep. 188; Jager, *Histoire de Photius,* p. 263; MS Iviron 160, f. 215.

2. In contrast to the previous letter addressed to the bishops in exile, this letter is short and easy to follow. It has a cheerful tone and is full of optimism. The letter begins with contradictions. Photios is using a number of antitheses here. In one breath we have reality speaking, in the next, Photios. "Heavy is the persecution but sweet the promise of blessedness by the Master. Painful is the exile, but delightful the Kingdom of Heaven." The theme of the athlete and the race, on the one hand, and the expected rewards—not on this earth but in Heaven—is present here again. Patriarch Photios during the difficult period of persecution and hardships is trying the best way he knows how—through his pen—to sustain the faith and courage of his fellow priests. He concludes the letter in the name of the Theotokos and all the Saints.

3. Matt. 5:10.

4. II Tim. 4:7-8.

Letter 10

1. Val. Ep. 148; PG 102.821; Mont. Ep. 9; Jager, p. 243; MS Iviron160, f. 55. This letter begins with a strong attack—*ephodos.* "You are complaining about your sufferings," Photios writes, "because you are ignorant of ours." Photios is trying to remind Ioannes that he (the Patriarch) has lost much also; nevertheless, he is writing to the Metropolitan to console him. He suggests that if Ioannes were aware of the sufferings of Photios and the other exiled priests, he would spend less time lamenting his own loss. The theme of prizes and rewards not of this life but of the next is present at .the conclusion of this letter.

Letter 11

1. Val. Ep. 149; PG 102.864; Mont. Ep. 218; MS Iviron 160, f. 246. This letter addressed to Ioannes is less didactic. The Patriarch is giving his friend a lesson in patience. The success of Christ, he reminds the Metropolitan, was not through the exercise of His power, which He had, but through His sufferings and His humiliation.

Letter 12

1. Val. Ep. 150; PG 102.836; Mont. Ep. 126; MS Iviron 160, f. 118. Both Euschemon of Caesarea and Georgios of Nicomedia were special friends and faithful followers of Patriarch Photios. While to the other exiled clergymen Photios has to send words of encouragement, to these two he has only words of praise and pride. This letter ends with the promise of rewards in Heaven. The example of Job is pointed out again by the Patriarch as it is in a number of consolatory letters.

2. Τόν καθηγητήν refers to the Devil. The demonstrative τουτουί bears the connotation of "present-day" or contemporary, while ἐκείνου refers back to τόν καθηγητήν (the Devil). The phrase "τόν καθηγητήν αὐτῶν πεπονθότα" has caused its readers difficulty of interpretation. Its meaning, however, is clearly established if three things are taken into account: (1) αὐτῶν exhibits the scribal error of appending a final "ν" to words ending in a vowel or a diphthong, an error of very frequent occurrence in manuscripts; therefore, αὐτῶν must be amended to αὐτῷ (sc. Job); (2) τόν καθηγητήν is an instance of a verbal noun, derived from καθηγέεσθαι, and it is being used as a substitute for the

participial construction (sc. τόν καθηγούμενον or καθηγησάμενον) with αὐτῷ as its object. Thus, τόν καθηγητήν refers to the Devil; (3) πεπονθότα is an instance of a participle with its substantive (καθηγητήν) corresponding to a verbal noun with the genitive. The amendment γεγονότα would also make sense, i.e., "him who had been the exerciser of authority (sc. Devil) over him (sc. Job)."

Letter 13

1. Val. Ep. 151; PG 102.860; Mont. Ep. 225; MS Iviron 160, f. 254. Michael in A.D. 870 also lost his metropolitan see and was replaced by another clergyman who was a follower of Ignatios. While in exile he received two letters from Patriarch Photios. See Letter 14 below. Both letters are of a consolatory nature. This letter ends in a tone of confidence that indicates that the Patriarch is sure of his friend's decision.

Letter 14

1. Val. Ep. 152; PG 102.860; Mont. Ep. 227; MS Iviron 160, f. 255. This letter is longer than the first one to Michael. Here Photios takes on the familiar theme of the instability and vanity of this world. The only place where things are stable and never change is in Heaven.

Letter 15

1. Val. Ep. 153; PG 102.840; Mont. Ep. 186; MS Iviron 160, f. 204. The Euschemon of this letter is the same person of the letter addressed to the Metropolitans Euschemon and Georgios (Letter 12 here). This letter is also a message of encouragement and consolation over the trials of the exiled priesthood.

2. Ps. 37:35-36.

3. Photios is presenting evil or sin as a woman with a painted face and uncovered head walking in the streets. According to the Bible only prostitutes made use of color on their faces: I Cor. 11:5 "uncovered woman"; II Kings 9:30 "painted woman—Jezebel"; Jeremiah 4:30 "adorning her face with paint"; Jeremiah 22:14 "paints with vermilion"; and Ezekiel 23:40 "you painted your eyes."

Letter 16

1. Val. Ep. 154; PG 102.897; Mont. Ep. 149.

2. The name of Metrophanes is first mentioned in the encyclical letter of Patriarch Photios to the patriarchs of the East. The Monk Metrophanes was among the group of priests in Italy who had signed an encyclical letter with redresses against the Pope. Photios names three of the signers, "Basil and Zosimas and Metrophanes, among others." While in Constantinople as an envoy Metrophanes met Photios and became one of his followers. In the midst of the struggle, however, Metrophanes changed his allegiance and joined the Ignatians; for this he is called an apostate by Photios (Val. Ep. 172; below Letter 41). Three more letter were written by the Patriarch to this monk after he deserted the Photian cause (Val. Epp. 172, 173, and 174; Ep. 173 is translated here as Letter 42).

Letter 17

1. Val. Ep. 218; PG 102.765; Mont. Ep. 97; Jager, pp. 254-58; MS Iviron 160, ff. 97-99; MS Parisiensis gr. 1335, ff. 221-240. This letter was written during Photios' exile to Skepi. At this time the Patriarch also wrote to Michael the Protospatharios repeating the same complaints (Val. Ep. 211; also the letter to the bishops in exile).

2. Photios had baptized Stephanos, the youngest son of Emperor Basil I.

3. *LXX* Amos 8:11.

4. Athanasios, Patriarch of Alexandria, ca. 293-373.

5. Eustathios, Bishop of Antioch, exiled to Trajanopolis by Emperor Constantine I, ca. 331.

6. Paulos, Patriarch of Constantinople, 641-653.

7. John of Antioch, 428-441.

8. Flavianos, Patriarch of Constantinople, 446-449.

9. Emperor Constantine I, the Great, 324-337.

10. Eusebios, Bishop of Caesarea, 335.

11. Nestorios, Patriarch of Constantinople, 428.

12. Dioskoros, Patriarch of Alexandria, 444-451.

13.   Petros, the monophysite patriarch of Alexandria, 477; and 482-489.

14. Severus, Patriarch of Antioch, 512-518.

15. Emperor Leo V, 813-820.

16. Nikephoros, Patriarch of Constantinople, 806-815.

Letter 18

1.   Val. Ep. 219; PG 102.772; Mont. Ep. 98; MS Iviron 160, f. 99.

Letter 19

1. Val. Ep. 162; PG 102.833; Mont. Ep. 116; MS Iviron 160, f. 112.

Letter 20

1.   Val. Ep. 220; PG 102.994; Mont. Ep. 78; MS Marc. 575, ff. 283-285; MS Iviron 160, f. 90.

Letter 21

1. Val. Ep. 122; PG 102.949; Mont. Ep. 91; MS Iviron 160, f. 94.

Letter 22

1. Val. Ep. 163; PG 102.833; Mont. Ep. 115; MS Iviron 160, f. 111.

Letter 23

1. Val. Ep. 169; PG 102.840; Mont. Ep. 175; MS Iviron 160, f. 194.   Patriarch Photios had to replace Paulos, the Archbishop of Caesarea, by Euschemon, in November of 861.

Letter 24

1. Val. Ep. 206; PG 102.968; Mont. Ep. 226; MS Iviron 160, f. 254. Manuel was a member of the court and a high official. After the Eighth Synod, he asked Metrophanes, Metropolitan of Smyrna, to record the acts of the Council. Metrophanes wrote a very biased and anti-Photian account. Patriarch Photios writes to Manuel reprimanding him for his actions.

Letter 25

1. Val. Ep. 215; PG 102.965; Mont. Ep. 193; MS Iviron 160, f. 217.

Letter 26

1. Val. Ep. 164; PG 102.877; Mont. Ep. 113; MS Marc. 575, f. 294; MS Iviron 160, f. 110. Patriarch Photios wrote four letters to the same Gregorios: Val. Epp. 111, 112, 113, 164.

2. Patriarch Tarasios.

3. Ἀπό γῆς, *from the earth* (from among men).

Letter 27

1. Val. Ep. 112; PG 102.873; Mont. Ep. 100; MS Iviron 160, f. 100. On January 9, 870 before the end of the anti-Photian council in Constantinople, a strong earthquake occurred. Many churches and homes were knocked down. The following October, after the condemnation of Photios another even stronger quake shook the city. The roof of the Patriarchal building fell; also a great obelisk in the hippodrome was destroyed. Photios, while in exile, heard of the damages and wrote this letter and the following one (Letter 28).

Letter 28

1. Val. Ep. 111; PG 102.873; Mont. Ep. 101; MS Iviron 160, f. 101.

Letter 29

1. Val. Ep. 202; PG 102.944; Mont. Ep. 73; MS Iviron 160, f. 82.

Letter 30

1. Val. Ep. 173; PG 102.885; Mont. Ep. 66; MS Iviron 160, f. 84.

Letter 31

1. Val. Ep. 200; PG 102.944; Mont. Ep. 60; MS Iviron 160, f. 83.

Letter 32

1. Val. Ep. 158; PG 102.624; Mont. Ep. 4; MS Iviron 160, f. 52. After the enthronement of the new Patriarch Photios, many partisans of the old Patriarch Ignatios, under the leadership of Metrophanes of Smyrna and Stylianos of Neo-Caesarea, according to Niketas, met for forty consecutive days from 2 February to 12 March. At the conclusion of their meeting, they pronounced the election of Photios void. In order to punish them, Caesar Bardas began an attack on all the partisans of Ignatios. Photios, wishing to put an end to the enmities, sent a letter to Bardas on behalf of Christodoulos around 20 March 858. Bardas, however, paid no attention to the pleas of the new Patriarch and continued his attacks on the Ignatians with even more zeal. A second letter to Bardas by Photios followed in mid-April, prompted by the news that the monk Blasios had had his tongue cut out at the order of the Caesar. The tone of the second letter leaves no doubt as to the feelings of the Patriarch.

2. Matt. 7:2; Mark 4:24; and Luke 6:38.

Letter 33

1. Val. Ep. 159; PG 102.624-25; Mont. Ep. 6; MS Iviron 160, f. 52. Photios writes to Bardas on behalf of a monk, the keeper of the archives whose life had been endangered during the persecutions against Photios.

Letter 34

1. Val. Ep. 222; PG 102.720; Mont. Ep. 19; MS Iviron 160, f. 59.

Letter 35

1. Val. Ep. 110; PG 102.872; Mont. Ep. 88; MS Iviron 160, f. 91. This letter shows the humorous side of Patriarch Photios, as well as his love for good food.

Letter 36

1. Val. Ep. 126; PG 102.952; Mont. Ep. 109; MS Iviron 160, f. 108.

Letter 37

1. Val. Ep. 138; PG 102.937; Mont. Ep. 51; MS Iviron 160, f. 185. ´

Letter 38

1. Val. Ep. 86; PG 102.825; Mont. Ep. 40; MS Iviron 160, f. 72.

Letter 39

1. Val. Ep. 91; PG 102.845; Mont. Ep. 194; MS Iviron 160, f. 218.

Letter 40

1. Val. Ep. 99; PG 102.864; Mont. Ep. 32; MS Iviron 160, f. 68.

Letter 41

1. Val. Ep. 233; PG 102.861; Mont. Ep. 207; MS Iviron 160, f. 230.
2. The Basil referred to here is St. Basil the Great.
3. Photios here refers to Gregory of Nyssa, the brother of St. Basil.

Letter 42

1. Val. Ep. 239; PG 102.828; Mont. Ep. 96; MS Iviron 160, f. 96.

Letter 43

1. Val. Ep. 172; PG 102.885; Mont. Ep. 65; MS Iviron 160, f. 84.

Letter 44

1. Val. Ep. 256; PG 102.929; Mont. Ep. 16; MS Iviron 160, f. 56.

Letter 45

1. Val. Ep. 257; PG 102.953; Mont. Ep. 122; MS Iviron 160, f. 56.

Letter 46

1. Val. Ep. 107; PG 102.897; Mont. Ep. 122; MS Iviron 160, f. 116.

Letter 47

1. Val. Ep. 228; PG 102.837; Mont. Ep. 169; MS Iviron 160, f. 170. This letter confirms the information we have that Patriarch Photios had a good knowledge of medicine. It seems that Metropolitan Georgios was ill and was cured by Photios' medicines.

2. He also refers to the word *akestorides* referring to the first doctor Asklepios.

Letter 48

1. Val. Ep. 100; PG 102.865; Mont. Ep. 142; MS Iviron 160, f. 130.

2. Anios was the son of Apollo and Kreoussa, as well as King of Delos and a priest.

3. *Iliad* iii. 222.

4. Ibid., i. 248; ii. 246.

Letter 49

1. Val. Ep. 17; *Amphilochia,* Question 218; Mont. Ep. 138; MS Iviron 160, f. 28.

2. Luke 22:44.

Letter 50

1. Val. Ep. 201; PG 102.937; Mont. Ep. 49; MS Iviron 160, f. 71; *Myriobiblon,* ed. Hoeschel, p. 914. The Angurians or Angyrians were the inhabitants of the city of Angyra in Asia Minor, which was also the Metropolitan see of the diocese of Galatia. Five letters addressed to the same Ioannes have survived. Two have been translated in this study (see letter 29). All the letters have strong, castigating language. From Photios' reference to the story of Attis, we can conclude that Ioannes was a eunuch. According to this story, Attis, the son-in-law of the king of Pessinos, was born a eunuch and became a priest of Cybele. Another version of the life story of Attis, however, maintains that he had pledged himself to Rhea. Rhea became very jealous when she imagined that Attis had become enamored of Adgestis (another name for Cybele). Rhea then cast a spell on Attis that caused him, in a maniacal rage, to castrate himself. Mimicking Attis, the priests of Rhea, who were called Galli, voluntarily mutilated themselves.

Letter 51

1. Val. Ep. 193; PG 102.939; Mont. Ep. 46; MS Iviron 160, f. 69.

2. Only Photios attributes this saying to Alexander. Others connect it with Titus and Traian.

Letter 52

1. Val. Ep. 240; PG 102.877; Mont. Ep. 170; MS Iviron 160, f. 185; *Myriobiblon,* ed. Hoeschel, p. 909. Anastasios participated as ambassador for King Louis in the Synod of 869 in Constantinople which condemned Patriarch Photios.

SELECTED BIBLIOGRAPHY
Primary Sources

Acta Consilii Constantinopolitani IV (869-870), ed. J. Domenico Mansi. 16.1-208. Versio Latina, Anastasio Bibliothecarii. 16.300-413. Versio Graeca, Mansi.

Acta Consilii Constantinopolitani V (879-900), ed. J. D. Mansi. 17.365-525.

Acta Consiliorum Oecumenicorum, 4 vols., ed. Eduard Schwartz. Frankfurt am Main, 1927.

Agapius (Mahboud) de Menbilj. *Histoire universelle,* ed. A. A. Vasiliev. Paris, 1909-1915.

Anastasius Bibliothecarius. *Epistolae.* MGH 7. 395-412.

Assemanus, Josephus S. *Bibliotheca Iuris Orientalis Canonici et Civilis,* 5 vols. Rome, 1762-1766.

Cedrenus, George (Skylitzes). *Historiarum Compedium,* ed. de Boor. PG 121.23-1166.

Cinnamus, John. *Historia,* ed. August Meiniki. CSHB. Bonn, 1836.

Constantinos Porphyrogenitus. Emperor of the East (905-959). De Administrando Imperio. PG 113.327-588.

────────────────. *De Cerimoniis Aulae Byzantinae,* ed. Migne. PG 112.33-1464.

────────────────. *Le Livre des Cérémonies,* 2 vols., ed. and trans. Albert Vogt. Paris, 1935.

Ducas, Michael. *Historia Byzantina,* ed. I. Bekker. CSHB. Bonn, 1834.

Einhardi. *Annales 741-788.* MGH 32.135-148.

Formosus, Papa. *Letters to Stylianos,* ed. J. D. Mansi. 16:439-456.

Genesius, Joseph. *Regna,* ed. C. Lachmon. CSHB. Bonn, 1834.

Georgius Monachus cognoment Hamartolus. *Vitae recentiorum imperatorum 813-894.* PG 109.536-585.

Hadrianus, Papa. *Epistolae.* MGH Ep. 6, 691-765.

Holy Canons of the Seven Oecumenical Synods. Trans. John Thomas. London, 1867.

Leo Grammaticus. *Chronographia.* PG 108.1037-1164.

Leo Imperator. *Panegyric of Basil I,* eds. A. Vogt and I. Hausherr. "L'Oraison funèbre de Basile Ier," *Orientalia Christiana* 25 (1931).

────────. *Panegyric of St. Elias,* ed. Akakios. Λέοντος τοῦ Σοφοῦ, Πανηγυρικοί Λόγοι. Athens, 1868.

Liber Pontificalis, 3 vols., ed. L. Duchesne. Paris, 1886-1892.

Mansi, J. D., ed. *Sacrorum Consiliorum Nova et Amplissima Collectio,* 31 vols. Florence and Venice, 1759-1798.

Metrophanes of Smyrna. *Letters to the Logothete Manuel,* ed. J. D. Mansi, 16:413-20.

MGH. Epistolae Scriptores, ed. Georgius Heinrichus Pertz. Hanover, 1826.

Nicholas I, Pope. *Epistolae.* MGH Ep. 6, 257-690.

Niketas Choniata. *Thesaurus Orthodoxae Fidei.* PG 140.10-282.

Niketas-David. *Vita Ignatii.* PG 105.487-574.

Papadopoulos-Kerameus, A. *Epistolae of Photios 45.* Ex Codibus montis Athos. Petropolis, 1899.

————————————————. *Monumenta Graeca et Latina ad Historiam Photii Patriarchae Pertinentia,* 2 vols. Petropolis, 1901.

Photios. *Ad Amphilochium,* ed. Sophocles Oikonomou. Athens, 1858.

————. *Collationes Accurataeque Demonstrationes de Episcopis et Metropolitis,* ed. F. Fontani. *Novae Eruditorum Deliciae.* Florence, 1786. PG 104.1220-1232.

————. ΕΠΙΣΤΟΛΑΙ, ed. S. Valettas. London, 1864. PG 102. 585-990.

————. ΕΡΩΤΗΜΑΤΑ ΔΕΚΑ ΚΑΙ ΙΣΑΙ ΑΠΟΚΡΥΣΕΙΣ. Rome, 1785.

————. *The Library of Photios,* ed. J. H. Freese. London, 1920.

————. *Myriobiblon (Bibliothiki),* ed. D. Hoeschel. Geneva, 1612.

————. *Mystagogia.* PG 102.279-400.

————. ΟΜΙΛΙΑΙ ΚΑΙ ΛΟΓΟΙ, ed. S. Aristarchos. Constantinople, 1901.

————. *Photiaca,* ed. A. Papadopoulos-Kerameus. St. Petersburg, 1897.

————. *Photii sanctissimi patriarchae Constantinopolitani Epistolae,* ed. Richard Montague. London, 1651.

————. *Photios Patriarche de Constantinople, Nomocanon.* Comentare, Theodore Balsamonis, ed. Christophe Justellus. Paris, 1615.

————. *Ponimata,* ed. A. Papadopoulos-Kerameus. Petropolis, 1892.

Simeon Logothete (Pseudo-Simeon). XPONIKON. Bonn, 1838. *Theoph. Cont.* 603-760.

Stylianos of Neo-Caesaria. *Letter to Pope Stephen V,* ed. J. D. Mansi, 16.426-435. MGH Ep. 7, 375-382.

Synaxarium Constantinopolitanum. A. S. Nov., ed. H. Delehaye. Brussels, 1902.

Synodicon Vetus, in Johann Albert Fabricius and G. C. Harles, *Bibliotheca Graeca,* 12. Hamburg, 1809.

ΣΥΝΤΑΓΜΑ ΙΕΡΩΝ ΚΑΝΟΝΩΝ ΤΩΝ ΤΑΙ ΑΓΙΩΝ ΑΠΟΣΤΟΛΩΝ ΚΑΙ ΤΩΝ ΙΕΡΩΝ ΟΙΚΟΥΜΕΝΙΚΩΝ ΚΑΙ ΤΟΠΙΚΩΝ ΣΥΝΟΔΩΝ ΚΑΙ ΤΩΝ ΑΓΙΩΝ ΠΑΤΕΡΩΝ, eds. G. Ralles and M. Potles. Athens, 1852-1859.

Theodorus Studita. *Epistolae.* PG 99.904-1670.

————————. *Naratio de Beatis Patriarchis Tarasio et Nicephoro.* PG 99.1849-54.

Theognostos. *Libellus,* ed. J. D. Mansi, 16:296-301.

Theophanes Continuatus, ed. Immanuelis Bekker. Bonn, 1838.

Theophanes Continuatus, ed. C. de Boor. Lipsiae, 1887.

Vita Euthymii, ed. C. de Boor. Berlin, 1888.

Vita S. Methodii. PG 100.1244-1261.

Vita S. Nicephori, by Ignatios the Deacon, ed. C. de Boor. Lipsiae, 1880.

Vita S. Tarasii, by Ignatios the Deacon. PG 108.1369-1520.

Vita S. Theodorae. Reginae. PG 127.903-908.

Vita S. Theodorus Studita. PG 104.139-420.

Wolf von Glanvell, ed. *Die Kanonensammlung des Kardinals' Deusdedit.* Paderborn, 1905.

Zonaras, J. *Annales.* PG 137. Bonn, 1841.

————————. *Commentaria in Conones.* PG 137, 138.

Secondary Sources, Modern Works, Periodicals and Journals

Abel, A. "La lettre polémique d'Aréthas à l'Emir de Damas," *B* 24 (1954), 343-370.

Adontz, N. "L'âge et l'origine de l'empereur Basile Ier," B 8 (1933), 475-550; 9 (1934), 223-60.

————————. "La portée historique de l'oraison funèbre de Basile Ier par son dils Leon le Sage," B (1933). 501-13.

Alexander, Paul J. "The Iconoclastic Council of St. Sophia (815) and its Definition (Horos)," *DOP* 7 (1953), 35-66.

Alfoldi, A. "Insignien und Tracht der romischen Kaiser," *Mitteilungen des Deutschen Archaologischen Instituts, Romisches Abteilung* 50 (1935), 117-20.

Amann, Emile. "Photius," *Dictionnaire de Théologie catholique,* 15 vols. 12 (1933-1935): 1536-1604.

Amantos, Konstantinos. ΙΣΤΟΡΙΑ ΤΟΥ ΒΥΖΑΝΤΙΝΟΥ ΚΡΑΤΟΥΣ *395-867 A.D.,* 2 vols. (2nd edition). Athens, 1953.

Amari, Michel. *Bibliotheca arabo-sicula, Versione italiana,* 2 vols. Turino and Rome, 1880-1889.

Anderson, J. C. G. "The Campaigns of Basil I Against the Paulicians in 872 A.D., " *Classical Review* 10 (1896), 136-40.

Andreades, Andreas. *Le recrutement des fonctionnaires et les universités dans l'Empire Byzantin.* Paris, 1926.

Antoniades, Emmanuel. *Hagia Sophia.* Athens, 1907.

Arbargi, Martin George. "Byzantium in Latin Eyes: 800-1204." Dissertation, Rutgers and The State University, 1961.

Arhweiler, Helene. "Sur la carriere de Photius avant son patriarcat," *BZ* 58 (1965), 348-63.

Aristarches, Stavros. ΤΟΥ ΕΝ ΑΓΙΟΙΣ ΠΑΤΡΟΣ ΗΜΩΝ ΦΩΤΙΟΥ ΠΑΤΡΙΑΡΧΟΥ ΚΩΝΣΤΑΝΤΙΝΟΥΠΟΛΕΩΣ ΛΟΓΟΙ ΚΑΙ ΟΜΙΛΙΑΙ. Constantinople, 1901.

Arnakis, George. "Captivity of Gregory Palamas by the Turks and Related Documents as Historical Sources," *Speculum* (January, 1951), pp. 104-18.

Bach, E. "Les lois agraires byzantines du Xᵉ siecle," *Classica et Mediaevalia* 5 (1942), 70-91.

Barisic', F. "Genesios et le Continuateur de Theophane," *B* 28 (1958-1959), 119-33.

_____. "Les sources de Génésios et du Continuateur de Théophane pour l'histoire du règne de Michel II (820-829)," *B* 31 (1961), 257-71.

Barker, Ernest. *Social and Political Thought in Byzantium from Justinian I to the Last Palaeologus.* Oxford, 1957.

Baronius, Caesar. *Annales Ecclesiastici, una cum critica Historico-chronologica.* Lucae, 1738-1759.

Basnage, Jacques Mons. *Histoire de l'Eglise depuis Jésus Christ jusqu'à présent.* Rotterdam, 1699.

Baynes, Norman H. *The Byzantine Empire.* London, 1925.

_____. *Byzantine Studies and Other Essays.* London, 1955.

_____ and H. St. L. B. Moss, eds. *Byzantium: An Introduction to East Roman Civilization.* Oxford, 1948.

Beck, H. G. *Kirche und theologische Literatur im byzantinischen Reich.* Munich, 1959.

Becker, P. *De Photio et Aretha lexicorum scriptoribus.* Bonn, 1909.

Bees, A. "Eine unbeachtete Quelle uber die Abstammung des Kaisers Basilios I, des Mazedoniers," *Byzantinisch-neugriechische Jahrbucher* 4 (1932), 76-87.

_____. "Un manuscrit des Météores de l'an 861-2," REG 26 (1913), 58-67.

Benediktsson, Jacob. "Ein fruhbyzantinishes Biblio-lexicon," *Classica et Mediaevalia* 1 (1938), 243-80.

Blake, R. P. "Note sur l'activité litteraire de Nicéphore Ier patriarche de Constantinople," *B* 14 (1939), 1-15.

Brehier, Louis. "Attempts at Reunion of the Greek and Latin Churches," *CMH* 4 (1923), 594-626.

_____. "Iconoclasm," *Histoire de l'Eglise* 5 (1938), 431-70.

_____. *La civilisation byzantine.* Paris, 1950.

_____. *La querelle des images, VIIIe-IXe siecles.* Paris, 1904.

_____. "L'enseignement classique et l'enseignement religieux a Byzance," *RHPR* 21 (1941), 34-69.

_____. "L'origine des titres impériaux à Byzance," *BZ* 15 (1906), 161-72.

_____. "Normal Relations Between Rome and the Churches of the East before the Schism of the Eleventh Century," *CQ* 4 (1916), 669-75.

_____. "Notes sur l'histoire de l'enseignement supérieur à Constantinople," *B* 3 (1927), 73-94; 4 (1929), 13-28.

_____. "The Greek Church: Its Relations with the West up to 1054," *CMH* 4 (1923), 246-73.

_____. "Un patriarche sorcier à Constantinople," *ROC* 10 (1904), 261-68.

_____. *Vie et mort de Byzance.* Paris, 1950.

Brown, Peter. "A Dark-Age Crisis: Aspects of the Iconoclastic Controversy," *EHR* 88.346 (1973), 1-34.

Bryce, James. "Life of Justinian by Theophilos," *EHR* 2 (1887), 657-84.

—————————. *The Holy Roman Empire.* New York, 1896.

Bury, John Bagwell. "Roman Emperors from Basil I to Isaak Komnenos," *EHR* 4 (1889), 41-64, 251-85.

—————————. "The Ceremonial Book of Constantine Porphyrogennetos," *EHR* 22 (1907), 209-27, 417-39.

—————————. "The Embassy of John the Grammarian," *EHR* 24 (1909), 296-99.

—————————. "The Great Palace," *BZ* 21 (1912), 210-25.

—————————. "The Relationship of Photios to the Empress Theodora," *EHR* 5 (1890), 255-58.

—————————. "The Treatise de Administrando Imperio," *BZ* 15 (1906), 517-77.

—————————. *The Constitution of the Later Roman Empire.* Cambridge, 1910.

—————————. *A History of the Eastern Roman Empire from the Fall of Irene to the Accession of Basil I, A.D. 802-867.* London, 1912.

—————————. *A History of the Later Roman Empire from Arcadius to Irene.* London, 1889.

—————————. *The Imperial Administrative System in the Ninth Century, with a revised text of the Kleterologion of Philotheos.* London, 1911.

Callistos, Archimandrites. Ο ΘΡΟΝΟΣ ΤΗΣ ΚΟΝΣΤΑΝΤΙΝΟΠΟΛΕΩΣ ΚΑΙ ΤΑ ΔΙΚΑΙΩΜΑΤΑ ΚΑΙ ΠΡΟΝΟΜΟΙΑ ΑΥΤΟΥ ΕΠΙ ΤΩΝ ΛΟΙΠΩΝ ΕΚΚΛΗΣΙΩΝ ΤΗΣ ΑΝΑΤΟΛΗΣ. Alexandria, 1920.

Canard, M. "Byzantium and the Muslim World to the Middle of the Eleventh Century," *CMH* 4 (1966), 697-736.

—————————. "Les expéditions des Arabes contre Constantinople dans l'histoire et dans la légende," *JA* 208 (1926), 61-121.

Canisus, Hanricus. *Lectiones Antiquae,* ed. Jacobus Basnage, 4 vols. Antwerp, 1725.

Carwithen, J. B. S. and Rev. A. Lyall. *History of the Christian Church.* London, 1856.

Casper, Erich L. *Geschichte des Papsttums von den Anfangen bis zur hohe der Weltherschast.* Tubingen, 1930, 1933.

Charanis, P. "The Armenians in the Byzantine Empire," *Byzantino-slavica* 22 (1961), 196-240.

_____. "Some Aspects of Daily Life in Byzantium," *GOTR* 8 (1962-1963), 53-70.

_____. "The Monastic Properties and the State in the Byzantine Empire," *DOP* 4 (1948), 51-118.

Chatzes, A. C. "Ἱστορία τοῦ Βυζαντινοῦ Κράτους," *Practica of the Academy of Athens* 4 (1929), 746-48.

Chrysos, Evagelos. Η ΕΚΚΛΗΣΙΑΣΤΙΚΗ ΠΟΛΙΤΙΚΗ ΤΟΥ ΙΟΥΣΤΙ-ΝΙΑΝΟΥ. Thessalonike, 1969.

Conrat, M. "Romisches Recht Bei Papst Nikolaus I.," *Neus Archiv* 46 (1911), 29-52.

Costa-Louillet, G. da. "Saints de Constantinople aux VIIIe, IXe et Xe siecles," *B* 24 (1954), 179-263, 453-512; 25-27 (1955-1957), 783-852.

Dain, Alphonse. "La transmission des textes littéraires classiques de Photius à Constantin Porphyrogénète," *DOP* 8 (1954), 31-47.

De Boor, C. "Der Angriff der Rhos auf Byzanz," *BZ* 4 (1895), 445-66.

_____. "Die Chronik des Logotheten," *BZ* 6 (1897), 233-84.

Deer, J. "Der Globus des spatromischen und der byzantinischen Kaisers. Symbol oder Ensigne?" *BZ* 54 (1961), 53-85.

Deissmann, A. *Forschungen und Funde im Serai.* Berlin-Leipzig, 1933.

Delehaye, Hippolyte. *The Legends of the Saints.* New York, 1962.

_____. *Mélanges d'agiographie grecque et latine.* Brussels, 1966.

_____. *Synaxarium Constantinopolitanum.* Brussels, 1902.

Demetrakopoulos, Andronikos K. ΕΚΚΛΗΣΙΑΣΤΙΚΗ ΒΙΒΛΙΟΘΗ-ΚΗ. Leipzig, 1866.

_____. ΙΣΤΟΡΙΑ ΤΟΥ ΣΧΗΣΜΑΤΟΣ. Leipzig, 1867.

_____. ΟΡΘΟΔΟΞΟΣ ΕΛΛΑΣ. Leipzig, 1872.

Devreese, Robert. *Introduction à l'étude des manuscrits grecs.* Paris, 1954.

Diehl, Charles. "La légende de l'empereur Théophile," *Annales de l'Institut Kondakov* 4 (1931), 33-37.

—————. "Le Sénat et le peuple byzantin aux IXe et XIIe siecles," *B* 1 (1924), 201-18.

—————. *Byzantium: grandeur et decadence.* Paris, 1919.

—————. *Etudes sur l'administration byzantine dans l'Exarchat de Ravenne.* Paris, 1888.

Dikigoropoulos, Andreas. "The Constantinopolitan Solidi of Theophilus," *DOP* 18 (1964), 353-61.

Diller, Aubrey. "Photios' Bibliotheca in Byzantine Literature," *DOP* 16 (1962), 189-240.

Dinneen, Lucilla. *Titles of Address in Christian Greek Epistolography.* Washington, D.C., 1929.

Dolger, Franz. *Byzance und die Europaische Staatenwelt von 565 bis 1453.* Ettal, 1953.

—————. *Regesten der Kaiserkunden des ostromischen Reiches von 565-1453.* Volume I of Corpus der griechischen Urkunden des Mittelalters und der neuren Zeit, 3 vols. Munich-Berlin, 1924-1932.

Draeseke, J. "Die Syllogismen des Photios," *ZWT* 44 (1901), 553-89.

Duchesne, Louis M. O. *Etude sur le Liber Pontificalis.* Paris, 1886.

Du Gange, C. du Fresne. *Glossarium ad scriptores mediae et infimae Graecitatis,* 2 vols. Lyons, 1688.

Dujcev, I. "Au lendemain de la conversion du peuple bulgare. L'épitre de Photios," *Melanges de science religieuse* 8 (1951), 211-26.

Dvornik, Francis. "Etudes sur Photius," B 11 (1936), 1-19.

—————. "Le second schisme de Photius. Une mystiphication historique," B 8 (1933), 425-74.

—————. "Lettre à Henri Gregoire," *B* 10 (1935), 1-5.

—————. "Lettre à M. H. Gregoire à propos de Michel III," *B* 10 (1935), 5-9.

—————. "Patriarch Ignatios and Caesar Bardas," *Byzantinoslavica* 27 (1966), 7-22.

—————. "Patriarch Photios, Scholar and Statesman," *Classical Folia* 13 (1959), 3-18.

—————. "Photios et la réorganisation de l'Académie Patriarcale," *AB* 68 (1950), 108-25.

—————. "The Patriarch Photios and Iconoclasm," *DOP* 7 (1953), 69-97.

_____. "Sur la carrière universitaire de Constantin le Philosophe," *Byzantinoslavica* 3 (1931), 59-67.

_____. "The Patriarch Photios in the Light of Recent Research," *Berichte zum XI Internationalen Byzantinisten-Kongress* 3 (1958), 1-56.

_____. "The Circus Parties in Byzantium," *BM* 1 (1946), 119-33.

_____. *Byzantine Missions among the Slavs.* New Brunswick, N.J., 1970.

_____. *Byzantium and the Roman Primacy.* New York, 1964.

_____. *Early Christian and Byzantine Political Philosophy: Origins and Background.* Washington, D.C., 1966.

_____. *The Idea of Apostolicity in Byzantium and the Legend of the Apostle Andrew.* Cambridge, Mass., 1958.

_____. *Les légendes de Constantin et de Méthode vues de Byzance.* Hattiesburg, Miss., 1969.

_____. *The Making of Central and Eastern Europe.* London, 1949.

_____. *The Photian Schism: History and Legend.* Cambridge, 1948.

_____. *Les Slavs, Byzance et Rome au IXe siècle.* Hattiesburg, Miss., 1970.

_____. *The Slavs: Their Early History and Civilization.* Boston, 1956.

Exler, F. X. J. *A Study in Greek Epistolography.* Washington, D.C., 1923.

Fanez, C. *La consolation latine chrétienne.* Paris, 1937.

Faucher, Crisostome P. *Histoire de Photius patriarche-schismatique de Constantinople suivie d'observations sur le fanatisme.* Paris, 1772.

Festa, Nicolas. *Theodori Ducae Lascaris Epistolae CCVII.* Florence, 1898.

Finlay, George. *History of the Byzantine and Greek Empire, from DCCXIV to MLVII,* 2nd edition. Edinburg and London, 1855.

Fischer, F. *De Patriarcharum Constantinopolitanorum Catalogis et de Chronologia octo primorum patriarcharum.* Leipzig, 1884.

Fleury, Claude. *Histoire du christianisme,* 6 vols. Paris, 1836-1837.

Fowler, H. W. and F. G. Fowler. *The Works of Lucian of Samosata,* 4 vols. Oxford, 1905.

Freese, J. H. *The Library of Photius.* London, 1920.

Fuchs, Friedrich. "Die ökumenische Akademie von Konstantinopel in frühen Mittelalter," *Bayerische Blaetter fur des gymnasialschulwesen* 49 (1923), 177-92.

——————. *Die höheren Schulen von Konstantinopel im Mittelalter.* (Byzant. Archiv 8) Leipzig and Berlin, 1926.

Gardner, Alice. *Theodore of Studion, His Life and Times.* London, 1905.

Gasquet, Amedee Louis Ulysse. *De l'autorite imperiale en matière religieuse a Byzance.* Paris, 1879.

Geanakoplos, Deno. "Erasmus and the Aldine Academy of Venice: A Neglected Chapter in the Transition of Greco-Byzantine Learning to the West," *Greek, Roman and Byzantine Studies* 3 (1960), 107-34.

——————. "On the Schism of the Greek and Roman Churches. A Confidential Papal Directive for the Implementation of Union," *GOTR* 1 (1954), 16-24.

——————. *Byzantine East and Latin West. Two Worlds of Christendom in the Middle Ages and Renaissance.* New York, 1966.

Gelzer, H. *Abriss der byzantinischen Kaisergeschichte.* Munich, 1897.

Gennadios, Metropolitan. "Τά ἰδιαίτερα δικαιώματα τοῦ Οἰκουμενικοῦ Πατριαρχείου καί ἡ Θέσις αὐτοῦ ἔναντι τῶν ἄλλων Ὀρθοδόξον Ἐκκλησιῶν," ΘΡΘΟΔΟΞΙΑ 6 (1931), 404-52.

Gerland, E. "Photius und der Angriss der Russen auf Byzanz," *Neue Jahrbucher fur das klassische Altertum* 11 (1903), 718-22.

Gibbon, Edward. *The Decline and Fall of the Roman Empire,* vol. VII. London, 1848.

Gouillard, J. "Art et littérature théologique à Byzance au lendemain de la querelle des images," *Cahiers de civilisation medievale* 12 (1969), 1-13.

——————. "Deux figures mal connues du second iconoclasme," *B* 31 (1961), 371-401.

Gregoire, Henri. "Digénes Akritas," *B* 4 (1929), 45-90.

——————. "Du nouveau sur le patriarche Photius," *Bulletin de la classe des lettres de l'Academie royale de Belgique* 20 (1934), 36-53.

_____. "Etudes sur le IXe siècle," *B* 8 (1933), 515-50.

_____. "Michel III et Basile le Macédonien dans l'inscription d'Ancyre," *B* 5 (1929-1930), 327-46.

_____. "Le peuple de Constantinople," *B* 11 (1936), 617-716.

_____. "Les sources de l'histoire des Pauliciens," *Bulletin de la classe des lettres de l'Académie royale de Belgique* 22 (1936), 95-114.

Grivec, F. "Cyrilli et Methodii amicitia dubia cum Photio," *Orientalia Christiana* 17 (1951), 382-92.

Grumel, V. "Formose ou Nicolas Ier dans la Mystagogie de Photius," *EO* 33 (1934), 194-5.

_____. "La liquidation de la querelle photienne," *EO* 33 (1934), 257-88.

_____. "L'encyclique de Photius aux Orientaux," *EO* 34 (1935), 129-38.

Guilland, R. "La noblesse byzantine: remarques," *REB* 24 (1966), 40-57.

_____. "Le droit divin à Byzance," *EO* 42 (1947), 160-61.

_____. "La noblesse de race à Byzance," *Byzantinoslavica* 9 (1948), 307-14.

_____. "Le Synodicon de l'Orthodoxie: edition et commentaire," *Travaux et memoires du Centre de Recherche d'Histoire et de Civilisation byzantines* 2 (1967), 1-316.

Habert, H. *Archieratikon Liber Pontificalis Ecclesiae Graece,* 3 vols. Paris, 1643.

Haight, Elizabeth H. *Essays on Greek Romances.* Washington, D.C., 1943.

Halkin, F. "Trois dates historiques précises grâce au Synaxaire," *B* 24 (1954), 7-17.

Hefele, K. J. von. *Histoire des conciles,* IV, ed. H. Leclerc et al. Paris, 1911.

Heisenberg, A. "Das Probleme der Renaissance in Byzanz," *Historische Zeitschrift* 133 (1926), 393-412.

Henry, René. *La bibliothèque de Photius,* 6 vols. Collection G. Budé. Paris, 1959-1969.

_____. "Proclos et le vocabulaire technique de Photius," *Revue belge de philologie et d'histoire* 13 (1934), 615-27.

Henze, W. "Uber den Brief Kaiser Ludwigs II an dem Kaiser Basilius I," *Neus Archiv des Gesallschaft für ältere deutsche Geschichtskunde* 35 (1910), 661-76.

Hergenröther, Joseph, Cardinal. *Handbuch den Allgemeinen Kirchengeschichte.* Freiburg im Bresgau, 1884-1886.

——————————————————. *Photius, Patriarch von Konstantinopel: sein Leben, seine Schriften und das griechische Schisma,* 3 vols. Regensburg, 1867-1869.

Hertzberg, G. F. *Geschichte der Byzantiner und des osmanischen Reiches bis genen Ende des XVI en Jahrhunderts.* Berlin, 1883.

Hesseling, D. C. *Essai sur la civilisation byzantine.* Paris, 1907.

Hirsch, F. *Byzantinische Studien.* Leipzig, 1876.

Hitti, P. K. *History of the Arabs,* 6th edition. London, 1958.

Honigmann, E. *Die Ostgrenze des byzantinischen Reiches von 363 bis 1071.* Brussels, 1935.

Hopf, K. *Griechische Geschichte.* Leipzig, 1867.

Hussey, J. M., ed. *The Byzantine Empire.* Vol. 4 of *The Cambridge Medieval History.* Cambridge, 1966.

——————————. *The Byzantine World,* 2nd edition. New York, 1961.

Impellizzeri, Salvatore. "Il Umanesimo Bizantine del IX Secolo e la Genesi della Bibliotheca de Fozio," *Studi Bizantini e Neoellenici* 17 (1969), 70-114.

Iorga, Nicolae. *Histoire de la vie byzantine, Empire et civilisation,* 3 vols. Bucharest, 1934.

——————————. "Médaillons d'histoire littéraire byzantine, Photius," *B* 3 (1926), 18-30.

Jacobs, F., ed. *Palatine Anthologie,* 9 vols. Heidelberg, 1794-1817.

Jaffe, Philippus. *Regesta Pontificum Romanorum.* Leipzig, 1885-1888.

Jager, J. N. Abbe. *Histoire de Photius et du schisme des Grecs,* 2nd edition. Paris, 1854.

Jenkins, R. J. H. "The Classical Background of the *Scriptores Post Theophanem,*" *DOP* 8 (1954), 11-30.

——————————. "Constantine VII's Portrait of Michael III," *Bulletin de la classe des lettres de l'Academie royale de Belgique* 34 (1948), 71-77.

——————————. "Symeon the Logothete," *DOP* 19 (1965), 91-112.

——————————— and P. Grierson. "The Date of Constantine VII's Coronation," *B* 32 (1962), 133-38.

———————— and Cyril Mango. "The Date and Significance of the Tenth Homily of Photios," *DOP* 10 (1956), 123-40.

Jugie, M. *Le schisme byzantin.* Paris, 1941.

Kalliphron, B. D. ΣΥΛΟΓΗ ΕΚΚΛΗΣΙΑΣΤΙΚΩΝ ΛΟΓΟΝ ΚΑΙ ΑΛΛΩΝ, 3 vols. Constantinople, 1857.

Kalokyris, Constantine. *The Essence of Orthodox Iconography,* trans. Peter A. Chamberas. Brookline, Mass., 1971.

Karlin-Hayter, P. "New Aretha Texts," *B* 31 (1961), 273-307.

Klibausky, Robert. *The Continuity of the Platonic Tradition During the Middle Ages.* London, 1939.

Kondakoff, N. *Histoire de l'art byzantin,* 2 vols. New York, 1970.

Koraes, Adamantios. ΠΡΟΔΡΟΜΟΣ ΕΛΛΗΝΙΚΗΣ ΒΙΒΛΙΟΘΗΚΗΣ, 2 vols. Paris, 1805.

Kougeas, Socrates. Ο ΚΑΙΣΑΡΙΑΣ ΑΡΕΘΑΣ ΚΑΙ ΤΟ ΕΡΓΟΝ ΑΥ-ΤΟΥ. Athens, 1913.

Koustas, G. "The Literary Criticism of Photius: A Christian Definition of Style," *Hellenika* 17 (1962), 132-69.

————————. "Function and Evolution of Byzantine Rhetoric," *Viator* 1 (1970), 55-73.

Krumbacher, Karl. *Geschichte der byzantinischen Litteratur von Justinian bus zem des Ostromischen Reiches, 527-1453.* New York, 1958.

Kyriakis, M. J. "The Unviersity: Origin and Early Phases in Constantinople," *B* 41 (1971), 161-82.

Ladner, G. B. "The Concept of the Image in the Greek Fathers and the Byzantine Iconoclastic Controversy," *DOP* 7 (1953), 1-34.

Laemmer, Hubert. *Papst Nicolaus der erste und die byzantinische Staatskirche seiner Zeit.* Berlin, 1857.

Lampros, S. P. "Χρονολογία Βασιλείου Μακεδόνος," ΝΕΟΣ ΕΛΛΗ-ΝΟΜΗΜΩΝ 20 (1926), 292-93.

————————. "Zu Symeon Magister," *BZ* 6 (1897), 506-08.

Laourdas, Basil. "The Codex Ambrosianus Graecus 81 and Photius," *BZ* 44 (1951), 370-72.

————————. "Ἐπιγραφή τῆς πρός τόν Βασιλέα τῶν Βουλγάρων Μιχαήλ, Πρώτης Ἐπιστολῆς τοῦ Φωτίου," ΘΕΟΛΟΓΙΑ 23 (1952), 3-6.

————————. "Ἑρμενευτικά εἰς Φώτιον," ΕΛΛΗΝΙΚΑ 14 (1955), 168-70.

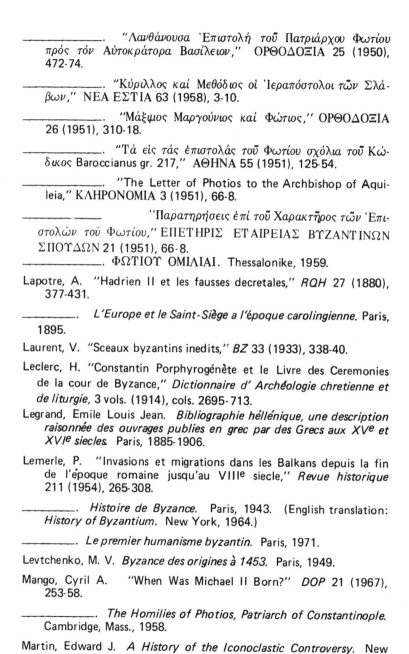

——————. "Λανθάνουσα Ἐπιστολή τοῦ Πατριάρχου Φωτίου πρός τόν Αὐτοκράτορα Βασίλειον," ΟΡΘΟΔΟΞΙΑ 25 (1950), 472-74.

——————. "Κύριλλος καί Μεθόδιως οἱ Ἱεραπόστολοι τῶν Σλάβων," ΝΕΑ ΕΣΤΙΑ 63 (1958), 3-10.

——————. "Μάξιμος Μαργούνιος καί Φώτιος," ΟΡΘΟΔΟΞΙΑ 26 (1951), 310-18.

——————. "Τά εἰς τάς ἐπιστολάς τοῦ Φωτίου σχόλια τοῦ Κώδικος Baroccianus gr. 217," ΑΘΗΝΑ 55 (1951), 125-54.

——————. "The Letter of Photios to the Archbishop of Aquileia," ΚΛΗΡΟΝΟΜΙΑ 3 (1951), 66-8.

—————— "Παρατηρήσεις ἐπί τοῦ Χαρακτῆρος τῶν Ἐπιστολῶν τοῦ Φωτίου," ΕΠΕΤΗΡΙΣ ΕΤΑΙΡΕΙΑΣ ΒΥΖΑΝΤΙΝΩΝ ΣΠΟΥΔΩΝ 21 (1951), 66-8.

——————. ΦΩΤΙΟΥ ΟΜΙΛΙΑΙ. Thessalonike, 1959.

Lapotre, A. "Hadrien II et les fausses decretales," RQH 27 (1880), 377-431.

——————. L'Europe et le Saint-Siège a l'époque carolingienne. Paris, 1895.

Laurent, V. "Sceaux byzantins inedits," BZ 33 (1933), 338-40.

Leclerc, H. "Constantin Porphyrogénète et le Livre des Ceremonies de la cour de Byzance," Dictionnaire d' Archéologie chretienne et de liturgie, 3 vols. (1914), cols. 2695-713.

Legrand, Emile Louis Jean. Bibliographie héllénique, une description raisonnée des ouvrages publies en grec par des Grecs aux XVe et XVIe siecles. Paris, 1885-1906.

Lemerle, P. "Invasions et migrations dans les Balkans depuis la fin de l'époque romaine jusqu'au VIIIe siecle," Revue historique 211 (1954), 265-308.

——————. Histoire de Byzance. Paris, 1943. (English translation: History of Byzantium. New York, 1964.)

——————. Le premier humanisme byzantin. Paris, 1971.

Levtchenko, M. V. Byzance des origines à 1453. Paris, 1949.

Mango, Cyril A. "When Was Michael II Born?" DOP 21 (1967), 253-58.

——————. The Homilies of Photios, Patriarch of Constantinople. Cambridge, Mass., 1958.

Martin, Edward J. A History of the Iconoclastic Controversy. New York, 1930.

Maximos, Metropolitan of Sardis. ΤΟ ΟΙΚΟΥΜΕΝΙΚΟΝ ΠΑΤΡΙ-
ΑΡΧΕΙΟΝ ΕΝ ΤΗ ΟΡΘΟΔΟΞΩ ΕΚΚΛΗΣΙΑ. Thessalonike, 1972.

Meyendorff, J. "Byzantine News of Islam," *DOP* 18 (1964), 115-32.

Moravcsik, G. "Sagen und Legenden uber Kaiser Basilios I," *DOP* 15
(1961), 61-126.

_____ and R. J. H. Jenkins, eds. *Constantine Porphyrogennetos: De Administrando Imperio.* Budapest, 1949 and London,
1962.

Mosin, V. "Les Khazars et les Byzantins d'aprés l'anonyme de Cambridge," *B* 6 (1931), 309-25.

_____. "The Origin of Russia: The Normans in Eastern Europe,"
Byzantinoslavica 3 (1931), 38-58, 285-307.

Mouratides, K. ΣΧΕΣΕΙΣ ΕΚΚΛΗΣΙΑΣ ΚΑΙ ΠΟΛΙΤΕΙΑΣ. Athens,
1965.

Muller, Herbert J. *The Uses of the Past.* New York, 1969.

Naber, S. A. *Photius Lexicon,* 2 vols. Leiden, 1864-1865.

Nauck, A. *Lexicon Vindobonense.* St. Petersburg, 1867.

Niederle, Lubor. *Manuel de l'antiquité slave,* 2 vols. Paris, 1923-
1926.

Norden, E. *Die Antike Kunsprosa von VI Jahrhundert V. Ch. bis im
die Zeit der Renaissance,* 2 vols. Leipzig, 1898.

Obolensky, Dimitri. "The Empire and its Northern Neighbors 565-
1018," *CMH* 4 (1966), 473-518.

_____. *The Byzantine Commonwealth: Eastern Europe
500-1453.* London, 1971.

Oekonomos, Sophocles. ΦΩΤΙΟΥ ΑΜΦΙΛΟΧΙΑ. Athens, 1858.

Ostrogorsky, George. "The Byzantine Background of the Moravian
Mission," *DOP* 19 (1965), 1-18.

_____. "The Byzantine Emperor and the Hierarchical
World Order," *Slavic and East European Review* 35 (1956), 1-14.

_____. *History of the Byzantine State.* New Bruns-
wick, N.J., 1969.

_____. *Studien zur Geschichte des byzantinische Bil-
derstreites.* Breslau, 1929.

Papadopoulos, Chrysostomos. ΠΕΡΙ ΤΗΣ ΕΠΙΣΤΗΜΟΝΙΚΗΣ ΔΡΑ-
ΣΕΟΣ ΤΟΥ ΜΕΓΑΛΟΥ ΦΩΤΙΟΥ ΠΑΤΡΙΑΡΧΟΥ ΚΩΝΣΤΑΝ-
ΤΙΝΟΥΠΟΛΕΩΣ. Athens, 1912.

Papadopoulos-Kerameus, A. "Ὁ Πατριάρχης Φώτιος ὡς Πατήρ Ἄγιος τῆς Ὀρθοδόξου Καθολικῆς Ἐκκλησίας," *BZ* 8 (1899), 647-71.

——————————. Ὁ ΑΚΑΘΙΣΤΟΣ ΥΜΝΟΣ ΟΙ ΡΟΣ ΚΑΙ Ο ΠΑΤΡΙΑΡΧΗΣ ΦΩΤΙΟΣ. Athens, 1903.

Paparigopoulos, Konstantinos. ΙΣΤΟΡΙΑ ΤΟΥ ΕΛΛΗΝΙΚΟΥ ΕΘ-ΝΟΥΣ, 8 vols. Athens, 1925.

Parels, Ernst. *Papst Nikolaus I und Anastasius Bibliothecarius.* Berlin, 1920.

Phillimore, J. S. "The Greek Romances," *English Literature and the Classics* (1912), pp. 108-15.

Politis, L. "Die Handschriftesammlung des Klosters Zavorda und die neuaufgefundene Photios Handschrift," *Phililogus* 105 (1961), 136-44.

Ralli—Potli. ΣΥΝΤΑΓΜΑ ΙΕΡΩΝ ΚΑΝΟΝΩΝ, 4 vols. Athens, 1852-1859.

Rambaud, Alfred N. *L'Empire grec du Xe siècle: Constantin Porphyrogenete.* Paris, 1870.

——————————. *De Byzantino Hippodromo et circensibus factionibus.* Paris, 1870.

Rattenbury, Robert M. *Les Ethiopiques, Théagènes et Chariclee,* 3 vols. Paris, 1939-1943.

Reese, Gregory. *Music in the Middle Ages.* New York, 1945.

Regel, W., ed. "Vita Sanctae Theodorae Imperatricis (893)," *Analecta Byzantino-Russica* 10 (1891), 1-44.

Reitzenstein, R. *Geschichte der griechischen Etymologika, ein Beitrag zur Geschichte des Philologie in Alexandria und Byzanz.* Leipzig, 1897.

Reuss, J. "Die Matthaus-Erklarung des Photius von Konstantinopel," *Ostkirchliche Studien* 1 (1852), 132-34.

Rhode, E. *Der griechische Roman.* Leipzig, 1914.

Runciman, Steven. *Eastern Schism.* Oxford, 1955.

——————————. *First Bulgarian Empire.* London, 1930.

Scharf, J. "Photius und die Epanagoge," *BZ* 49 (1956), 385-400.

——————————. "Zur Echtheitsfrage der Manichaerbucher des Photius," *BZ* 44 (1951), 487-94.

Scheidweiler, F. "Paulikianer-probleme," *BZ* 43 (1950), 10-39, 366-84.

220 Patriarch Photios

Schlumberger, G. *L'épopée byzantine à la fin du Xe siecle,* 3 vols. Paris, 1896-1905.

_____. *Sigillographie de l'Empire byzantine.* Paris, 1955.

Schoell, M. *Histoire de philologie grecque,* VI. Paris, 1823.

Schroder, H. O. "Oribasius," *Paulys-Real Encyclopedie,* VII (1940), cols. 797-812.

Schwarzlos, K. *Der Bilderstreit, ein Kamp der griechischen Kirche und ihre Eigenhart und ihre Freiheit.* Gotha, 1890.

Setton, K. M. "On the Raids of the Moslems in the Aegean in the Ninth and Tenth Centuries, and their Alleged Occupation of Athens," *American Journal of Archaeology* 58 (1954), 311-29.

Shepard, A. M. "The Byzantine Reconquest of Crete," *U.S. Naval Institute Proceedings* 67:462 (1941), 1021-30.

Sherrard, Philip. *The Greek East and the Latin West.* London, 1959.

Smith, Sir William. *Dictionary of Greek and Roman Biography and Mythology.* London, 1880.

Soulis, G. "The Legacy of Cyril and Methodios to the Southern Slavs," *DOP* 19 (1965), 19-43.

Spengel, L., ed. *Rhetores Graeci.* Leipzig, 1854.

Spinka, Matthew. *A History of Christianity in the Balkans: A Study in the Spread of Byzantine Culture among the Slavs.* Chicago, 1933.

Staab, Karl. *Pauluskommentare aus der griechischen Kirche aus Katenanhandschriften gesammelt.* (*Neutestament Abhandlung* 15 [1933], 470-652.)

Stein, Ernest. *Gerschichte des Spatromischen Reiches,* I. Vienna, 1928.

_____. *Studien zur Geschichte des byzantinischen Reiches.* Stuttgart, 1919.

_____. "Ein Kapitel vom persischen und vom byzantinischen Staat," *Byzantinisch-neugriechische Jarhbucher* 1 (1920), 50-89.

Sycoutres, Ioannes. *Probleme der byzantinischen Epistolographie.* Athens, 1932.

Tantalides, Elias. ΙΔΙΩΤΙΚΑ ΣΤΙΧΙΟΥΡΓΛΗΜΑΤΑ. Trieste, 1869.

Tatakis, Basil. "Φώτιος ὁ Μεγάλος ᾽Ανθρωπιστής," ΚΥΡΙΛΛΩ ΚΑΙ ΜΕΘΟΔΙΩ ΤΟΜΟΣ ΕΟΡΤΙΟΣ ΕΠΙ ΤΗ ΧΙΛΙΟΣΤΙ ΚΑΙ ΕΚΑΤΟΣΤΙ ΕΠΕΤΗΡΙΔΙ. Thessalonike, 1966.

_____. Η ΣΥΜΒΟΛΗ ΤΗΣ ΚΑΠΠΑΔΟΚΙΑΣ ΣΤΗ ΧΡΙΣ-
ΤΙΑΝΙΚΗ ΣΚΕΨΗ. Thessalonike, 1959.

_____. ΘΕΜΑΤΑ ΧΡΙΣΤΙΑΝΙΚΗΣ ΚΑΙ ΒΥΖΑΝΤΙΝΗΣ
ΦΙΛΟΣΟΦΙΑΣ. Athens, 1952.

Ter-Mrkttschian, Karapet. *Die Paulicianer.* Leipzig, 1893.

Todd, F. A. *Some Ancient Novels.* Oxford, 1940.

Tomadakis, Nikolaos. ΒΥΖΑΝΤΙΝΗ ΕΠΙΣΤΟΛΟΓΡΑΦΙΑ : ΕΙΣΑ-
ΓΩΓΗ ΕΙΣ ΤΗΝ ΒΥΖΑΝΤΙΝΗΝ ΦΙΛΟΛΟΓΙΑΝ, 3 vols., 3rd
edition. Athens, 1969-1970.

_____. ΕΙΣΑΓΩΓΗ ΕΙΣ ΤΗΝ ΒΥΖΑΝΤΙΝΗΝ ΦΙ-
ΛΟΛΟΓΙΑΝ, 2 vols., 3rd edition. Athens, 1965.

_____. ΣΥΛΛΑΒΟΣ ΒΥΖΑΝΤΙΝΩΝ ΜΕΛΕΤΩΝ
ΚΑΙ ΚΕΙΜΕΝΩΝ: Ο ΙΕΡΟΣ ΦΩΤΙΟΣ. Athens, 1961.

_____. "Ἡ Δῆθεν Μεγάλη Σιγή τῶν Γραμμάτων ἐν
Βυζαντίῳ (650-850)." ΑΡΧΑΙΟΓΝΩΣΙΑ ΚΑΙ ΠΝΕΥΜΑΤΙΚΑΙ
ΕΚΔΗΛΩΣΕΙΣ. Athens, 1971.

Uspenskii, F., ed. *Synodicon for Orthodoxy Sunday.* Odessa, 1893.

Vakalopoulos, Alexandros. *History of Modern Hellenism.* Thessalonike, 1961.

Valettas, Ioannes. ΦΩΤΙΟΥ ΤΟΥ ΣΟΦΩΤΑΤΟΥ ΚΑΙ ΑΓΙΩΤΑ-
ΤΟΥ ΠΑΤΡΙΑΡΧΟΥ ΚΩΝΣΤΑΝΤΙΝΟΥΠΟΛΕΩΣ ΕΠΙΣΤΟΛΑΙ.
London, 1864.

Van de Ven. "La vie grecque de St. Jean le Psichaite," *Le Museon* 3
(1885), 90-110.

Vasiliev, Alexander A. *Byzance et les Arabes. I: la dynastie d'Amorium (820-867),* eds. H. Gregoire et. al. Brussels, 1935.

_____. *History of the Byzantine Empire,* 2 vols.
Madison, 1928.

_____. *The Russian Attack on Constantinople in 860.*
Cambridge, Mass., 1946.

Vogt, Albert. "Deux discours inedits de Nicetas de Paphlagonie,"
Oriental History 76 (1931), 223-450.

_____. "La jeunesse de Leon VI le Sage," *Revue historique*
174 (1934), 389-428.

_____. *Basile Ier Empereur de Byzance (867-886) et la civi-
lisation byzantine a la fin du IXe siecle.* Paris, 1908.

_____ and I. Hausherr, eds. "L'oraison funebre de Basile Ier
par son fils Leon le Sage," *Orientalia Christiana* 26 (1932), 502-13.

Weichart, V., ed. *Demetri et Libanii.* ΤΥΠΟΙ ΕΠΙΣΤΟΛΙΚΟΙ *et*
ΕΠΙΣΤΟΛΙΜΑΙΟΙ ΧΑΡΑΚΤΗΡΕΣ. Leipzig, 1910.

White, Despina. "Photios' Letter to the Bishops in Exile," *GOTR* 19
(1974), 113-29.

——————————. "Patriarch Photios' Letter to Mother Superior Eusebia," *Classical Folia* 29 (1975), 31-43.

——————————. "Patriarch Photios' Letter to his Brother Tarasios
on the Death of his Daughter," *GOTR* 18 (1973), 47-58.

Zakythenos, Dionysios. Η ΒΥΖΑΝΤΙΝΗ ΑΥΤΟΚΡΑΤΟΡΙΑ *324-
1071.* Athens, 1969.

——————————. ΒΥΣΑΝΤΙΝΑ ΚΕΙΜΕΝΑ. Athens, 1957.

——————————. ΟΙ ΣΛΑΒΟΙ ΣΤΗΝ ΕΛΛΑΔΑ : ΣΥΜΒΟΛΑΙ
ΕΙΣ ΤΗΝ ΙΣΤΟΡΙΑΝ ΤΟΥ ΜΕΣΑΙΩΝΙΚΟΥ ΕΛΛΗΝΙΣΜΟΥ.
Athens, 1945.

Zeigler, K. "Photios," *Paulys-Real Encyclopedie* (1941), cols. 667-
737.

Ziemann, F. *De Epistolarum Graecorum Formulis Sollemnibus: Quaestiones Selectae.* Halle, 1910.

INDEX

A

Aachen, Council of, 32

Abraham, 87, 123, 133, 178

Abridged History, 50

Academy, Patriarchal, 16

Achaeans, 173

Achilles, 57

Acragas, 178

Adam, 126

Adgestics, 205

Adrian II, Pope, 33, 36

Aeschines, 53

Aesop, 95

Aethiopica of Heliodoros, 56

Aetios, 55

Afutios, Armenian Prince, 108

Agapios, 54

Agatharchides, 49, 52

Ahrweiler, Hélène, 49

Aisne (Quierz), 29

Akakios the Monk, 83, 180

Alexander the Blacksmith, 96

Alexander the Comes, 81, 96, 184

Alexander the Great, 96, 184
  the Macedonian, 184

Alexander, son of Basil I, 36

Alexandria, 53, 54, 57
  Church of, 73
  Patriarch of, 22, 32, 75

Ambrose, Saint, 93

Amorian dynasty, 15

Amphilochia, 16, 68, 74, 77, 108

Amphilochios, metropolitan of
  Kythera, 60

Amphilochios, metropolitan of
  Kyzikos, 16, 76, 80, 187

Anakletes, Pope, 58

Anastasia, 42

Anastasios Bibliothekarios, 19, 20,
  35, 185

Anastasios, the Tax Collector, 69,
  168

Anchialos River, 27

Andocides, 53

Angura, city of, 195

Angurians, 183

Anios, 183, 184

Anna, Saint, 61

Annales Bertiniani, 24

Annunciation of the Virgin, 61

Anthimos, bishop of Remnicus,
  107

Antioch, Church of, 73
  Patriarch of, 22, 32, 75

Antiphon, 53

Antiquities of Rome, 52

Antonios, archbishop of Bosporos,
  171

Aphthonios, 53

Apollo, 95

Aphileia, metropolitan of, 74, 82,
  93

Arabs, 53; in Asia Minor, 24
  in Crete, 27
  in Mediterranean, 24, 27

Archelaos, Philopatris, King, 55

Arethas, archbishop of Caesarea,
  48, 49

Arian madmen, 91

Arianism, 90-91

Arianizers, 152

Arians, 91

Arios, 70, 90

Aristophanes, 95

Aristotle, 50, 53, 114, 178;
  categories, of, 17
  logic of, 17

223